Urban Economics

Second Edition

Urban Economics

Second Edition

Edwin S. Mills

Professor of Economics and Public Affairs
Gerald L. Phillippe Professor of Urban Studies
Princeton University

WITHDRAWN

Scott, Foresman and Company
Glenview, Illinois   Dallas, Tex.   Oakland, N.J.
Palo Alto, Cal.   Tucker, Ga.   London

For Susan and Alan

Cover photograph by Jean-Claude Lejeune

Acknowledgements:

From A. V. Kneese, et al., *ECONOMICS AND THE ENVIRONMENT*—A Materials Balance Approach, page 10. Copyright © 1970, by Resources for the Future, Inc.

From Edwin S. Mills and Katsutoshi Ohta, "Urbanization and Urban Problems," in *Asia's New Giant—How the Japanese Economy Works,* page 691. Copyright © 1976, The Brookings Institution.

From John L. Palmer and Joseph J. Minarik, "Income Security Policy," in *Setting National Priorities—The Next Ten Years,* page 508. Copyright © 1976, The Brookings Institution.

From Morgan Reynolds and Eugene Smolensky, "Further Results: Gini Concentration Ratios and Lorenz Curves," from *Public Expenditures, Taxes, and the Distribution of Income—The United States, 1950, 1961, 1970,* page 74. Copyright © 1977 by the Regents of the University of Wisconsin System on behalf of the Institute for Research on Poverty.

Library of Congress Cataloging In Publication Data
Mills, Edwin S
Urban economics.
Includes bibliographies and index.
1. Urban economics.   I. Title.
HT321.M53   1980   330.9173'2   80–13385
ISBN 0–673–15264–2

1 2 3 4 5 6 - VHJ - 85 84 83 82 81 80

Preface to the Second Edition

The purpose of the second edition of *Urban Economics,* as of the first, is to introduce the study of urban economics. Part One provides a conceptual and historical background for analyzing the urban economy. Part Two provides basic theoretical models of urban spatial structure, linking urban economics to the content of microeconomics courses. Part Two also presents the elements of welfare economics needed to analyze urban problems. Part Three applies the tools of analysis developed in Part Two and the background presented in Part One to several of the most urgent urban problems of the 1980s.

In the second edition, as in the first, my intention has been to present a unified thread of analysis useful in understanding a variety of urban phenomena and problems. I believe it is important, in a textbook, to present a coherent view of the subject. The price paid for the strategy adopted is that students are left with an inadequate sense of the richness and diversity of the urban economics literature. Thus, I have kept the book short, so that it can be supplemented with readings that present alternative viewpoints. Some suggestions for additional readings, with brief annotations, are listed at the end of each chapter.

This book is intended to be used as a core text in upper-division undergraduate courses in urban economics. It can also be used as a supplementary text in graduate-level urban economics courses. If desired, the book can also be used for supplementary reading in intermediate microeconomics courses. Chapters in Part Two systematically apply to an urban context most of the important topics in the microeconomic theories of production, consumer behavior, and equilibrium.

Any student who has mastered a modern microeconomics text should be able to understand the book without difficulty. With help from an instructor, students who have had only a one-semester introduction to microeconomics should also be able to use the book. High school algebra and diagrammatic analysis are used freely, but calculus is restricted to the Appendix. Students with an understanding of elementary calculus can follow the Appendix, but those without a calculus background should skip it.

In gathering material for the second edition, I have been impressed with the progress of urban economics since the first edition was published in 1972. Much new theoretical analysis has appeared, but most of it is too advanced for an introductory text. What is of fundamental importance is that every applied topic has been the subject of important new research during the 1970s. Poverty, housing, and other urban problems have by now been much better documented and analyzed than they had been when *Urban Economics* was first written. Thus, each chapter of Part Three has been substantially rewritten, partly to bring census data, etc., up to date, but mostly to incorporate results of recent research.

The book has been slightly reorganized for the second edition. Part One now consists of three chapters. Chapter 3, which is new, presents historical background on the sizes and spatial structures of urban areas. In Part Two, some rewriting has been undertaken to improve the presentation, but the major change is the removal of what was formerly Chapter 5 to the Appendix. In Part Three, Chapter 12 is new and presents welfare and government policy analysis of issues relating to sizes and spatial structures of urban areas.

In writing and rewriting this book I have of course drawn on the work of many scholars. I hope I have properly acknowledged my debt to them in the appropriate places. I have also learned much from students to whom I have taught urban economics at Johns Hopkins and Princeton. Many professors and students who used the first edition have kindly sent suggestions for the second edition. Most importantly, I would like to thank the following reviewers for their valuable suggestions:

> Gordon Bagby, University of Illinois, Urbana
> Jerald Barnard, University of Iowa
> Louis Cain, Loyola University, Chicago
> Leslie Daniels, Washington University, St. Louis
> John Gemello, San Francisco State University
> Vernon Henderson, Brown University
> David Marcinko, College of Saint Rose, New York
> John McDonald, University of Illinois, Chicago Circle
> Richard Muth, Stanford University
> James Prescott, Iowa State University
> Jon Sonstelie, University of California, Santa Barbara
> W. Edward Whitelaw, University of Oregon
> Anthony Yezer, George Washington University

Thomas Raubach provided assistance in updating the material in the first edition, and Arthur Sullivan provided helpful critiques of recent literature on urban problems. I am indebted to George Lobell of Scott, Foresman and Company for his efficiency and patience in every aspect of the revision. Annmarie Ritz Carney has typed this edition with her usual intelligence and skill.

Princeton, N.J.   Edwin S. Mills
January 1980

Contents

PART 2
THEORETICAL FOUNDATIONS   43

PART 3

URBAN PROBLEMS AND THE PUBLIC SECTOR   99

7

The Problem of Poverty   100

8

Housing, Slums, and Race   117

12

Government Policies Toward Urban Sizes and Structures   201

13

Government and Urban-Area Prospects   218

Appendix:

A Simplified Mathematical Model of Urban Structure   222

1
Basic Ideas and Historical Background

"WHAT ARE URBAN AREAS AND WHY DO THEY EXIST?" IS CER- tainly the most fundamental question an urban specialist can ask. Most people make intuitive distinctions between urban and rural, and between big cities and small towns. For many purposes, the intuitive distinctions are adequate. Nevertheless, it is worthwhile to start with some careful definitions and distinctions, because data sources depend on them. The second part of the question is much harder to answer than the first, and answers given by scholars in one academic discipline are likely to be disputed by scholars in other disciplines. But ideas about the reasons for the existence of urban areas color all thoughts about their organization and functions, and about the causes and cures of their problems. It is important to ask to what extent economic concepts can account for the existence of urban areas. Then, after a review in the rest of Part One of historical and statistical trends in urbanization and urban size and structure, it will be possible to proceed to the theoretical analysis presented in Part Two.

1

The Nature of Urban Areas

WHAT ARE URBAN AREAS?

There are many urban concepts: town, city, metropolitan area, and megalopolis are examples. Some have legal definitions. Towns, municipalities, and cities are built-up areas designated as political subdivisions by states, provinces, or national governments. Practices in designating urban government jurisdictions vary greatly from country to country and, in the United States, from state to state. What is designated a city in one country or state may be designated a town in another. More important, the part of an urban area included in a city or other political subdivision varies from place to place and from time to time. In 1970, the city of Boston contained only 23 percent of the 2.8 million people in the metropolitan area, whereas the city of Austin contained 85 percent of the 295,000 people in its metropolitan area. In U.S. metropolitan areas, the largest city contains only about half the residents of the metropolitan area on the average. In other countries, the tendency is to expand city boundaries as the metropolitan area expands so that the city includes all or nearly all of the metropolitan area.

To the political scientist studying local government, the legal definitions of local government jurisdictions are of primary importance. They are also important to the economist studying economic aspects of local government. Much of Chapter 10 is about causes and effects of arrangements of local government jurisdictions. But local government jurisdictions were chosen largely for historical and political reasons, and they have little to do with the economist's notion of an urban area. They are therefore of secondary concern in urban economics.

Much more fundamental for urban economists than legal designations is variability in population and employment density from one place to another. A country's **average population density** is the ratio of its population to its land area. In 1970, average population density was about 57 people per square mile in the United States. It is conceivable that every square mile in the country might have about the same number of residents. The beginning of urban economics is the observation that population density varies enormously from place to place.

In 1970, there were about 250 places in the United States where population density reached extremely high levels relative to the average and relative to levels a few miles away. In New York City, to take the most dramatic example, population density was more than 26,000 people per square mile. Fifty miles away, in Sussex County, New Jersey, it was 147. A less dramatic, but instructive, example is Wichita, Kansas. In 1970, its population density was 3197 people per square mile. The remainder of Sedgwick County, which contains Wichita, had a population density of 81. The adjoining county of Kingman had a density of only 10. New York and Wichita are clearly urban areas. Such places contain more than half the country's population and constitute the popular image of a metropolitan area. But they do not exhaust the list of urban areas. There are hundreds of small cities and towns many of whose population densities exceed those of surrounding rural areas by factors of 50 or 100. They are also urban areas.

Thus, the fundamental and generic definition of an **urban area** is a place with a much higher population density than elsewhere. At least a few urban areas have existed since the beginning of recorded history, and they are now found in every country in the world. For some purposes, this crude definition is adequate. But for purposes of data collection and analysis, more careful definitions are needed.

The generic definition of an urban area is a relative concept. A place whose population density is high relative to average density in one region or country might not be high relative to the density in another region or country. To take an extreme example, the average population density in Japan was 755 people per square mile in 1970. That is higher than the densities of many metropolitan areas in the United States. Thus, a minimum density that would define an urban area would need to be higher in Japan than in the U.S. Similar problems arise within the United States. The average population density in the Phoenix metropolitan area is less than one third that of the entire state of New York. Thus, urban areas cannot be defined exclusively by population density.

To be designated urban, a place must have not only a minimum density but also a minimum total population. An isolated half-acre lot lived on by a trapper and his family in Alaska may have as great a density as many urban areas, but no one would call it a one-family urban area. There are many small places with densities that are high relative to surrounding areas. Official statistics necessarily employ an arbitrary population cutoff in defining urban areas, usually between 2500 and 25,000.

A final problem arises in counting urban areas. As urban areas grow, they frequently come to encompass places that were formerly separate urban areas. Metropolitan areas come to encompass what were formerly separate small towns. On a larger scale, metropolitan areas gradually grow together. The New York–Northeastern New Jersey area encompasses several metropolitan areas, and the Chicago–Gary area encompasses two metropolitan areas. Such amalgamations give rise to no problems in counting the urban population, but they do cause problems in counting the number of urban areas. When metropolitan areas grow together, the U.S. Census Bureau wisely presents data separately for each metropolitan area, so that users can put the data together as they please. Then the Census Bureau also uses its criteria as to what metropolitan areas are sufficiently integrated so that they can be thought of as one large area, and it publishes the combined data. For example, several metropolitan areas across the Hudson River from New York are closely related to the New York metropolitan area, although they are in some ways distinct.

A NOTE ON STATISTICAL DATA

Much of the U.S. data available to the urban economist, and most of that which is comparable among urban areas on a nationwide basis, comes from the U.S. censuses of population and housing, manufacturers, business, and government. Every student of urban economics should get to know these data sources. Despite their many inadequacies, there are none better in the world.

Most U.S. federal government data pertaining to urban areas are now based on the same set of definitions regarding the area covered. But the federal government distinguishes among several urban concepts, depending on the way data became available and the purposes for which measures are intended.

An **urban place** is any concentration, usually in an incorporated town, borough, or city, of at least 2500 people. But since an urban place is usually defined by political boundaries, it does not correspond to the economist's notion of an urban area. Data pertaining to urban places are therefore of relatively little value to the urban economist. In fact, an urban area usually contains many urban places. In the 1970 U.S. census of population, there were 7062 urban places containing 149 million people, about 73 percent of the country's population of 203 million at that time.

The concept that corresponds to the economist's notion of an urban area is called an **urbanized area** by the federal government. An urbanized area consists of one central city (or sometimes two) of at least 50,000 residents, and the surrounding closely settled area. The urbanized area is thus the physical city, defined without regard for political boundaries. In 1970, the U.S. census identified 246 urbanized areas in the United States. They contained 118 million people, or 58 percent of the country's population.

A geographically more inclusive concept is the **standard metropolitan statistical area**, or SMSA. An SMSA includes one central city (or possibly two) of at least 50,000 residents, and one or more contiguous counties that are metropolitan in character, as determined by the percentage of the labor force that is nonagricultural and by the amount of commuting between the county and the city. Thus SMSAs do not include parts of counties. Although the list of SMSAs is virtually the same as the list of urbanized areas, the SMSAs include nonurbanized parts of contiguous metropolitan counties. Not surprisingly, SMSAs have somewhat greater populations than urbanized areas and much more land. In 1970, 139 million people, 69 percent of the country's population, lived in 243 SMSAs —18 percent more people than in urbanized areas. But the SMSAs contained 11 times as much land. Some SMSA counties, particularly in the west, contain large amounts of land, although their nonurbanized parts contain few people. A dramatic example is the San Bernardino SMSA in California, which extends through the desert to the eastern boundary of the state.

The urbanized area corresponds much more closely to the generic concept of an urban area than does the SMSA. Then why should an economist be interested in SMSA data? The answer is easy: more data are available for SMSAs than for urbanized areas, because some data become available by county and can therefore be put together for SMSAs, but not for urbanized areas.

The largest urban concept recognized by the federal government is the **standard consolidated statistical area**, or SCSA, which consists of several contiguous SMSAs. By the mid-1970s, the government had recognized 13 SCSAs. The largest were the New York–New Jersey–Connecticut and Los Angeles–Long Beach–Anaheim SCSAs, which contained 17.2 million and 10.2 million people in 1974. The smallest were the Cincinnati–Hamilton and Milwaukee–Racine SCSAs, each containing 1.6 million people. The largest SCSAs are larger than the largest SMSAs, but many SMSAs are larger than the smallest SCSAs.

The term **megalopolis** is sometimes applied to the part of the eastern seaboard from Boston to Washington or Richmond. It is also applied to the Pacific coast of Japan from Tokyo to Osaka and to the stretch of England from London to Manchester. The term is popular and somewhat descriptive, but it is unofficial. It is also somewhat unreal. The three megalopolises do indeed contain many people. The Japanese megalopolis is the largest of the three, with more than 40 million residents. Yet the term is unreal in that the metropolitan areas within a megalopolis are not united by the usual criteria of commuting from one to another. It is also unreal in that each of the three megalopolises, especially the U.S. one, contains large amounts of rural land.

That the urbanized area is a significant urban concept is indicated by overall density data. In 1970, population density for the United States was 57 people per square mile. In urbanized areas it was 3376. By contrast, in SMSAs it was 360.

In this book the term **urban area** refers generically to places of high population density. The term **city** refers to the legal city. The terms **urban place, urbanized area, SMSA,** and **SCSA** refer to the concepts used in federal government data sources.

WHY URBAN AREAS?

If the urban area is defined by dramatically high population densities relative to those found elsewhere, the next question is, "Why do we have urban areas?" There is no single answer. Historians, geographers, sociologists, political scientists, and economists tend to emphasize different sets of causes in explaining why urban areas exist. We can begin with the proposition that urban areas exist because people have found it advantageous to carry on various activities in a spatially concentrated fashion.

Most of the differences of opinion about the reasons for urban areas result from the fact that these activities may be of very different kinds: military activities, religious practice or religion administration, government, and private production and distribution of goods and services. At various times in history, many urban areas had defense as their major function. It was simply more economical and effective to defend a large group of people if they were spatially concentrated. The word "was" is used intentionally, because weapons technology in the nuclear age may make it easier to defend a dispersed than a concentrated population. In such urban areas, people commuted out of the city to carry on the predominant economic activity, farming. Some urban areas began as cathedral towns or centers for religion administration. Finally, some cities grew because they were seats of civil government. Washington, D.C., is the most obvious U.S. example.

However, most urban areas do not owe their existence or size to military, religious, or governmental activities. In countries where economic decisions are mainly privately made, *the sizes of most urban areas are mainly determined by market forces.* Households have found that income and employment opportunities, and prices and availability of consumer goods, are more favorable in urban than in other areas. And business firms have found that returns are higher on investments made in urban than in rural areas.

In the United States, seats of government are almost the only substantial exceptions to the determination of urban sizes by market forces. Washington, D.C., is a clear exception. So, to some extent, are most state capitals. But most state capitals were intentionally located in small towns away from major centers, and many have remained small towns. European national capitals, such as London, Paris, and Rome, are harder to classify. They certainly owe part of their size to their being seats of government. But the opposite is also true. They were made seats of government partly because they were major cities.

People unsympathetic to economic location theory sometimes claim that historical, rather than economic, forces have determined the locations of major urban areas. They claim, for example, that a certain urban area is where it is because some settlers happened to land there first. But this idea assumes that settlers or other founders were unresponsive to the advantages and disadvantages of alternative locations. Much more important, the map is dotted with places where settlers happened to settle. Some became major urban centers, but most remained just dots on the map, despite elaborate local plans and efforts to make them metropolitan centers. Those that developed into major centers did so because their economic potential induced thousands of people and institutions to decide to work, live, and produce there. The best assumption is that economic factors affect location decisions to about the same extent that they affect other types of decisions, such as pricing by firms and demand for goods and services by consumers. Employers who locate in wrong places find that they cannot compete for employees or customers. Workers who make poor locational choices find that their living standards suffer.

Scale Economies

How do market forces generate urban areas? We have said that most urban areas arise mainly because of the economic advantages of large-scale activities. The economist's term for this phenomenon is **indivisibilities** or, more generally, **scale economies.** General price theory says that a firm's production function displays scale economies if a proportionate change in all inputs leads to a greater proportionate change in output. In this book we say that scale economies exist at any level of output at which, with all input prices constant, long-run average total cost is falling. Thus, **diseconomies** of scale exist if long-run average cost is rising.

What is the relationship between scale economies and spatial concentration? Economists usually assume that most scale economies are realized within a plant, which is usually a contiguous set of production facilities. But even if they are contiguous, they may be more or less concentrated; that is, the ratios of capital or other inputs to land may be high or low. Which ratio entails lower costs?

In some cases, the mechanism by which proximity provides scale economies is clear. When a raw material is subject to several processing stages, greater spatial separation of the stages entails more movement of the material. This is particularly significant for cases where material must be at extreme temperatures during processing: to move molten steel over substantial distances would be highly impractical. But contiguity does not always seem to be a requirement for scale economies. It is easy to imagine that a firm with two plants might find it economical to provide a service facility, such as maintenance, for its plants, and that it might therefore have lower average costs than a firm with one plant that either bought maintenance services from another firm or produced them itself. Although examples are easy to come by, economists have to date paid relatively little attention to the spatial aspects of scale economies.

Scale economies are important for the existence of urban areas. Consider a simple model of a country in which there are no scale economies. In the economy a finite, but possibly large, number of different goods is produced. Inputs in each industry are: the outputs of other industries; several kinds of labor, which are mobile; and a single nonproduced natural resource, which is distributed uniformly over the land. Suppose that all input and output markets are competitive, and that there are neither economies nor diseconomies of scale at any output in any industry. Thus production can take place on however small a scale is necessary to meet local demands. There is no loss of efficiency, so no need for transportation from one area to another. Each small area would contain the same mix of production and the same mix of people with different tastes. Markets would be in equilibrium because population and employment densities were uniform, with all demands satisfied by local production.

The density of population or employment in any one area could not be greater than elsewhere: competition for land in a high-density area would drive its land values above the land values in areas of lower density, so households and businesses in the high-density area would move to an area of lower density with lower land costs. They would not be held back by lower production costs or lower prices of consumer goods and services resulting from economies of scale in the high-density area.

The crux of the argument here is that, if there are no scale economies, production can take place on a very small scale near each consuming location, and population and production density—and land values—will thus be uniform.

Now change the model by supposing that one industry *(S)* does have scale economies, at least at small outputs. Now it pays for a firm to concentrate spatially the production of industry *S* in a large plant in order to obtain a lower average cost. The amount produced in one place depends on the extent of the scale economies, on the nature of demand, and on transportation cost. In addition, workers in industry *S* live near their place of work to avoid commuting costs. Moreover, it is advantageous to other industries—without scale economies—to locate nearby if they sell their products to industry *S* or to its employees. It is also advantageous to their employees to live nearby. Again, the same advantages apply to industries selling to these industries and their employees, and so on.

The process produces a spatial concentration of economic activity that legitimately can be called an urban area. Although the description of the process makes it appear that everything might end up in one urban area, at some size the advantages of proximity are balanced by high transportation and land costs, and the urban area's growth ceases. Thus, there will be several urban areas, each of which has one firm of industry *S*. In addition, the urban areas do not trade with each other, although industry *S* may export its output to the surrounding countryside. Each urban area satisfies its own demands for the product of industry *S* and for the products of all industries without scale economies. So there is as yet no specialization among urban areas.

The foregoing description is perhaps the simplest model of urban areas. Such models, based on scale economies, are referred to as **central place theory,** which has had a long and distinguished history. (One of the curiosities of that history is that, until after World War II, most contributions were made by German-speaking writers, and central place theory was practically unknown to English-speaking economists. August Lösch, the father of modern location theory, was the most important contributor. The English translation of his *The Economics of Location,* published in 1954, did a great deal to familiarize English-speaking economists with central place theory.)

Specialization of a kind results from the next step toward reality in our model. Economists tend to think of scale economies mainly in manufacturing. In terms of absolute scale, that may be appropriate. In a manufacturing plant, scale economies may not be exhausted until employment numbers in the hundreds. But scale economies are pervasive in all industries, at least at low levels of output. In retailing, wholesaling, and services, scale economies also exist, but may be exhausted when employment reaches only a dozen or a few dozen. It is not the absolute scale at which economies are exhausted, but rather *the scale relative to market demand* which determines whether there can be one, two, or a hundred firms in an industry. Many service industries, for example, are highly specialized and have extremely low per capita demands. Scale economies may prevent such industries from locating in towns and small cities, or may permit so few firms that they have substantial monopoly power. Thus, large urban areas provide specialized cultural, legal, medical, financial, and other services that are not available in small urban areas.

The fact that scale economies exist in all industries rather than in just one, and that scale economies may be exhausted at different levels of output or employment in different industries, greatly enriches our hypothetical landscape. All industries tend to concentrate spatially to some extent, and transportation costs can be kept low if they concentrate near each other. Thus, it is now possible to account for variety among urban area sizes, and for a certain kind of trade between large and small urban areas. The small urban areas would contain only those industries whose scale economies were exhausted by the demands of small populations. The larger urban areas would contain, in addition to small-scale industries, industries whose scale economies were exhausted only by the demands of a larger population. The larger urban areas would supply such products not only to their own residents but also to residents of small urban areas. The largest urban areas would contain all types of industries, and would be the only urban areas to contain those industries whose scale economies required the demands of the largest population to exhaust them.

Thus, urban areas of a given size would export to urban areas of smaller sizes, but there would be no other kind of trade between urban areas. In particular, it is not yet possible to account for mutual trade, in which one urban area both exports to and imports from another.

Lösch used a model of the foregoing kind to explain not only a hierarchy of urban area sizes, but also their spatial distribution. But his results are based on an assumption that, for our purposes here, is unduly restrictive. He assumed each industry's average cost curve to be L-shaped, which means that no output can be produced below a certain level, at any cost, and that there are no scale economies at outputs above that level. Such a model cannot accommodate the fact that some goods and services are produced in both large and small urban areas, but are produced on a larger scale or in more competitive industries in large urban areas than they are in small urban areas.

Agglomeration Economies

So far, the existence of urban areas has been explained entirely in terms of scale economies in production, a concept that economists understand relatively well. Urban economists also often refer to the **agglomeration economies** of urban areas. In part they mean by the term the advantages of spatial concentration resulting from scale economies. Of course, it must be remembered that scale economies exist not only in the private sector, but also in mixed public/private or regulated sectors, such as transportation, communication, and public utilities. Also, scale economies may exist in such public-sector activities as education, police protection, water supply, and waste disposal.

Urban economists also use the term "agglomeration economies" to refer to the advantages of spatial concentration that result from the scale of an entire urban area but not from the scale of a particular firm. The most important of such agglomeration economies is statistical in nature, and is an application of the law of large numbers. Sales of outputs and purchases of inputs fluctuate in many firms and industries for random, seasonal, cyclical, and secular reasons. To the extent that fluctuations are imperfectly correlated among employers, an urban area with many employers can provide more nearly full employment of its labor force than can an urban area with few employers. Likewise, a firm with many buyers whose demand fluctuations are uncorrelated will have proportionately less variability in its sales than a firm with few buyers. It can therefore hold smaller inventories and employ smoother production scheduling.

A second agglomeration economy is complementarity in labor supply and in production. Different kinds of labor are to some extent supplied in fixed proportions. Industries with large demands for female workers are attracted to areas where women live because of their husbands' workplaces. Complementarity in production works the same way. If two commodities can be produced more cheaply together than separately, then users of both commodities will be attracted to areas where they are produced.

A third agglomeration economy has been emphasized by Jane Jacobs. Although her argument is complex, it is based on the contention that spatial concentration of large groups of people permits a great deal of personal interaction, which in turn generates new ideas, products, and processes. She views urban areas generally as the progressive and innovative sector of society. Hers is a fascinating theory, which ties in with economists' interest in sources of technical progress, and deserves careful attention.

Other types of agglomeration economies have been claimed, but on analysis they usually turn out to be special cases of the mechanisms just described.

Comparative Advantage

The foregoing analysis has assumed a single, uniformly distributed, natural resource. It accounts for large and small urban areas, but for trade between urban areas of only a very special kind. Thus the last step in our argument is to recognize that regions have **comparative advantage** for certain products because of the variability of available natural resources. Land is a natural resource used in all economic activity, but its qualities vary from place to place. Although fertility is not important for most urban activities, other qualities are, such as drainage, grade, and the nature of subsoil formations.

In addition, most manufacturing and to some extent other industries directly or indirectly process mineral or other natural resources. The uneven occurrence of such resources produces regional comparative advantage for particular products. A characteristic of much technical progress is the increase in the number of processing stages to which natural resources are subjected. Presumably, proximity to the natural resource thereby becomes gradually less important relative to the other locational considerations already discussed. At the same time, increases in population and per capita income make greater demands on certain replenishable natural resources, especially air and water. The availability of pure air and water becomes increasingly important as a determinant of comparative advantage.

A final factor in comparative advantage is climate. Temperature and humidity affect heating, air conditioning, and construction costs. Rainfall affects drainage and water supply in complex ways, but is otherwise unimportant. Snowfall makes most kinds of transportation expensive, slow, and dangerous.

There is an obvious similarity between the factors that determine comparative advantages among urban areas and those that determine comparative advantages among countries. International trade specialists usually list differences in technology, costs and skills of labor, and costs and availability of capital, in addition to natural resources, as determinants of international comparative advantage. The state of technology obviously varies much less within than between countries. Labor is obviously much more mobile within than between countries. Within the United States, regional differences in wage rates and education of the labor force have become smaller through time. But they are not negligible, and they have persisted for long periods. Much existing physical capital is nearly immobile—although there are notable exceptions, such as airplanes and trucks. Investment of new capital, however, responds quickly to regional differences in rates of return, and such differences are therefore small in a growing economy. Thus, differences in natural resources are much more important, relative to other factors, in determining the comparative advantage of regions within a country than among countries.

Another determinant of urban size and location is proximity to economical interurban transportation. The transportation way may be manmade—a road, railroad, or airport, for example—or it may be of natural origin—a navigable river or an ocean port. The argument is that, other things being equal, goods for interurban shipment are produced near interurban transportation terminals to avoid extra unloading and reloading of goods. This argument must be used with care, however. Transportation access is a determinant of urban area size and location if there is some reason for interurban trade, but is not itself a reason for interurban trade. In the absence of regional comparative advantage or other reasons for interurban trade, proximity to interurban transportation routes would be irrelevant. In fact, *almost all large U.S. urban areas are located on navigable waterways,* evidence not only that waterways are valuable interurban trade routes, but also that comparative advantage is important. Furthermore, international trade resulting from international comparative advantage provides a reason for urban areas to be at ports of entry and exit. Most large urban areas on the eastern seaboard of the United States owe their prominence to international comparative advantage.

Up to this point, discussion of natural resources has been concerned with their effects on comparative advantage in production. But natural resources may have direct effects on people's welfare, and hence, indirect effects on production costs. Suppose that climate, topography, and other natural conditions cause workers and their families to prefer residence in some areas to residence in others. Then, workers would migrate until their welfare was the same in each location, making labor costs lower in the more desirable areas and leading production to concentrate there. It has been claimed by Perloff that such **amenity resources** have become increasingly important in recent decades, as industry has become less tied to locations near natural resources and therefore more "footloose." Parts of the country frequently claimed to have the best amenity resources are in the "sunbelt" stretching from Florida to Southern California. Much of the sunbelt has indeed grown rapidly since World War II, especially during the 1970s. Amenity resources can also help to account for the dispersed structure of Los Angeles and other sunbelt metropolitan areas. The amenity resources there are presumably climate, topography, and, in much of the sunbelt, proximity to ocean beaches. Such amenities pervade sunbelt metropolitan areas and generate no need for urban areas with high employment and residential densities.

To what extent does regional comparative advantage pertain to production and to what extent is it explained by effects on people's welfare through amenities available only in certain places? To answer this question, it would be necessary to know to what extent sunbelt firms have lower costs than they would have elsewhere because of lower costs of labor with given qualifications, and to what extent their costs are lower because of lower nonlabor costs. Costs of labor with given educational attainment and experience are lower in the sunbelt than in other regions of the country. Presumably, amenities are one reason for the situation, but there are probably others.

In summary, regional comparative advantages occur for a variety of reasons, most of which are related to natural resources. Regional comparative advantage accounts for mutual interurban trade, and for the tendency of major urban areas to be located near economical interurban transportation.

LIMITS TO URBAN SIZE

So far the discussion has centered on the reasons for the existence of urban areas. Only incidentally have the limits to the size of large urban areas been mentioned. One limit to urban area size is the demand for the products in which it specializes. In other words, *an urban area's size may be limited by the demand for its exports.* Another limit is the natural resources which provide its comparative advantage; if they run out, the comparative advantage disappears. Even if they are not depleted, their rate of extraction may be subject to diminishing returns. Alternatively, if natural resources are not extracted, they may be subject to congestion. Only so many ships can be handled economically by a port, and only so many people can live comfortably in the Los Angeles basin. Even replenishable resources, such as clean air and water, are limited in supply—as we are now becoming painfully aware—and if they are overused, they deteriorate.

Some writers have speculated that there is also an **intrinsic limit** to urban size in the sense that the entire urban area is subject to diminishing returns, at least beyond some point. Suppose that an entire urban area is in equilibrium. No change in the location or level of any activity can increase either consumer welfare or producer profits. Suppose that all industries, including local transportation, have constant returns to scale at outputs greater than those that exist. Suppose the output of each industry in the urban area is to be doubled. Can that be done by doubling the urban area's population and the labor and other inputs in each industry? To double inputs in all industries efficiently requires that floors be added to some buildings and that others be demolished to make way for increased transportation.

Doubling inputs in the transportation system produces twice as many passenger-miles and ton-miles of transportation services. However, transportation per person and per ton of output will be unchanged, since population and output have also doubled. Is this enough transportation for the larger urban area? The land area has doubled, so it seems reasonable to assume that trip lengths must increase. If so, transportation must grow faster than the urban area's population, and real income and output per capita must fall. Whether trip lengths increase—and diminishing returns therefore occur—depends on precisely how spatial arrangements change as urban areas grow. At present, too little is known to decide whether or not increased trip lengths are a significant cause of diminishing returns to urban size. But the theoretical case seems persuasive.

Even if this analysis is correct, it does not imply that traffic congestion is inevitably worse in large than in small urban areas. Some congestion is desirable in large urban areas, as is explained in Chapter 11. In addition, some congestion occurs in large urban areas because, as traffic increases, not enough land is taken from buildings and other uses to handle the increased transportation without increased congestion. But failure to tear down buildings for more transportation is not perfidy on the part of public officials. It results from the fact that, once buildings have been put in place, it is often prohibitively expensive to tear them down. Thus, one reason for downtown congestion is the historical fact that the land-use decisions for structures and transportation were made in an earlier era when transportation needs were slight.

This fact illustrates a common characteristic of urban problems. Important aspects of many problems can be understood by long-run equilibrium analysis. But many are made more serious and complex by the fact that *structures have long lives, and thus, urban spatial relationships are strongly influenced by decisions made long ago.*

SUMMARY

The subject matter of urban economics is the generic urban area, not the legal central city or other local government jurisdiction. The basic characteristics of urban areas are high population densities, high ratios of other inputs to land, and high land values.

Urban areas exist because of the advantages of scale and proximity in the production and exchange of goods and services. Economies of scale in manufacturing and in other productive activities are the most important reasons for urban areas. Other agglomeration economies result from statistical averaging of fluctuations, from complementarity in labor supply and production, and from the rapid generation and spread of new ideas that can occur in large urban concentrations. The sizes and locations of urban areas are also affected by regional comparative advantage resulting from uneven distribution of natural resources and from locations of economical interregional transportation networks.

Theoretical analysis suggests that the limit to the size of an urban area may be set by limits on demands for products produced in the urban area or from decreasing returns to production and transportation activities in the urban area.

QUESTIONS AND PROBLEMS

1. Suppose there are economies of large-scale production so that large urban areas export to small urban areas, but not vice versa. How can small urban areas pay for their imports?

2. From 1950 to 1970, most of the rapidly growing U.S. metropolitan areas were near the edges of the country, with easy access to ocean transportation (this includes the Great Lakes ports). How do you explain this in a country in which international trade is relatively unimportant?

3. Commuting times and distances are greater in large than in small urban areas. Is this evidence of diminishing returns in large urban areas?

4. Suppose urban areas produce just one commodity, X. Each urban area produces $x = AN^\alpha$ units, where N is the labor force in an urban area and A and $\alpha > 1$ are constants. Thus, there are increasing returns in producing a large amount of X in each urban area. But each urban area must supply X to the rural residents who live closer to it than to another urban area. Rural residents have a fixed density D, and each consumes a fixed amount $\bar{x}$ of X. If urban areas are too small, the advantages of large-scale production are missed; if they are too large, scale economies will be more than offset by the costs of transporting X from urban areas to rural consumers. Find the optimum size of each urban area. (Assume each unit-mile of transportation of X requires γ workers. The optimum-size urban area minimizes the sum of workers needed to produce and ship units of X.)

REFERENCES AND FURTHER READING

Martin Beckmann, *Location Theory*, 1968. *A short and elementary, but very abstract, statement of modern location theory.*

Jane Jacobs, *The Economy of Cities*, 1969. *A wise and perceptive essay by a non-economist on economic aspects of urban life.*

August Lösch, *The Economics of Location,* 1954. *Probably the most important contribution ever made to location theory. Very difficult in some places.*

Harvey Perloff and others, *Regions, Resources and Economic Growth,* 1960. *An influential study of the causes and consequences of differences in economic growth rates among regions of the U.S.*

U.S. Census Bureau, *Census of Population. Published for every year ending in zero. Presents the most complete urban data available anywhere. Provides careful definitions of concepts.*

VERY POOR COUNTRIES ARE, WITHOUT EXCEPTION, LARGELY agricultural, since food is the prime requirement for life. Economic development consists in part of the transfer of labor and other inputs from predominantly rural agriculture to the predominantly urban manufacturing and service industries. Economic growth is thus everywhere associated with urbanization. During the nineteenth century, rapid economic growth in Europe and North America resulted in rapid urbanization. The United States, having industrialized somewhat later than Western Europe, also lagged in urbanization. Much of Europe was highly urbanized by the early decades of the twentieth century. Since about 1925, even more rapid industrialization and urbanization have taken place in some countries in Asia and South America.

2

Urbanization and Economic Growth in the United States

Although the pattern of urbanization and economic growth has not differed greatly in the United States from that observed in Europe, its scale and speed have been as dramatic here as anywhere. During a period of less than two centuries, the United States was transformed from a rural and agricultural society into an urban and industrial society. Urbanization has been one of the most prominent, widely studied, and controversial trends throughout U.S. history. In this and the next chapter, the broad trends of urban growth and the sizes and structures of urban areas are discussed. The purpose of these chapters is to present a historical context for the analytical chapters that follow in Part Two and for the policy chapters in Part Three.

TABLE 2.1.   URBAN AND RURAL POPULATION OF THE COTERMINOUS UNITED STATES, 1790–1970 (POPULATION FIGURES IN MILLIONS)

Year	Total Population	Urban Population		Rural Population	
1790	3.9	0.2	5.1%	3.7	94.9%
1800	5.3	0.3	6.1	5.0	93.9
1810	7.2	0.5	7.3	6.7	92.7
1820	9.6	0.7	7.2	8.9	92.8
1830	12.9	1.1	8.8	11.7	91.2
1840	17.1	1.8	10.8	15.2	89.2
1850	23.2	3.5	15.3	19.6	84.7
1860	31.4	6.2	19.8	25.2	80.2
1870	38.6	9.9	25.7	28.7	74.3
1880	50.2	14.1	28.2	36.1	71.8
1890	63.0	22.1	35.1	40.9	64.9
1900	76.2	30.2	39.6	46.0	60.4
1910	92.2	42.1	45.6	50.2	54.4
1920	106.0	54.3	51.2	51.8	48.8
1930	123.2	69.2	56.1	54.0	43.9
1940	132.2	74.7	56.5	57.5	43.5
1950	151.3	90.1	59.6	61.2	40.4
1960	179.3	113.1	63.0	66.3	37.0
1970[a]	203.2	149.3	73.5	53.9	26.5

a) Based on new urban place definition; not comparable with earlier data. See the source for definitions.

Source: United States Censuses of Population, 1960 and 1970.

LONG-TERM TRENDS

The simplest statistical picture of the growth and urbanization of the U.S. population is presented in Table 2.1, which shows the growth of the urban and rural population from 1790, the time of the first U.S. census, to 1970. The urban population consists of people living in urban places. It was pointed out in Chapter 1 that most urban areas consist of many urban places, so the population of an urban place is not an indication of the size of an urban area. But the population of all urban places is the proper measure of the urban population of the entire country. It should be remembered that an urban place can contain as few as 2500 people, and urban places therefore include many villages and small towns.

Total U.S. population grew from 3.9 million in 1790 to more than 200 million in 1970. In 1790, only 5 percent of the country was urban, even under the inclusive measure reported in Table 2.1. In 1960, 63 percent was urban. Since 1950 the Census Bureau has used a new and somewhat broader definition of urban places that increases the urban percentages for 1950 and 1960 in Table 2.1 by about 7 percentage points. Only data based on the new definition are available in the 1970 U.S. census.

The percentage of the U.S. population that is urban has grown steadily from 1790 to 1970, with the exception of an insignificant drop between

1810 and 1820. But the country's total population has grown fast enough that the number of people in rural areas has also grown each decade, even though its percentage of the total population has declined. Indeed, the number of rural residents in 1960 exceeded the country's entire population in each census year up to 1900.

Table 2.1 also suggests the close historical relationship that has existed between urbanization and industrialization. Historians place the beginning of rapid U.S. industrialization at about 1840. Table 2.1 shows that, between 1790 and 1840, the urban percentage of the population increased by about 1.1 percentage points per decade. Between 1840 and 1930, the increase averaged about 5 percentage points per decade. Urbanization thus proceeded very rapidly during the second half of the nineteenth century and the early part of the twentieth century, when industrial employment and output were also increasing rapidly.

It is not widely appreciated that *urbanization has decelerated since about 1930.* Between 1930 and 1960 the percentage of the population that was urban increased by an average of only 2.3 percentage points per decade. Industrialization has become more widespread, and the growth rate of employment in manufacturing has slackened relative to that in other sectors. Also, despite the massive urbanization of society, rural areas are by no means drained of people. Even under the new urban place definition, more than 50 million people still live in rural areas. Another popular misconception is that most rural people live on farms. In 1970, the U.S. farm population was less than 10 million.

In the early years of U.S. history, the cities and towns in which the urban population lived were very small indeed. In 1790, only 62,000 people lived in the only two cities (New York and Philadelphia) whose populations exceeded 25,000. By 1840, three cities (New York, Baltimore, and New Orleans) had populations in excess of 100,000, but the three cities together contained little more than half a million people. In 1840, Chicago had fewer than 5000 people. During the last half of the nineteenth century, statistics on the growth of cities become difficult to interpret because of the common tendency to annex suburban areas to the central city. For example, between 1890 and 1900, New York City's population increased from 1.5 million to 3.4 million, mostly as a result of the consolidation of the five boroughs that now constitute the city. But by 1900, six cities (New York, Chicago, Philadelphia, Baltimore, St. Louis, and Boston) had at least half a million people each. Los Angeles, now the nation's second largest metropolitan area, had little more than 100,000 people.[1]

Employment data are fragmentary for the early years of the nation's

1.   All statistics in this paragraph are from the U.S. Census of Population, 1960.

Table 2.2.   INDUSTRIAL DISTRIBUTION OF GAINFUL WORKERS, 1820–1977
(EMPLOYMENT FIGURES IN THOUSANDS)

Year	Total	Agriculture		Manufacturing		Other and Not Allocated	
1820	2,880	2,070	71.9%	350[a]	12.2%	460	16.0%
1840	5,420	3,720	68.6	790[a]	14.6	910	16.8
1860	10,530	6,210	59.0	1,930[a]	18.3	2,390	22.7
1880	17,390	8,610	49.5	3,170	18.2	5,610	32.3
1900	29,070	10,710	36.8	6,340	21.8	12,020	41.3
1920	41,610	11,120	26.7	10,880	26.1	19,610	47.1
1940	45,070	8,449	18.7	10,650	23.7	25,951	57.6
1950	56,435	6,909	12.2	14,685	26.0	34,841	61.7
1960	64,639	4,257	6.6	17,513	27.1	42,869	66.3
1970	78,627	3,462	4.4	19,369	24.6	55,796	71.0
1977	90,546	3,244	3.6	19,555	21.6	67,747	74.8

a) Includes construction.

Sources: 1820–1920: *Historical Statistics of the United States.* 1940–1960: United States Census of Population, 1960. 1970, 1977: *Survey of Current Business,* 1971 and 1978.

history, but they make it possible to trace the rough outlines of the industrialization process. Table 2.2 shows the number of gainful workers in the total labor force and in agriculture and manufacturing for selected years from 1820 to 1977.

Table 2.2 shows vividly the transformation of the U.S. economy. Farm workers fell from 71.9 percent of all workers in 1820 to a mere 3.6 percent in 1977. Manufacturing workers increased from 12.2 percent to 21.6 percent during that period. It can be seen that, even in 1820, many rural people were nonfarm. In that year, as seen in Table 2.1, 92.8 percent of the population was rural, but only 71.9 percent of the workers were on farms. Table 2.2 also shows that the period of rapid industrialization was between about 1840 and 1920. During that period, the percentage of all workers employed in manufacturing increased by an average of 1.4 percentage points per decade. But between 1920 and 1960, the percentage of all workers in manufacturing hardly changed. By 1970, it had fallen below its 1920 value. (The 1940 figure is strongly influenced by the large amount of unemployment that still existed that year. The figures in Table 2.2 are workers, not labor force, and employment fell much more in manufacturing than in agriculture during the depression. Therefore, the 23.7 percent of the workers in manufacturing would be closer to the 1920 and 1970 percentages had there been full employment in 1940.)

Table 2.2 shows the magnitude of the agricultural revolution that has been in progress for fifty years. As a result of mechanization and other changes, productivity per farm worker has risen at an unprecedented rate. Despite the fact that food consumption has increased substantially, agricultural workers have decreased, not only as a percentage of all workers, but also in numbers. Between 1950 and 1970, about half the jobs in agriculture disappeared. Since the rural population grew or, under the new definition, remained about constant during the period, nonfarm people have become an increasingly large percentage of the rural population.

Provision of food has the highest priority in every society. A poor society must devote most of its labor force to production of food or of exports to get the foreign exchange needed to import food. But in wealthy societies, high productivity in agriculture and low income elasticities of demand for food free much of the labor force to produce other goods and services. In such societies, increases in agricultural productivity come from technical progress both in agriculture and in industry. In the United States, large increases in agricultural productivity have resulted from technical progress in the design and production of farm machinery, which is part of the manufacturing sector. The process of freeing workers from food production has gone much further in the United States than in other countries that produce enough food to nourish their population, and the United States is a large net exporter of agricultural products.

But nonagricultural workers can, and often do, find rural employment in manufacturing and other sectors. Rapid urbanization has occurred because manufacturing and other employers found it increasingly advantageous to locate in large population centers. Since about 1920 there has been a deceleration of growth in manufacturing employment. One consequence has been deceleration in the growth of urban areas. Another consequence has been that urban employment has grown more rapidly in other sectors.

RECENT TRENDS

SMSA Population

Much more accurate and comprehensive data regarding urbanization are available for the period since 1940. Most important has been publication by the Census Bureau of comprehensive demographic and economic data for SMSAs (see Table 2.3). These data confirm the observation that the populations of urban places and SMSAs are of similar magnitude. Some urban places are outside SMSAs, and some parts of each SMSA are rural. But there is a large overlap between SMSA and urban-place populations, and the two nonoverlapping groups approximately cancel out.

The SMSA data provide the best picture of the metropolitan character of the U.S. population. Table 2.3 shows that in 1975 almost three fourths of the U.S. population lived in metropolitan areas. This places the United States among the world's most urbanized countries. Almost certainly, the percentage of the population living in SMSAs will increase only slowly during the coming decades.

Table 2.3.   POPULATION OF THE UNITED STATES AND SMSAs, 1940–1975
(POPULATION FIGURES IN MILLIONS)

Year	U.S. Population	SMSA Population	SMSA Population as a Percentage of U.S. Population
1940	131.7	72.8	55.3%
1950	150.7	89.3	59.3
1960[a]	179.3	112.9	63.0
1970	203.2	139.4	68.6
1975[b]	213.1	156.1	73.3

a) 1960 and subsequent data include Alaska and Hawaii.
b) Estimate.

Sources: 1940–1970: U.S. Census of Population, 1970. 1975: Current Population Reports, series P-25, no. 709.

SMSA Employment

By and large, SMSAs are labor-market areas. Most people who work in an SMSA also live there, and vice versa. In fact, there is some commuting between SMSAs. Some people live in Gary and work in Chicago, and some people live in Newark and work in New York. It is for this reason that the Census Bureau has defined SCSAs. But there is relatively little commuting between SMSAs and non-SMSA areas. The number of workers employed in SMSAs is therefore about the same as the number of workers living in SMSAs. Another way to say this is to say that it is not necessary to distinguish workers by place of employment from workers by place of residence, although the distinction is crucial in discussing data on suburbanization (Chapter 3).

Table 2.4 shows U.S. and SMSA employment in 1950 and 1970 for 12 major industry groups. Aside from those who did not report the industry in which they were employed, the groups are exhaustive; that is, they include all workers. The names of the groups are self-explanatory. Not all SMSAs are included in Table 2.4, unlike Table 2.3. Table 2.4 includes only those SMSAs with at least 100,000 population. They should be called medium and large SMSAs, but for brevity they can be referred to as large SMSAs. In 1950, 151 of the 168 SMSAs were in this category; in 1970, it was 217 out of 243 SMSAs. The percentage of workers living in large SMSAs increased from 58.2 in 1950 to 69.6 in 1970. For each year, Table 2.4 shows the percentage distribution of total U.S. and large-SMSA employment by industry; it also shows the percentage of all workers found in large SMSAs in each industry.

For any industry and either year, the percentage figure in the last column of Table 2.4 exceeds the national total at the bottom of the table if, and only if, the percentage figure in the SMSA column exceeds the percentage figure in the U.S. column. In other words, if the percentage of

Table 2.4. INDUSTRY GROUPS OF EMPLOYED PERSONS: UNITED STATES AND SMSAs WITH AT LEAST 100,000 POPULATION, 1950 AND 1970 (EMPLOYMENT FIGURES IN THOUSANDS)

Industry	1950 U.S.		1950 SMSA		Percentage in SMSAs	1970 U.S.		1970 SMSA		Percentage in SMSAs
Agriculture, forestry, fisheries	7,034	12.5%	826	2.5%	11.7%	2,840	3.7%	782	1.5%	27.5%
Mining	931	1.6	251	0.8	27.0	631	0.8	240	0.5	38.0
Construction	3,458	6.1	2,004	6.1	58.0	4,572	6.0	2,978	5.6	65.1
Manufacturing	14,685	26.0	10,021	30.5	68.2	19,837	26.0	13,722	25.8	69.2
Transportation, communication, utilities	4,450	7.9	2,911	8.9	65.4	5,186	6.8	3,832	7.2	73.9
Wholesaling, retailing	10,507	18.6	6,834	20.8	65.0	15,373	20.1	11,026	20.7	71.7
Finance, insurance, real estate	1,920	3.4	1,508	4.6	78.5	3,838	5.0	3,129	5.9	81.5
Business and repair services	1,308	2.3	888	2.7	67.9	2,395	3.1	1,904	3.6	79.5
Personal services	3,465	6.1	2,154	6.6	62.2	3,537	4.6	2,356	4.4	66.6
Entertainment, recreation	493	0.9	382	1.2	77.5	631	0.8	492	0.9	78.0
Professional & related services	4,826	8.6	2,899	8.8	60.1	13,511	17.6	9,606	18.0	71.1
Public administration	2,514	4.5	1,727	5.3	68.7	4,202	5.5	3,175	6.0	75.6
Not reported[a]	843	1.5	435	1.3	51.6	na	na	na	na	na
Total	56,435	100.0%	32,840	100.1%	58.2%	76,553	100.0%	53,243	100.1%	69.6%

a) "Not reported" category not applicable to 1970 data.

Sources: United States Censuses of Population, 1950 and 1970.

the workers in a certain industry who are in large SMSAs exceeds that for all workers, then that industry's workers must constitute a larger percent of SMSA than of U.S. workers. For example, in 1950, 68.2 percent of manufacturing workers were in large SMSAs, which exceeds the 58.2 percent of all workers who were in large SMSAs. Therefore, manufacturing workers constitute a larger percentage of large SMSA workers, 30.5 percent, than of U.S. workers, 26.0 percent.

It should be expected that some industries are predominantly located in SMSAs, whereas others are predominantly outside SMSAs. In 1970, the percentage of workers living in large SMSAs ranged from less than 28 percent in agriculture, forestry, and fisheries to more than 81 percent in finance, insurance, and real estate. Although manufacturing is the largest employer in both the United States and in large SMSAs, it is not, contrary to popular belief, among the most highly urbanized industries by the measure in Table 2.4. In 1970, seven industries had larger percentages of their employment in large SMSAs than did manufacturing. Manufacturing was slightly less urbanized than total employment. Not surprisingly, agriculture, forestry, fisheries, and mining are the least urbanized industries, whereas the service industries are most urbanized.

If 1950 is compared with 1970, the percentage of total employment that was in large SMSAs rose from 58.2 to 69.6. Manufacturing employment fell from 30.5 percent of large-SMSA employment in 1950 to 25.8 percent in 1970. But the percentage of manufacturing employees who were in SMSAs rose slightly from 68.2 to 69.2. In percentage terms, the largest growth in both United States and large-SMSA employment was in service industries: finance, insurance, and real estate; business and repair services; professional services; and public administration. Not only did these industries grow rapidly; they also became increasingly urbanized. We now see clearly what is suggested by the data presented in the foregoing section on "Long-Term Trends": recent growth in SMSA employment has taken place to a considerable extent outside manufacturing.

The major lesson of Table 2.4 is that manufacturing and other industrial jobs (construction, transportation, communications, and utilities) are no longer the major sources of SMSA employment growth. A secondary lesson is that highly urbanized service industries are not only major sources of increased SMSA employment; they are also becoming more urbanized. The shift of employment toward services parallels the national trend, and results mainly from high income elasticities of demand and the slow growth of productivity in service industries. One reason for the increased urbanization of service industries is that they find it increasingly advantageous to locate near hospitals, medical laboratories, law courts, financial markets, and other institutions found mainly in large population centers. Another reason is that improved transportation and communication have increased the ability of service industries to provide services to customers whose residences are far away.

An anomaly in Table 2.4 is that the percentage of agricultural, forestry, and fishery employment in large SMSAs rose from 11.7 percent in 1950 to 27.5 percent in 1970. There was a smaller drop in large-SMSA than in U.S. employment in this sector, probably caused by three factors. First, land prices in the rural parts of SMSAs have probably risen relative to prices of other factors of production in agriculture, so SMSA agriculture became increasingly labor-intensive. Second, there was probably a tendency near population centers to substitute production of labor-intensive agricultural products. Third, nurseries are part of agriculture, and the rise in SMSA employment in agriculture probably reflects the growth of nurseries in suburbs.

SMSA Manufacturing Employment

Most U.S. federal government industrial statistics are now based on a consistent industrial classification scheme. The data in Table 2.4 are based on what is called the one-digit standard industrial classification (SIC) code. The next level of detail is the two-digit level. For example, all manufacturing industries are in one-digit groups two and three. Two-digit numbers are numbers from 20 to 39 that represent twenty more-detailed categories of manufacturing industries.[2] These two-digit groups are successively divided into three-, four-, five-, and seven-digit groups. For example, food processing is the two-digit manufacturing industry bearing the SIC code 20. Within the food-processing category, there are several three-digit industries, one of which is meat products, given the three-digit code 201. Within the three-digit meat products category, there are several four-digit industries, one of which is slaughterhouses, given the four-digit code 2011. Altogether there are 149 three-digit industries and 427 four-digit industries. There are also five- and seven-digit codes. Disclosure rules limit the detail that government agencies can publish. In addition, most five- and seven-digit data are too detailed for economists' purposes. Only at the two-digit level are comprehensive data available for large SMSAs.

Table 2.5 provides complete two-digit data for the largest industry, manufacturing. The table shows U.S. and large-SMSA employment data for all two-digit manufacturing industries for 1947 and 1972. The set of SMSAs included consists of those with at least 40,000 manufacturing employees. The set contains only about a third of the SMSAs included in Table 2.4.

It should not be surprising to find that some two-digit manufacturing

---

2. In 1963, a new two-digit industry (ordnance, with SIC code 19) was added, but it is not included in data discussed in this section.

Table 2.5.   MANUFACTURING EMPLOYMENT IN THE UNITED STATES AND IN LARGE SMSAs BY SIC INDUSTRY GROUPS, 1947 AND 1972 (EMPLOYMENT DATA IN THOUSANDS)

SIC Code	Industry	1947 Employment			1972 Employment		
		U.S.	SMSA	Percent- age in SMSAs	U.S.	SMSA	Percent- age in SMSAs
20	Food	1442	717	49.7%	1569	764	48.7%
21	Tobacco	112	33	29.5	66	4	6.1
22	Textiles	1233	384	31.1	953	327	34.3
23	Apparel	1082	759	70.1	1386	721	52.0
24	Lumber products	636	87	13.7	691	143	20.7
25	Furniture	322	158	49.1	462	219	47.4
26	Paper	450	207	46.0	633	300	47.4
27	Printing	715	511	71.5	1056	747	70.7
28	Chemicals	632	370	58.5	837	482	57.6
29	Petroleum refining	212	133	62.7	140	68	48.6
30	Rubber products	259	176	68.0	618	342	55.3
31	Leather	383	159	41.5	273	84	30.8
32	Stone, clay, glass products	462	203	43.9	623	305	49.0
33	Primary metals	1157	839	72.5	1143	727	63.6
34	Fabricated metals	971	698	71.9	1493	1001	67.0
35	Nonelectrical machinery	1545	1018	65.9	1828	1107	60.6
36	Electrical machinery	801	614	76.7	1662	974	58.6
37	Transportation equipment	1182	901	76.2	1719	747	43.5
38	Instruments	232	184	79.3	454	257	56.6
39	Miscellaneous	464	339	73.1	446	296	66.4
		14,292	8490	59.4	18,034	9615	53.3

Sources: Compiled from data in the U.S. Censuses of Manufacturers, 1947 and 1972. Source withheld data for a small number of entries.

industries are much more urbanized than others. In 1972, large-SMSA employment ranged from a low of 6.1 percent of total employment in tobacco products to a high of 70.7 percent in printing. Generally, the least urbanized industries are those whose major material inputs originate in rural areas. Food processing, tobacco products, textiles, lumber products, furniture, paper, chemicals, petroleum refining, and leather, stone, clay, and glass products fall in this category. The most urbanized industries tend to be those in which material inputs have already gone through several processing stages. For example, the printing industry buys one of its major inputs from the paper industry, which has already processed the raw materials. Other industries in this category are machinery and instruments.

It is not surprising that industries that process materials grown in or extracted from the ground tend to locate near the predominantly rural sources of such materials. Industries that mainly process the products of other industries tend to locate near centers of population where they find their customers and their labor force.

Table 2.5 shows a drop of 6 points in the percentage of manufacturing employment in large SMSAs. This finding is in contrast with Table 2.4, which shows an increase in the percentage of manufacturing employment in large SMSAs. Neither the years nor the SMSAs are the same in the two tables. Table 2.4, which represents the larger set of SMSAs, shows that the percentage of manufacturing employment that is in SMSAs has been stagnant, while the percentage of the population in SMSAs has grown. The contrast between Tables 2.4 and 2.5 shows a dramatic shift of manufacturing from large to smaller SMSAs.

If changes in urbanization among particular two-digit industries are considered, an interesting pattern emerges. The percentage of employment that was in large SMSAs fell in most two-digit industries and in those employing most manufacturing workers. The percentage fell in 16 of the 20 two-digit industries. In 1947, the 16 industries employed 89.6 percent of manufacturing workers in large SMSAs and 80.5 percent of manufacturing workers in the country. Furthermore, the percentage decreases are much larger in the industries that became less urbanized than in industries that became more urbanized.

How can it happen that most manufacturing industries became substantially less urbanized at a time when the total changed relatively little? This apparent paradox occurs frequently in economic statistics, and it is worthwhile to explore it. Although it did not happen, it is logically possible for urbanization to decrease in every manufacturing industry at a time when urbanization increases in total manufacturing employment. An example will make the phenomenon clear. Suppose a country has two industries, *A* and *B*, and that SMSA and total employment data for years one and two are as shown in Table 2.6. Between years one and two, urbanization decreased from 80 percent to 71 percent in industry *A* and from 20 percent to 7 percent in industry *B*. Yet urbanization of total employment increased from 50 percent to 52 percent. This peculiar pattern is made possible by a shift in employment in the direction of the more highly urbanized industry. Thus, even though a smaller percentage of workers is in SMSAs in year two than in year one in each industry, the percentage of all workers in SMSAs has increased because the more urbanized industry employs a larger percentage of all workers in year two than in year one.

A less extreme form of the phenomenon is illustrated in Table 2.5. In 1947, 39.7 percent of manufacturing employees were in two-digit industries whose urbanization was below the national average of 59.4 percent. By 1972 these particular industries employed only 33.9 percent of manufacturing employees. Thus, as in the example of Table 2.6, manufacturing employment has shifted in the direction of relatively urbanized two-digit industries.

So much for the apparent statistical paradox. Why did employment shift toward the more highly urbanized industries? The answer involves a

Table 2.6.   INCREASING/DECREASING URBANIZATION

Industry	Year One			Year Two		
	National Employment	SMSA Employment	Percentage in SMSA	National Employment	SMSA Employment	Percentage in SMSA
A	25	20	80%	35	25	71%
B	25	5	20	15	1	7
Totals	50	25	50	50	26	52

certain amount of guessing, but appears to be as follows. Technical change is pervasive and rapid in manufacturing. An inevitable characteristic of technical progress is an increase in the number of processing stages through which raw materials go before they reach the final consumer. Indeed, the Industrial Revolution itself imposed the factory between the farmer as producer and the farmer as consumer. And current technical change continues to create further stages of raw-material processing. The greater is the number of processing stages, the greater is the number of workers who will be found in those two-digit industries representing later processing stages. But, as has been seen, industries engaged in later stages of processing are precisely those that are not tied to location near predominantly rural sources of raw materials.

Increased fabrication of raw materials explains the shift of employment toward urbanized two-digit industries, but it does not explain the decreased urbanization of these industries. All two-digit industries have substantial employment outside urban areas. There is no reason to expect that the percentage of employment in large SMSAs will remain constant in any industry. But the particular pattern of decreased urbanization of the most highly urbanized industries calls for study and explanation.

There are of course special explanations for the changes in particular industries. The decreased urbanization of the textile industry is part of the migration of that industry from New England to predominantly rural parts of the South. The movement has been extensively studied. Decreased urbanization in the apparel industry is partly explained by the movement of that industry out of New York City. There are undoubtedly reasons that are peculiar to other industries. But it would be interesting to know the importance of factors that are common to most industries.

The pattern observed in this section is one of rather modest increases since World War II in the percentages of population, total employment, and manufacturing employment found in SMSAs. But there is evidence in all three categories of slowing down in urbanization. Nobody knows what future censuses will show, but it seems likely that the trends since 1940 will persist during the remainder of the twentieth century.

SUMMARY

In less than two hundred years, the United States has been transformed from a country in which 95 percent of the population was rural to one in which three fourths is urban. In broad outlines, the transformation has been associated with dramatic decreases in agricultural employment and with industrialization of the economy. Since about 1920, urbanization has proceeded steadily, even though the percentage of the labor force in manufacturing has remained constant.

There is great variation in the extent of urbanization among industries. Manufacturing is more urbanized than most industries, but less urbanized than many service industries. Within manufacturing, industries that process raw materials are least urbanized, whereas those that process materials previously processed are more urbanized. Since World War II there has been a shift in manufacturing employment toward more highly urbanized industries, but a decrease in urban location in most manufacturing industries.

QUESTIONS AND PROBLEMS

1. Do you think that manufacturing industry will be less urbanized in the year 2000 than it is now? Why?

2. What part of the population do you think will live in SMSAs in the year 2000? Do you expect the service sector to urbanize more rapidly than the population during the remainder of the century?

3. In the late 1970s about two thirds of the population of industrialized countries was urban, whereas only about one third of the population of less developed countries was urban. How will these figures change by the end of the century?

4. In many industrialized countries, a larger fraction of the nonfarm population is urban than in the U.S. How would you explain that fact?

REFERENCES AND FURTHER READING

Davis Kingsley, "The Urbanization of Human Populations," *Scientific American*, Vol. 213, No. 3 (September 1965), 41–53. *A provocative survey of long-term trends in urbanization in industrialized and less developed countries.*

Oscar Handlin and John Burchard (editors), *The Historian and the City*, 1963. *Papers by historians and other scholars on urban history.*

Harvey Perloff and others, *Regions, Resources and Economic Growth*, 1960. *An influential study of the causes and consequences of regional shifts in population and production.*

Stephan Themstron and Richard Sennett (editors), *Nineteenth-Century Cities*, 1969. *Fascinating historical essays on life in nineteenth-century cities.*

THE LAST CHAPTER PRESENTED THE BROAD OUTLINES OF trends in the urbanization of people and jobs during two hundred years of U.S. history. In this chapter the historical survey is completed by discussion of two other important characteristics of urbanization: the sizes of urban areas and suburbanization.

3

Trends in Sizes and Structures of Urban Areas

Urban areas vary enormously in total population. Many millions of people live in the largest metropolitan areas; only a few hundred in each of dozens of small towns. Documenting and explaining the facts has been a favorite pastime of urban specialists for decades. With significant qualifications, the facts are easy to come by. Total populations of cities are published by more national censuses and for more years than are almost any other data except for national population totals. The important qualification is that the most common data are populations of legal cities, and it has been seen that they often do not include the entire urban area. Persuasive explanations of the observed data are much more difficult to come by. This chapter concentrates mainly on the data; comments on explanations are reserved for Chapter 13.

Also important, but outside the scope of economics, is the effect of the size of the urban area on attitudes and life-styles. Life in New York City or Los Angeles differs in many ways from life in Broken Bow, Nebraska or Monroeville, Alabama. Anyone raised in one place or the other is forever stamped by the experience. Yet in terms of economists' measures, such differences are less important than previously. Incomes are lower in small towns than in metropolitan areas, but living standards vary less by size of urban area than they did in earlier times. The kinds and brands of products we buy and the work we do also differ much less from place to place than previously.

Suburbanization refers generically to the dispersion of population from the centers to the peripheries of urban areas. Americans associate the phenomenon with outward movement of people across central-city boundaries. That is indeed an important aspect of the phenomenon. It profoundly affects the ways local governments function in urban areas. This public-finance aspect of the issue will be analyzed in Chapter 10. But the generic notion of suburbanization or dispersion of population does not depend on the locations of central-city boundaries. Careful measurement of the phenomenon will be discussed in Chapter 12. This chapter relies on jurisdictional data.

However measured, suburbanization is one of the most pervasive and important urban phenomena of the twentieth century. It is pervasive in that it has been important in all industrialized countries and has proceeded since at least the beginning of the twentieth century—and since well before that, at least in countries where the phenomenon is documented. Thus, the first lesson about suburbanization is to stop thinking of it as exclusively a post-World War II U.S. phenomenon resulting from racial turmoil, high taxes, and poor public schools in central cities. The phenomenon also occurs when and where these causes are absent. They are undoubtedly important in the U.S. context, but are hardly fundamental causes.

Nevertheless, suburbanization has proceeded far in postwar U.S. urban areas. The final task of this chapter is to trace this process and to point out some of its implications.

SIZES OF U.S. URBAN AREAS

The two most important measures of the size of an urban area are its total population and its total land area. The former is more important and better documented than the latter. In this section, the size of an urban area always refers to its total population.

The primary characteristic of the sizes of urban areas is diversity. In most countries large enough to have more than a few urban areas, the largest urban areas are a hundred or a thousand times (two or three orders of magnitude) as large as the smallest. In the United States, the largest urban area is the New York SCSA, with about 17 million inhabitants. It is 1,000 times as large as a medium-sized town of 17 thousand inhabitants. The world's largest urban area is the Tokyo metropolitan area, with about 25 million residents. It is four orders of magnitude as large as a Japanese hamlet of 2,500 people.

Table 3.1 provides data on sizes of selected U.S. cities at 20-year intervals from 1790 to 1970. The table contains data for the 10 cities that were largest in 1970, and for a few other cities. The left-hand column shows each city's 1970 rank. The data refer to legal cities, not urban areas,

Table 3.1.   POPULATION OF SELECTED CITIES FOR SELECTED YEARS, 1790–1970 (POPULATION IN THOUSANDS)

	Rank in 1970	Population									
		1790	1810	1830	1850	1870	1890	1910	1930	1950	1970
New York	1	49	120	242	696	1,478	2,507	4,767	6,930	7,892	7,895
Chicago	2	—	—	—	30	299	1,100	2,185	3,376	3,621	3,367
Los Angeles	3	—	—	—	2	6	50	319	1,238	1,970	2,816
Philadelphia	4	29	54	80	121	647	1,047	1,549	1,951	2,072	1,949
Detroit	5	—	—	2	21	80	206	466	1,569	1,849	1,511
Houston	6	—	—	—	2	9	28	79	292	596	1,233
Baltimore	7	14	47	81	169	267	434	558	805	950	906
Dallas	8	—	—	—	—	—	38	92	260	434	844
Washington	9	—	8	19	40	109	189	331	487	802	757
Cleveland	10	—	—	1	17	93	261	561	900	915	751
Boston	16	18	34	61	137	251	448	671	781	801	641
Pittsburgh	24	—	5	13	47	86	239	534	670	677	520
Miami	42	—	—	—	—	—	—	5	111	249	335

Source: U.S. Census of Population, 1970.

but the distinction is mostly unimportant before World War II. Even with the restricted number of cities included in the table, one can see the great range of sizes. The tenth-largest city in 1970, Cleveland, is less than 10 percent as large as the largest city, New York.

Although all the cities in the table grew a great deal during the country's history, there is great persistance among ranks. New York was the nation's largest city in 1790 and has been ever since. Chicago, the nation's second-largest city, has occupied that rank for about 100 years. Ranks do change, but slowly. Philadelphia was the second-largest city in 1790, but fell to third place about a century ago and to fourth place after World War II. In 1790 Baltimore was the fourth-largest city; it was seventh in 1970. Los Angeles, Dallas, and Miami are relative newcomers to the ranks of large cities and have moved up in rank rapidly during the twentieth century.

Although cities change ranks only slowly, there is even greater persistence in the relative sizes of cities of particular ranks. The largest city may continue to be twice as large as the second-largest city even though the ranks come to be occupied by different cities. In fact, New York was 2.28 times as large as the second-largest city in 1870, and 2.34 times as large as the second-largest city a century later in 1970, although a different city had come to occupy second place. More will be said about the relative sizes of cities of different ranks at the end of this section.

The final important observation about the data in Table 3.1 is that a majority of the cities included had population declines between 1950 and 1970. Population decreases in central cities have been common during the postwar period, reflecting massive suburbanization. Even metropolitan areas that have grown rapidly throughout the postwar period have had declining central cities. Chicago is an example. In fact, many central cities that have recorded postwar growth have done so by annexing land adjacent to the city as population grows. Annexation is especially common in southwestern states like Texas. The tendency to annex land in certain regions of the country makes comparisons difficult. The subject of suburbanization and its measurement will be discussed at the end of the chapter.

As has been pointed out, comprehensive SMSA data are available only since 1940. Table 3.2 shows rank and population of each of the 10 largest SMSAs for 1950 and 1970. Ranks of SMSAs are of greater interest than are ranks of central cities, since SMSAs correspond more nearly to the notion of the generic urban area. Table 3.2 also indicates considerable stability of ranks, at least during the relatively brief period covered. New York was the largest SMSA throughout the period. Chicago and Los Angeles switched places between second and third. Philadelphia and Detroit retained their ranks. Four of the five smallest SMSAs in 1950 lost rank by 1970. One, San Francisco, rose. Cleveland dropped out of the ten largest SMSAs by 1970, whereas Washington entered.

As Table 3.1 showed for cities, Table 3.2 shows for SMSAs: there is greater persistence in the relative sizes of SMSAs of given ranks than in the identities of the SMSAs that occupy those ranks. New York was 1.85 times as large as the second-largest SMSA in 1950 and 1.65 times as large in 1970. Likewise, the fifth-largest SMSA was 1.78 times as large as the tenth-largest in 1950, and 1.65 times as large as the tenth-largest in 1970. In fact, these ratios suggest that the largest SMSAs have grown less rapidly than somewhat smaller SMSAs during the postwar period.

ESTIMATES OF SMSA SIZE DISTRIBUTIONS

The best way to think systematically about sizes of urban areas is to think of them as a frequency distribution. One can array urban area sizes in various categories from the largest to the smallest just as one can display a frequency distribution of incomes or of almost any economic variable. Such frequency distributions are published in every population census. It has been shown that the size distribution of cities or SMSAs is characterized by a small number of very large cities or SMSAs and much larger numbers of small cities or SMSAs. In other words, the frequency decreases continuously as sizes of urban areas increase. Such distributions are said to be *"skewed to the right."* They contrast with the more familiar normal or Gaussian distribution, which is symmetrical around its highest point. Many economic variables have been found to follow distributions that are skewed to the right: incomes, firm sizes, and urban area sizes. Statisticians

Table 3.2.   RANK AND POPULATION OF 10 LARGEST SMSAs, 1950 AND 1970 (POPULATION IN THOUSANDS)

Rank	SMSA	1950 Population	SMSA	1970 Population
1	New York	9,556	New York	11,572
2	Chicago	5,178	Los Angeles	7,032
3	Los Angeles	4,152	Chicago	6,979
4	Philadelphia	3,671	Philadelphia	4,818
5	Detroit	3,016	Detroit	4,200
6	Boston	2,414	San Francisco	3,110
7	Pittsburgh	2,213	Washington	2,861
8	San Francisco	2,136	Boston	2,754
9	St. Louis	1,755	Pittsburgh	2,401
10	Cleveland	1,533	St. Louis	2,363

Source: U.S. Census of Population, 1970.

and economists have studied carefully the properties of several such distributions.

The distribution most commonly employed to study urban sizes is the **Pareto distribution.** It can be written

$$G(x) = Ax^{-a} \tag{3.1}$$

where $G(x)$ is the number of urban areas with at least x people, and A and a are constants to be estimated from the data. Thus, $G(x)$ is the rank of an urban area with x people. For some reason, the Pareto distribution is usually written as in Equation 3.1, which is a cumulative distribution, cumulated from the top. That is, $G(x)$ is the number of observations *at least as large as x*, whereas the usual way to write a cumulative distribution is the number of observations at least as *small as x*.

Scholars in many disciplines have estimated Equation 3.1 from data on urban populations taken from U.S. and many other national censuses. Frequently, a is estimated to be about one. Then, the Pareto distribution can be written

$$G(x) = Ax^{-1} \tag{3.2}$$

which is known as the **rank-size rule.** Putting $G(x) = 1$, we see that $x = A$; that is, A is the population of the largest urban area. Multiplying both sides of Equation 3.2 by x,

$$xG(x) = A \tag{3.3}$$

That is, the product of an urban area's rank and population is a constant equal to the population of the largest urban area. Thus, the rank-size rule

Table 3.3. POPULATION AND RANK OF A SAMPLE OF U.S. URBANIZED AREAS, 1970

Urbanized Area	Rank	Population (Thousands)	Rank × Population
New York-Northeastern New Jersey	1	16,207	16,207
Pittsburgh, PA	11	1,846	20,306
Cincinnati, OH	21	1,111	23,321
Columbus, OH	31	790	24,491
San Bernardino-Riverside, CA	41	584	23,927
Salt Lake City, UT	51	479	24,446
Tampa, FL	61	369	22,493
Tucson, AZ	71	294	20,887
Des Moines, IA	81	256	20,722
Aurora-Elgin, IL	91	233	21,195
Rockford, IL	101	206	20,814
Utica-Rome, NY	111	180	20,019
Stockton, CA	121	160	19,405
Kalamazoo, MI	131	152	19,923
Eugene, OR	141	139	19,635
Green Bay, WI	151	129	19,495
Port Arthur, TX	161	116	18,752
Petersburg-Colonial Heights, VA	171	101	17,206
Springfield, OH	181	94	16,951
Lake Charles, LA	191	88	16,858
Anderson, IN	201	81	16,222
Fort Smith, OK	211	76	15,934
Laredo, TX	221	70	15,514
Pittsfield, MA	231	63	14,523
Simi Valley, CA	241	57	13,722

Source: U.S. Census of Population, 1970.

implies that the second-largest urban area is half the size of the largest, that of the third-largest urban area is one third that of the largest, and so on. There is no theoretical reason to expect the rank-size rule to hold with precision for urban sizes. But it is such a simple distribution that it is remarkable how close the fit is for urban area sizes in very different countries and at many different times in history.

An indication of the accuracy of the rank-size rule can be obtained from the data in Table 3.3. It shows the population, rank, and rank times population for every tenth entry in the census list by size of urbanized areas for 1970. Do those data confirm or refute the rank-size rule? Of course, no theory in economics is exactly confirmed by significant bodies of evidence. The most that can be hoped for is that deviations of actual from theoretical values are small and random.

There is a tendency for the product of rank and size of urbanized areas in the table to cluster, and the average of the entries in the last column is 19,319. But there are also substantial and apparently systematic departures. The smallest entries are at the top and bottom of the column. Entries rise smoothly from the top to the fourth entry, and they fall almost continuously after the sixth entry. The best way to test the rank-size rule is to return to the Pareto distribution, Equation 3.1. Taking logs of both sides yields

$$\log G(x) = \log A - a \log x \tag{3.4}$$

The Pareto distribution can be estimated by computing the least-squares regression[1] of Equation 3.4. Equation 3.5 presents an estimate of Equation 3.4 calculated, not from the data in Table 3.3, but from the full census list of ranks and populations of the 248 urbanized areas,

$$\log G(x) = 15.5085 - 0.8976\log x \qquad R^2 = 0.984 \tag{3.5}$$
$$(0.0893) \quad (0.0073)$$

The numbers in parentheses are estimated standard deviations of the coefficients above them. In a sample as large as this one, the probability is less than 0.05 that the true and estimated coefficients differ by at least as much as twice the standard deviation. R^2 in Equation 3.5 is the squared correlation coefficient between log $G(x)$ and log x. The reported R^2 means that the regression equation explains 98.4 percent of the variance of log $G(x)$.

Two important observations should be made about Equation 3.5. First, the Pareto distribution provides a very accurate description of the distribution of population sizes of urbanized areas. An R^2 of 0.984 means that the data all lie very close to the estimated Pareto distribution. It is remarkable that, in country after country and in decade after decade, the Pareto distribution fits urban area size distribution data so well. Second, the rank-size rule can be rejected for the U.S. 1970 data. The previous paragraph implies that the true value of a is unlikely to be above 0.9122 (= 0.8976 + 2(0.0073)). That is still well below the unit value of a implied by the rank-size rule.

The estimated value of a of 0.8976 in Equation 3.5 means that populations of urbanized areas far down in the size distribution are smaller than is indicated by the rank-size rule. This is a reflection of the fact that, in Table 3.3, the product of rank and population falls, through most of the table, as one moves down the final column. Unfortunately, few countries have measures of urban size as good as those provided by the U.S. urbanized area data. In a recent study employing data on legal cities, Rosen and Resnick estimated Pareto distributions of city sizes for

---

1.   The least-squares regression means using as estimates of log A and a values that minimize the sum of squared differences between values of log $G(x)$ calculated from Equation 3.4 and those in a sample of data. See any good textbook on statistical methods for more details.

all countries in the world that had a substantial number of cities and published the needed data. Their estimated value of a for the U.S. was somewhat above the average estimated a in the worldwide sample, indicating that city sizes are somewhat more evenly distributed here than in most countries. But the most important of Rosen and Resnick's findings from the U.S. data is that U.S. city sizes are distributed in a manner that is typical of many countries.

SUBURBANIZATION

Despite its familiarity, suburbanization is not really a simple concept. As has been stated, Americans tend to think of it in terms of numbers or percentages of people living or working in central-city and suburban jurisdictions of urban areas. But the concept is more basic than locations of jurisdictional boundaries. A basic definition is that an urban area is more **suburbanized** the more dispersed are residences and jobs around the center of the urban area. That definition does not rely on jurisdictional boundaries but still admits of several possible quantitative measures of the concept.

Jurisdictional measurements of suburbanization are unavailable in most countries because central-city boundaries are moved out as population expands, thus keeping all or nearly all the urban area within the boundaries of the central city. During the period of rapid urban growth in the nineteenth century, it was common to expand central-city boundaries as population expanded, even in the United States. In the twentieth century, the process of boundary movement stopped in much of the country, thus permitting measurement of suburbanization by concentration of people and jobs in central-city and suburban jurisdictions. By this measure, an urban area is said to have suburbanized between years one and two if a larger percent of the urban area's residents live or work in suburban jurisdictions in year two than in year one. That measure will be exploited in this section. Data are easily available and, for that reason, jurisdictional measures of suburbanization are almost always used in popular discussions of the subject in newspapers and magazines. More sophisticated measures will be introduced in Chapter 12 after their theoretical basis has been laid in intervening chapters.

It is important to keep in mind several limitations of jurisdictional measures as they are discussed in this section. First, jurisdictional measures do not permit careful cross-sectional comparisons. If one urban area has a larger percentage of its population living or working in the central city than another, it may indicate no more than where central-city boundaries happen to have been drawn many decades ago. Second, even time-series comparisons are imprecise, because some central-city boundaries are still

ble 3.4.   SUBURBANIZATION OF POPULATION AND EMPLOYMENT IN SELECTED SMSAs, 1950–1970 (POPULATION AND EMPLOYMENT FIGURES IN THOUSANDS)

| | 1950 | | | | 1960 | | | | 1970 | | | |
	Central City		Suburban Ring		Central City		Suburban Ring		Central City		Suburban Ring	
ɔulation	32,625	57.3%	24,281	42.7%	36,135	49.2%	37,267	50.8%	38,272	43.1%	50,617	56.9%
ployment[a]												
Manufacturing	4,523	63.3	2,625	36.7	4,392	56.5	3,382	43.5	4,566	51.0	4,387	49.0
Retailing	2,457	74.4	846	25.6	2,445	65.3	1,300	34.7	2,641	52.2	2,422	47.8
Service	889	80.8	211	19.2	1,072	75.2	353	24.8	1,534	64.2	857	35.8
Wholesaling	1,151	87.1	171	12.9	1,217	80.4	296	19.6	1,305	65.5	687	34.5
al	9,020	70.1%	3,853	29.9%	9,126	63.1%	5,331	36.9%	10,046	54.6%	8,353	45.4%

Employment data are averages of data for census years from the relevant employment censuses.

rces: U.S. Censuses of Population, 1950, 1960, and 1970; of Manufacturers, 1947, 1954, 1958, 1963, 1967, and 1972; of Business, 8, 1954, 1958, 1963, and 1967; of Retail Trade, 1972; of Selected Service Industries, 1972; and of Wholesale Trade, 1972.

moved outward as population and employment expand, especially in the South and Southwest. Each census presents population data within central-city boundaries as they existed at the time of the previous census, but making the comparison among several decades is laborious and approximate.

Table 3.4 contains some comprehensive data on postwar suburbanization, making use of jurisdictional data. It must be kept in mind that the data understate postwar suburbanization since they take no account of boundary movements. The problem of differing central-city boundary locations was avoided by basing Table 3.4 on the same set of SMSAs for each year included. SMSAs included are the 168 SMSAs defined by the census in 1950, less the SMSAs in the three SCSAs that had been defined by 1970. The reason for eliminating the SCSAs is that one SMSA may in a sense be a suburb of another within an SCSA. The exclusions leave 135 SMSAs which contained nearly two thirds of total SMSA population in 1970.

Despite the limitations of the data, Table 3.4 shows the massive suburbanization that has taken place in the United States since World War II. In 1950, 57.3 percent of the residents of the metropolitan areas included in the table lived in central cities. The percentage had fallen to about 50 in 1960 and 43.1 by 1970. Although many central cities lost population during the 20-year period, total central-city population increased in the metropolitan areas included in the table. But suburban population more than doubled during the period.

The employment data included in Table 3.4 are incomplete. Some private service jobs are excluded from the service category included in the table, but the most important exclusion is government service employment. Government employment is probably more concentrated in central cities than total employment, so its exclusion may give an exaggerated impression of employment suburbanization in the table.

Employment is less suburbanized than population, as should be expected. The implication is that more people commute inward than outward across central-city boundaries on the way to work in the mornings. Like population, employment has become much more suburbanized during the postwar period. In 1950, 70.1 percent of jobs in the metropolitan areas included in the table were in central cities. By 1970, the percentage had fallen to 54.6. By the 1980 census, the majority of metropolitan jobs may be in suburbs.

Among employment sectors, manufacturing is the most suburbanized. Retailing is a close second, with services and wholesaling being much less suburbanized. All four employment sectors have suburbanized a great deal since 1950. By one measure, the four employment sectors have come to be more nearly equally suburbanized since 1950. In 1950, almost 24 percentage points separated the percentage of jobs in central cities of the wholesaling and manufacturing sectors. By 1970, the range was less than 15 percentage points. This implies that postwar suburbanization has been most rapid in the employment sectors that were least suburbanized in 1950.

A final point is worth noting in Table 3.4. In 1950, there were 0.276 central-city jobs per central-city resident. By 1970, the figure had fallen only slightly to 0.262. Thus, although both jobs and people have suburbanized, the number of central-city jobs per central-city resident has hardly changed. This means that central-city jobs have not become notably scarcer relative to population during the postwar period.

Suburbanization has been among the most dramatic and widely discussed phenomena of recent history. Analyzing its causes and consequences will occupy a large part of both the theoretical and applied chapters of this book. This section has presented only the crudest measures of suburbanization. But they are adequate to show that it has occurred on a large scale.

SUMMARY

This chapter has reviewed trends in the sizes and structures of urban areas. It has been seen that there is great persistence in the ranks of metropolitan areas. There is even more persistence in the relative populations of metropolitan areas that occupy particular ranks in the metropolitan size distribution. The Pareto distribution was found to approximate closely the metropolitan size distribution for many countries and times in history. Furthermore, the exponents of the Pareto distribution are found to cluster around one.

The decentralization of residences and employment around the centers of metropolitan areas is also characteristic of many countries and many times in history. Metropolitan dispersion has proceeded especially far and fast in post-World War II U.S. metropolitan areas. By 1970, U.S. metropolitan areas were probably as dispersed as metropolitan areas anywhere in the world.

QUESTIONS AND PROBLEMS

1. Find out what government data are available on incomes, prices, and consumption patterns for particular metropolitan areas. What additional data do you think the government should collect and publish?

2. Would you expect greater persistence in relative sizes of central cities or of SMSAs of particular ranks?

3. Would you expect the exponent in the Pareto distribution of metropolitan populations to become larger or smaller as time passes? Why?

4. Do you think employment suburbanization has caused population suburbanization or vice versa? What do you think has caused whichever movement you think caused the other?

5. Which regions of the country do you think have the most suburbanized metropolitan areas? Why? Check your guess with census data.

REFERENCES AND FURTHER READING

Martin Beckmann and John McPherson, "City Size Distributions in a Central Place Hierarchy: An Alternative Approach," *Journal of Regional Science*, Vol. 10 (1970), 25–33. *A theory of city size distributions based on the work of Lösch. Provides an explanation why the distribution is approximately Pareto.*

Benjamin Chinitz, *City and Suburb*, 1965. *A collection of essays on the causes and consequences of suburbanization.*

August Lösch, *The Economics of Location*, 1954. *A classic on location theory. Parts are highly technical.*

Leon Moses and Harold Williamson, "The Location of Economic Activity in Cities," *American Economic Review*, Vol. LVII, May 1967, 211–222. *A fine empirical study of employment suburbanization in Chicago.*

Kenneth Rosen and Mitchel Resnick, "The Size Distribution of Cities: An Examination of the Pareto Law and Primacy," forthcoming, *Journal of Urban Economics*. *An analysis of city size distributions for many of the world's countries.*

2
Theoretical Foundations

IT WAS SHOWN IN CHAPTER 1 THAT URBAN AREAS ARE PLACES where market activities result in much higher production and employment densities than are observed elsewhere. Tall, closely spaced buildings and crowded streets and sidewalks are visible manifestations of high densities. But to the urban economist, urban land, buildings, and human labor are inputs in producing commodities and services. The observation that population and employment densities are high in urban areas translates into the economic statement that ratios of capital and labor to land inputs are high there. Thus, the key observation in urban economic model building is that input proportions in urban areas are systematically and dramatically different from those elsewhere.

4

Introducing Land and Land Rents into Price Theory

Analysis of input proportions and input prices is part of the microeconomic theory of production and supply.[1] However, modern price-theory textbooks hardly mention land, land prices, or land rents except in the context of agricultural examples. Hence, the first task is to incorporate land into production theory. That task is carried out in this chapter. The second task is to use the theory of production, modified by inclusion of land, to analyze the particular spatial relationships that characterize urban areas. That task is carried out in Chapter 5. Together with the discussion of welfare economics in Chapter 6, these chapters provide a broad theoreti-

---

1. For review, Mansfield offers a good discussion of production theory.

cal framework within which urban problems can be analyzed in Part Three.

Just as the wage is the price of labor services, so land rent is the price of land services. And just as a large part of labor-market theory is concerned with wage determination, so much of land-market theory is concerned with land-rent determination. Prices are of course instruments for rationing uses of inputs and outputs in a market economy. It is no less true of land than of any other commodity or service. But the special character of land rent as the price of a nonproduced input has stimulated some of the most interesting scientific and political controversy in history. Some comments on this controversy are made later in this chapter.

SOME TERMS

It is necessary here to define carefully several closely related terms. **Land value** and **land rent** are related in the way that the price of any asset is related to the price of the service that it yields. Stocks of physical assets are valuable because they yield flows of services during many years. Land rent is the price of the services yielded by land during a specific time period, such as a year. Land rent therefore has the dimension of the time period as well as of the unit in which land is measured. For example, land rent might be quoted as dollars per acre per year. The price of an asset is the present value, or capitalized value, of the rent the asset will yield during its useful life. For example, if a tract of land will yield a rent of R dollars per year in perpetuity, and if the appropriate interest rate to use in discounting is $100i$ percent per year, the price (P) of the land is[2]

$$P = R/i \qquad (4.1)$$

The asset price P has the dimension only of the unit in which the asset is measured (e.g., dollars per acre).

Man-made assets, such as buildings and machinery, inevitably deteriorate with time and use, and eventually cease to be valuable. Land used —or rather abused—in agriculture may also deteriorate. But most urban land uses do not cause physical deterioration, and the land therefore yields a perpetual stream of services, as assumed in Equation 4.1.

---

2.   The present value at time zero of a stream of R dollars per year in perpetuity, discounted at interest rate i, is

$$P = \sum_{t=1}^{\infty} \frac{R}{(1+i)^t} = \frac{R}{i} .$$

The second set of terms to define are **unimproved** and **improved land values.** Most urban land uses require that structures be built on the land. In other words, the urban production of goods and services normally requires both land and capital, among other factors of production. Unimproved land value means the price of the land with no structure on it, whereas improved land value means the price of the land and the structure on it. Since structures are usually expensive to move or demolish, it is often difficult to estimate the unimproved value of land that has a structure on it. Furthermore, in many urban areas very little unimproved land appears on the market, especially near city centers. There are therefore few transactions from which to estimate unimproved land values, which are among the scarcest and poorest of the data needed by urban economists.

There are also many ways to improve land in addition to building on it, if the term "improve" is taken literally. It can be drained and graded, provided with pipes for water supply and waste disposal, and planted with or cleared of trees. These are simply different kinds of capital investment in land, and like buildings, they can affect its market value. Some of the ambiguity of unimproved-land-value data results from the fact that various amounts of nonbuilding capital may have been invested in it.

Although nonstructural land improvements present real problems in applied research, as well as in real-estate tax assessment, they are not important in this book. The terms **land value** and **land rent** refer here to the prices and rents of unimproved land, that is, before any capital has been invested in it. **Improved land values** include the value of buildings and other capital invested in the land. Much of the analysis here is concerned with equilibrium situations in which land values and land rents are proportionate to each other, as in Equation 4.1.

THEORY OF LAND RENT AND LAND USE

In this section and throughout much of the book *it is assumed that input and product markets are perfectly competitive*, that is, that each market participant can buy and sell unlimited quantities without affecting the price set by the market. There are two compelling reasons for this assumption. First, most urban phenomena and problems can be best understood and analyzed within the competitive framework. Although monopoly and oligopoly may worsen some urban problems, they are not important *explanations* of most urban phenomena. Racial discrimination, poverty, poor housing, congestion, and pollution would hardly be less serious problems in competitive than in noncompetitive markets. (The analysis to support this claim is presented in Part Three.) Second, spatial models, such as those used to analyze urban markets, are usually much simpler to formulate and analyze if perfect competition is assumed than if other market structures are considered. There are basic difficulties (discussed later on) which economists have not yet solved in formulating spatial relationships in noncompetitive markets.

It is also assumed, as it is in other branches of economic theory, that people own productive land and capital assets because of the return they yield. Owners therefore seek the use of the asset that yields the greatest return available.

These are powerful assumptions and they yield many insights. Among them is the inference that, in equilibrium, *all equally productive units of land command the same price*— which does not imply that all urban land has the same price or rent. Productivity may vary greatly from one unit of land to another within an urban area.

Suppose a firm in a competitive industry produces a single commodity with the aid of several inputs, say land, labor, and capital. The firm can vary its production continuously by appropriate variations in its inputs. The firm's production function represents input combinations that can be used to produce each output volume. Input and output prices are given to the firm, so it need only find the input and resulting output volumes that maximize its profit level at those prices. Intermediate price-theory text-books show that profit maximization requires input quantities that equate the value of the marginal product *(VMP)* of each input to its price or, in the case of an asset, to its rental rate. This important result can be established as follows.

The marginal product *(MP)* of an input is the change in output that results from a small change in the input quantity employed. *VMP* is the product price multiplied by the *MP* of the input. It shows the change in the firm's revenue resulting from a small change in the employment of an input, holding constant the amounts of other inputs. The input price shows the change in the firm's cost resulting from a one-unit change in the employment of the input. If the *VMP* exceeds the input price, it means that employment of additional units of the input would add more to revenue than to cost. Profit would therefore increase. If the *VMP* is less than input price, a decrease in employment of the input would reduce cost by more than revenue. Profit would therefore increase. It follows that profit is largest when an amount of the input is used that equates the *VMP* and the input price.

The result is illustrated in Figure 4.1. The term n stands for the amount of the input, say labor, employed. S_n is the perfectly elastic supply curve of labor, and w is the competitive wage rate. VMP_n decreases as n increases, because the labor *MP* falls as more labor is employed with fixed amounts of other inputs. The term $\bar{n}$ shows the profit-maximizing employment of labor for the firm, in that it equates VMP_n to w.

Figure 4.1

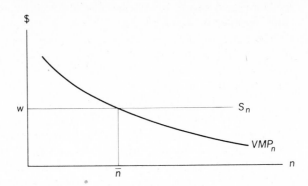

The result in Figure 4.1 can also be stated algebraically. Suppose three inputs—land, labor, and capital—are used to produce a product. Then the conditions for profit maximization can be written

$$p \cdot MP_l = R \qquad p \cdot MP_k = r \qquad p \cdot MP_n = w$$

or

$$MP_l = R/p \qquad MP_k = r/p \qquad MP_n = w/p \qquad (4.2)$$

where p is the price of the product, R is the rental rate of land, r is the rental rate of capital, w is the wage rate, and the MPs are the marginal products of the inputs indicated by the subscripts. By the assumption of perfect competition, the product price and each input price are given to the firm. Each MP depends not only on the quantity of the input designated, but also on quantities of the other two inputs. Thus, each of the equations involves all three input quantities, and they must be solved simultaneously to ascertain the profit-maximizing input levels, as shown in Figure 4.1.[3]

Until now, the discussion has been concerned entirely with the firm. In a competitive input market, input price is given to the firm and is

3.   As Figure 4.1 indicates, VMP is the firm's demand curve for the indicated input. It shows the profit-maximizing input quantity at each input price.

determined by industry supply and demand. To understand land-rent determination, we must therefore pass on to a discussion of the industry as a whole. In a competitive input market, each firm faces the same fixed input price. Industry demand is computed by adding the demands of all firms for the input at the fixed input price. The industry input demand schedule is obtained by repeating the procedure at each input price. Like the firm's *VMP* curve, it is downward-sloping. Although the input supply curve is horizontal for the firm, it is normally upward-sloping for the industry. The input price is determined by the equality of demand and supply for the input in the industry as a whole.

Input price determination is illustrated in Figure 4.2. N refers to labor employment in the entire industry. S_N and D_N are the labor supply and demand curves for the entire industry, w is the equilibrium wage rate, and $\bar{N}$ is total employment of labor in the industry. The term w equals the common value of VMP_n in all the firms in the industry.

The only peculiarity of land is that, being a nonproduced input, its total supply is fixed. Therefore its supply curve to the industry is vertical or perfectly inelastic. But the competitive supply to the individual firm is nevertheless horizontal or perfectly elastic. Thus, the foregoing analysis applies in full, and the appropriate diagram is Figure 4.3. L is land used by the entire industry, D_L is industry demand for land, and S_L is the vertical industry supply curve. R and $\bar{L}$ are the equilibrium land rent and land employed in the industry. As with labor or any other input, land rent equals the common value of its *VMP* in all land-using firms.

Figure 4.2

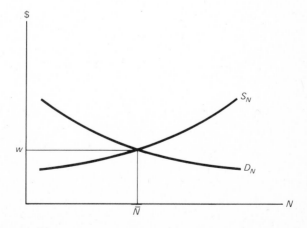

WELFARE AND ETHICAL ASPECTS OF LAND RENT

During the nineteenth century, some economists and social philosophers held passionate views about land rent. Many people still feel that land is basically different from other inputs and ought to be treated differently by governments. Two basic considerations account for these views. First, David Ricardo, Henry George, and others thought that land rents would absorb all the fruits of economic progress. Second is the view that land, not having been produced by people's efforts, should yield no return to its owners. Each view should be analyzed with care.

Ricardo's view rested on Malthus' population theory and on an inadequate appreciation of the importance of technical change. Ricardo believed that high birth rates would increase the labor supply and keep wage rates at the subsistence level in the long run. Land rent, being a residual, would absorb all revenues left over after paying workers—and perhaps capital owners—the input prices necessary to induce their supply. Thus, Ricardo believed, land rents would become an increasing share of total revenue as technical progress occurred. However important Malthusian theory may be for some parts of the world, it is not a threat for the foreseeable future in Western Europe, North America, and some other parts of the world. Birth rates there have fallen secularly for many decades and many countries now have virtually stationary populations. Thus, *wage rates have risen rapidly in real terms as capital accumulation and technical change have occurred.*

On the conceptual level, the relationship between land rents as a residual and land rents as a return to the owner of a productive input proceeds as follows. Suppose the production function has constant returns to scale and that input and output markets are competitive. Then, Euler's

Figure 4.3

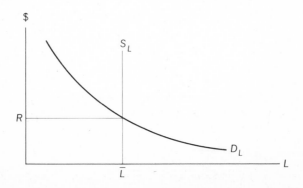

Figure 4.4

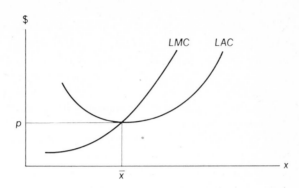

theorem[4] shows that all combinations of inputs and outputs satisfy the following identity:

$$x \equiv MP_l \cdot l + MP_k \cdot k + MP_n \cdot n \qquad (4.3)$$

Here, x is the output level, and l, k, and n are amounts of land, capital, and labor employed by the firm. Eliminating the MP terms from Equation 4.3 by substituting from Equations 4.2 and multiplying both sides by p, the result is

$$px = R \cdot l + r \cdot k + w \cdot n \qquad (4.4)$$

Equation 4.4 shows that the sum of competitive payments to the three inputs is equal to total receipts from the sale of the product on a competitive market. Thus, *the land rent that pays landowners the value of land's marginal product is precisely the amount left over after paying owners of other inputs the values of their marginal products.* This remarkable result shows that there is no conflict between the notion of land rent as a residual and the notion of land rent as a payment based on input productivity in the conditions stated. The result does not depend on the number of inputs.

Nor does the result depend on the restrictive assumption of constant returns to scale in the firm's production function. Suppose that input and output markets are competitive and that fixed competitive input prices yield a conventional U-shaped long-run average cost curve *(LAC)*, as

---

4.   Proved in many calculus and mathematical economics textbooks.

shown in Figure 4.4. *LMC* is the firm's long-run marginal cost curve, p is the industry's long-run equilibrium price and $\bar{x}$ is the firm's long-run equilibrium output. Then, price equals both average and marginal cost and competitively priced payments to inputs therefore exhaust revenues. Once again, land rent, or any other input payment, can be viewed as a productivity-based payment or as a residual.

Constant returns to scale and U-shaped average cost curves by no means exhaust the market situations that interest economists. But they exhaust those that are consistent with perfect competition. In recent decades, economists have greatly sharpened their tools for analyzing land rents in noncompetitive markets, but they appear to have lost interest in the subject.

In fact, the best evidence (see Keiper) is that the share of land rents in U.S. national income has been between 6 and 8 percent since the middle of the nineteenth century. The share probably fell slightly from 1850 to 1950. Thus, even if the Ricardo-George theory of a rising share of land rents were conceptually sound, it would be refuted by the facts.

Turn now to the second concern about land. Why should there be a return to landownership? Unlike labor and capital, land supply does not result from foregone leisure or consumption. No resources are used to produce land. Thus many writers have felt that landowners should not receive a return on this asset.

Henry George proposed a "single tax" on land. Since land supply is perfectly inelastic, he argued correctly that a tax equal to its entire rent would have no effect on its supply or use. He called it a "single" tax because he thought its yield would be sufficient to finance all government activity, making other taxes unnecessary. He was probably right at the time he wrote, but government now spends and taxes a much larger part of national income than the 6.4 percent that goes to land rent. Nevertheless, many economists believe that a 100 percent tax on land rent would be a good idea, and that it should replace other taxes to the extent that its yield would permit.

An analogy between land rent and wages may help to clarify some of the issues. Labor, like land, is a nonproduced input, in the sense that procreation is not undertaken mainly for the monetary return its issue provides to those who make the decision, the parents. Should income from land be taxed rather than that from labor? Not necessarily. First, ownership of land and other assets is much less equally distributed than ownership of labor. Therefore, an 8.5 percent tax on wages, which might have about the same yield as a 100 percent tax on land rent, would be a much less progressive tax. This argument is perfectly correct, but land redistribution is a considerably less drastic change in public policy than a 100 percent tax on land rent. Therefore, if inequality of landownership is the problem, land redistribution would seem preferable to a single tax.

Second, a large part of what we call "wage income" is really a return on investment in human capital, such as education and training. Taxes on wages reduce the return on investment in human capital and hence discourage it. But it is also difficult to separate the return on land from the return on capital investment, or improvements, on it. Thus, in principle, land and labor are similar. Both are typically "improved" by investments which should not be discouraged. It is much easier to separate the return on improved and unimproved land than the return on improved and unimproved labor. But the same kinds of problems are present in both cases.

Third, a major justification for competitive pricing of any input is to provide its owner with an incentive to use it efficiently. A central result of modern welfare economics (demonstrated in Chapter 6) is that if all inputs are priced competitively, and if their owners use them where the return is greatest, goods and services will be produced efficiently. Thus, if wages are taxed heavily, owners of labor (i.e., workers) lack incentive to find the occupation with the highest return.

Again the situation is nearly symmetrical with respect to land and labor. If central planners knew the best use for each plot of land and each unit of labor, they could allocate both without the help of market transactions. But central planners do not know the best use of each unit of each input. Market prices are therefore used as rewards to encourage input owners to find their best uses. An important difference between land and labor is that people are rightly much more bothered by bureaucratic controls over the use of labor than over the use of land. The former violates a human right, whereas the latter violates a property right. But the problem with the single tax remains.

To levy the right tax, the assessor must know the best use and the resulting rent for each plot of land. If he levies an excessively high tax, resource misallocation will result. Thus, *the single tax would assign to the tax assessor the task now assigned to real estate markets.* This is a serious matter, because urban land is a valuable resource and it is important that it be used efficiently. Whatever the deficiencies in the ways competitive markets allocate land (discussed in Chapter 8), it is clear that the job should not be given to the tax assessor. Tax assessors are skilled at tax assessment, not at urban land allocation.

A final point is that a 100 percent tax on land rent is, economically speaking, the same as land confiscation. It is not desirable public policy in the United States to institute such a tax without compensation of landowners at fair market values. But if government and landowners hold the same expectations of future land rents, compensation equals capitalized future land rents, and the government would be in no better financial position with the single tax than without it.[5]

---

5. This statement assumes that the government's discount rate equals the landowners' discount rate less the marginal income tax rate. It may not be quite true, because public and private risk premiums may differ.

The theoretical merits of the single tax seem slight. Most concern with land rents is probably based on concern with the distribution of asset or wealth ownership. If that is the case, asset redistribution is the appropriate reform, and one less drastic than adoption of the single tax.

Although the single tax may not be desirable, higher tax rates on land than on improvements may be justifiable. In the United States, real estate taxation is almost the exclusive preserve of local governments. They now tax both land and improvements at high rates, especially in urban areas. It can be argued that less distortion of resource allocation would result if land were taxed at higher rates and improvements at lower rates than they are at present. This practical policy issue is discussed in Chapter 10.

CONCLUSION AND SUMMARY

In Chapter 5, the basic theory of land rent and land allocation is used to develop the theory of urban structure. It is worth emphasizing here that land rent and allocation theory are tools to help us understand other urban phenomena, and are not themselves of primary concern. Reasons for direct concern with land rents are discussed above. Otherwise, land is merely one of several inputs used in urban production, and its remuneration certainly accounts for less than 10 percent of total incomes.

The theory and social implications of land rent were among the most hotly debated subjects in economics during the nineteenth century. David Ricardo, the father of land-rent theory, believed that land rent equals residual revenues remaining after other inputs are compensated at competitive prices. Modern economic theory shows that land rents, like other input prices, are set by marginal productivity. Marginal productivity and the residual theory are equivalent in competitive equilibrium.

Nineteenth-century writers were agitated about land rents because land is a nonproduced input and because they feared that land rents would absorb the fruits of technical progress, leaving wages at the subsistence level. Historical evidence shows that the second concern was misplaced, but the first is still a subject of controversy.

QUESTIONS AND PROBLEMS

1. Would you expect land rents to be a larger share of national income in the United States or in Japan?

2. What would be the effect of a single tax in Iowa on Iowa land values and corn prices?

3. Property income is more unequally distributed than earned income. Do you think landownership is more unequally distributed than ownership of other property?

4. Can you generalize Equation 4.4 to the case of a monopoly output market?

REFERENCES AND FURTHER READING

Henry George, *Progress and Poverty*, 1879. *Henry George's basic exposition of his theory of land rents and his defense of a single tax.*

Joseph Keiper and others, *Theory and Measurement of Land Rent*, 1961. *A fine survey of land-rent theories and estimates of land rents in U.S. economic history.*

David Ricardo, *Principles of Political Economy and Taxation*, 1951. *A definitive statement of the views of the famous nineteenth-century economist.*

Edwin Mansfield, *Microeconomics*, 1979. *A good undergraduate micro-theory text, which explains input-price determination in detail.*

THE GOAL IN THEORIZING ABOUT URBAN STRUCTURE IS TO understand how the urban economy "ticks." Why are certain goods and services produced in urban areas? Why are some produced downtown and some in suburbs? Why do suburbs grow more rapidly than central cities? Why are certain areas much more intensively developed than others? Most important, what are the causes and cures of problems that afflict urban areas?

5

Theoretical Analysis of Urban Structure

As shown in Chapter 1, urban areas are places where large amounts of labor and capital are combined with small amounts of land in producing goods and services. Intensive development of central cities is another way of saying that the ratio of nonland-to-land inputs is greater there than in suburbs. A major determinant of production location within an urban area is the extent to which large amounts of capital and labor can be combined economically with small amounts of land. Other things being equal, goods and services are produced downtown if their production functions permit substitution of capital and labor for land. If not, they are produced in suburbs or, as in the case of agriculture, outside urban areas altogether. Furthermore, goods and services produced both downtown and in suburbs are produced with higher ratios of nonland-to-land inputs downtown than in the suburbs. Therefore, understanding how the urban economy ticks is mainly a matter of understanding how markets combine land with other inputs in varying proportions at different places to produce goods and services.

This chapter presents the basic ingredients of models of urban structure, and puts them together in models of increasing complexity and realism.

AN URBAN AREA WITH A SINGLE INDUSTRY

Suppose there is a region with a comparative advantage in production of a certain commodity. The commodity is exported from the region at a certain point, which may be a port or a railhead. Wherever the commodity is produced in the region, it must be shipped to the point of export. It is therefore an advantage to produce it as close to the export point as possible.

A circle of radius u has a circumference of $2\pi u$ and an area of πu^2. Therefore, within u miles of the point of export, there are πu^2 square miles of space. Some of the space may be covered by water, or have other topographical features which make it unusable for production. And some space may be needed for intra or interurban-area transportation. But obviously the greater the distance from the point of export, the more space is available for production. Quite generally, the supply of such space can be represented by a function showing the square miles of land within u miles of the export point. For simplicity, suppose that ϕ radians of the circle are available for production at every distance from the point of export. Then the supply of land for production within u miles of the point of export is $(\phi/2)u^2$ square miles. Of course, ϕ cannot exceed 2π.

Production Conditions

Labor inputs and the production of housing services play no role in this model. They are introduced in the next section. Here it is assumed that only one commodity is produced in the urban area. Equivalently, it can be assumed that all commodities have the same production functions. The commodity can be sold locally as well as exported, but all units of the commodity are assumed to be shipped to the point of export for distribution in all cases. The demand for the commodity is a function of price at the point of export.

The commodity is produced with land and capital. The production function has constant returns to scale, and permits substitution between capital and land. Suppose a building has a certain number of floors and a certain number of rooms. Then the inputs and the output of usable floor space can be doubled by constructing an identical building adjacent to it.[1] This is the meaning of **constant returns to scale.** Now suppose the building is extended up rather than out to economize on land. Suppose, for example, that an identical second floor is added to a one-story building.

---

1. This is not quite true. Some economy is made possible by sharing common walls. But this economy becomes unimportant in a building with a modest number of rooms.

The land input is unchanged, but the amount of capital has more than doubled; although the second story requires the same amount of materials as the one-story building, the walls of the first story and the foundation must be strengthened to hold the second story, as well as the first. In addition, the output of usable floor space is less than double because part of the first story must be used for stairs to provide vertical transportation to the second story. Similar considerations apply to additional floors on the building. Thus, *capital can be substituted for land, but with diminishing returns to the use of additional capital with a fixed amount of land.*

It is assumed that input and output markets are perfectly competitive. A **competitive output market** means that all units of the commodity must be sold at the same price at the point of export, wherever they are produced. **Competitive input markets** mean that producers take rental rates on land and capital as given at each location. It is assumed that the supply of capital is perfectly elastic to the urban area as a whole, and that the rental rate on capital is the same throughout the urban area. Land rent, on the other hand, is determined by the model, and depends on distance from the point of export.

Finally, it is assumed that shipment costs of the commodity to the point of export depend only on the straight-line distance between the location of production and the point of export. This is an approximation, since shipments must follow the road network. But studies have shown that actual transportation time and distance are strongly correlated with straight-line distance in urban areas. Thus transportation cost per commodity unit per mile is assumed to be constant—independent of the distance shipped and of the point of origin.

The dependent variables in the model are the amounts of capital employed on different plots of land, the rental rates on the various plots, and the total output and price of the commodity. Since transportation cost to the point of export depends only on distance and not on direction, it follows that all the land available at a distance u from the export point has the same rent; that is, land rent also depends only on distance and not on direction.

As shown in Chapter 4, in any place that production of the commodity occurs, producers use amounts of capital and land inputs that equate the *VMPs* of the inputs to their rental rates. We can write these equations as

$$MP_{K(u)}(p - tu) = r \qquad (5.1)$$

$$MP_{L(u)}(p - tu) = R(u) \qquad (5.2)$$

$MP_{K(u)}$ and $MP_{L(u)}$ are the marginal products of the amounts of capital and land used at a distance u miles from the point of export. Each MP depends on the amounts of both factors used. The term p is the price of the

Figure 5.1

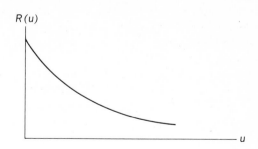

R(u)

u

commodity at the point of export, and *t* is the unit-mile shipment cost to the point of export. The term $p - tu$ is therefore the price at the point of production for units of the commodity produced *u* miles from the point of export, that is, the price net of shipment cost to the point of export. The terms *r* and *R(u)* are the rental rates per unit of capital and land.

We know from the discussion in Chapter 4 that a rent function *R(u)* that satisfies Equations 5.1 and 5.2 also makes profit exactly zero at each *u*. It is worthwhile to investigate carefully the shape of the rent function. If no input substitution were possible, then $MP_{L(u)}$ would be a constant, and Equations 5.1 and 5.2 would not have to be solved simultaneously. The rent that equated profit to zero at each *u* would decrease linearly as *u* increased. In that case, the only saving from locating production close to the export point is lower transportation cost. Therefore, to make profit just zero at each *u*, land rent increases just enough to offset the reduced transportation cost as *u* decreases. But in the model here, input substitution is possible. Then it is easy to show that *R(u)* must rise faster than linearly as *u* decreases; that is, *R(u)* must have the general shape shown in Figure 5.1.

To establish the result, suppose the contrary. Specifically, suppose *R(u)* is at a level that makes profit just zero at some large value of *u*, and that *R(u)* increases linearly as *u* decreases. Then profit would be just zero at a small value of *u*, if the same input proportions were used there as at a large value of *u*. But they would not be the same. At small values of *u*, land is more expensive relative to capital than at large values of *u*. This means that at small values of *u*, production cost is lower if a larger capital/land ratio is used than the ratio appropriate at a large *u*. Therefore, if *R(u)* increases linearly as *u* decreases, profit will be positive at small values of *u*. Thus, *R(u)* must increase faster than linearly as *u* becomes small, if profit is to be just zero at each *u*. Of course, the more rapidly *R(u)* rises at small *u*, the more capital is substituted for land. The urban area is in equilibrium when the capital/land ratio at each *u* is appropriate for *R(u)*, and $R(u)$ makes profit just zero at each u. $R(u)$ must satisfy both properties to be a solution of Equations 5.1 and 5.2.

Thus, $R(u)$ must increase faster than linearly as u becomes small. Of course, the ratio of capital to land inputs is an increasing function of the ratio of land rent to capital rent. Therefore, *as land rent rises rapidly and u decreases close to the city center, the capital/land ratio also rises rapidly.* The expression "rising capital/land ratio" is a graphic one, since it is precisely measured by the rising height of buildings.

The result is important. If it were not possible to substitute capital for land, urban rent functions would be linear, and land used for each purpose would be used with the same intensity in all parts of the urban area. But *land rent, population density, and capital/land ratios fall very rapidly with distance close to city centers, and flatten out in the suburbs.* The pattern is a consequence of input substitution, and the precise form of the rent function depends on the ease with which capital can be substituted for land. Nonlinear rent functions sometimes appear to be mysterious in models with linear transportation costs. Why should land rent increase more with a move from three to two miles toward the city center than with a move from nine to eight miles? After all, the saving in transportation cost is the same in the two moves. The answer, as we now see, is input substitution.

Market Equilibrium Conditions

So far, only the marginal-productivity conditions of Equations 5.1 and 5.2 have been discussed. The model is completed by several additional equations. First, all the land available within the urban area must be used to produce the commodity. It would never pay to use land at a certain distance from the point of export if closer land were unused. Thus, for each u within the urban area, we must have $L(u) = \phi u$.

Second, the production function tells us how much of the commodity is produced by the land and capital employed at each u.

Third, overall demand and supply for the commodity must be equal for the urban area as a whole. Overall supply is the sum, or integral, of the amounts produced at each u within the urban area. The overall demand equation shows the amount that can be sold, both locally and for export, at each p. Although each competitive producer in the urban area takes p as given, p depends on the total amount produced by the entire area. A decrease in p increases exports in two ways. The commodity is then cheaper in the area in which it was previously exported, and customers there buy more. In addition, a decrease in p increases the area in which the urban area's exports are competitive.

Finally, urban areas compete for land with nonurban users such as agriculture. Suppose, for simplicity, the nonurban land surrounding the urban area commands a rent of $\bar{R}$. Then the urban area includes only the land that can be bid away from nonurban users. The edge of the urban area occurs at a distance $\bar{u}$ miles from the export point, where urban land rent falls to the level $\bar{R}$. The urban area has a radius of u miles where $R(\bar{u}) = \bar{R}$.

This completes the model. The two marginal-productivity conditions, the equation relating land use to land available and the production function, give us four equations to determine land and capital inputs, output, and land rent at each u in the urban area. Then the equation of overall demand and supply and $R(\bar{u}) = \bar{R}$ determine the price of the commodity at the export point and the radius of the urban area.[2]

The model here cannot in any sense be thought of as a realistic model of urban structure. Its purpose is to introduce the use of land rent and allocation theory into models of urban structure. It is, however, possible to deduce from the model the single most pervasive characteristic of urban structure, namely, high land rents and intensive land use near the urban center, both falling rapidly near the center and much less rapidly in distant suburbs. Although there are many unrealistic simplifications in the model, the most significant is that the urban area here has no people in it. Labor does not appear as an input, and households do not appear as consumers of housing and other outputs.

HOUSEHOLDS IN AN URBAN SPATIAL CONTEXT

There are important similarities between the foregoing model of industrial location and the theory of household location. Firms are assumed to maximize profits by choosing a location for production, and shipping the commodity they produce to the urban center. Households are assumed to maximize their utility or satisfaction in choosing a residential location (among other goods and services). It is the worker himself who gets shipped, or rather commutes, to the urban center. Thus, production of housing services is analogous to industrial production, and commuting is analogous to the shipment of commodities. (Of course, not all workers actually work in the urban center, any more than all goods are really shipped to the urban center. More realistic assumptions along this line are introduced later. Here it is assumed that all commuting is to the urban center in order to maintain the parallelism of the model with the model of industrial location.)

Housing services, like other goods and services, are produced with

---

2.   Despite its drastic simplifying assumptions, computations with the model discussed here can be rather cumbersome. Nevertheless, a clearer understanding of it can be developed by working through the calculations of the more complex model in the Appendix, and then returning to this model and the other models in this chapter and working out some examples, using production and demand functions of your own invention or that you have studied in other courses.

land, labor, and capital inputs. The provision of housing services bears the same relationship to the housing construction industry that the downtown provision of legal services bears to the office construction industry. In both cases, the construction industry produces a capital good which is used as an input in the production of a service to consumers. The cost of housing services includes labor cost, for maintenance and repairs, plus the rent on the land and capital used. Provided that competitive markets supply the inputs to everyone on the same terms, the cost of a given amount of housing services at a given location is the same to all, and the distinction between ownership and rental of housing is immaterial. Real-estate mortgage markets are highly competitive, and mortgages are highly secure loans in that land and houses are durable, easily insured, and, unlike cars, virtually impossible to steal (in a physical sense). In this chapter we focus on the price per unit of housing services, which is a rental rate analogous to the rental rate on land.

In the United States, there are only two important reasons for the cost of a particular house in a particular location to vary from person to person. First, and most important, is racial discrimination. In many parts of most urban areas, whites sell or rent real estate to blacks only at premium prices, if at all. Second, mortgage interest payments and real-estate taxes are deductible for federal income tax purposes, whereas rent payments for housing are not. Thus, housing services are provided on more favorable terms to owners than to renters. (This is most important to people in a high marginal income-tax bracket.) More is said about racial discrimination and tax considerations in housing markets in Chapter 8. Here it is assumed that the cost of housing services is independent of tenure status.

Capital and land can be, and are, substituted for each other in the production of housing services in the same way as for commodity production. A downtown high-rise apartment has a high capital/land ratio. There is, however, an additional consideration, more important in the production of housing services than it is in commodity production. *The value of housing services is affected by the amount of uncovered land surrounding the house.* Presumably householders are as well off with a big house surrounded by a small amount of uncovered land as with a somewhat smaller house surrounded by a larger amount of uncovered land. That is, exterior and interior space can be substituted for each other. Although suburban industrial buildings sometimes have considerable amounts of uncovered land around them, it is usually held for parking, future expansion, or speculation.

Assumptions of the Model

We can formulate a theory of household-location choice as an extension of consumer behavior theory. Suppose that the household has a utility function or set of indifference curves for its tastes or preferences for housing services and for nonhousing goods and services. As is true of nonspatial consumer behavior theory, the theory presented here depends in only minor ways on the number of goods and services available. But to facilitate diagrammatic exposition, it is assumed that only one nonhousing commodity, called "goods" for short, is available.

The most general way to introduce location choice into the model would be to include u in the utility function. It could then represent all the subjective costs of commuting, such as time foregone from other activities, fatigue, strain, and boredom. Although little is known about some of these factors, it is reasonable to assume that the marginal disutility of additional time spent in commuting increases with the time spent commuting, at least beyond some number of minutes. (Some interesting research has been done on commuters' valuation of travel time; it is discussed in Chapter 9.) Almost no results can be demonstrated unless restrictions are placed on the way commuting affects utility. In this section, a very special assumption is used, that commuting costs enter linearly in the budget constraint but do not otherwise affect utility. The important restriction implied by this assumption is that the marginal disutility of additional time spent commuting is a constant. In the Appendix it is shown that the disutility of a given amount of commuting may nevertheless increase with income.

Households maximize their satisfaction with respect to the consumption of housing, goods, and commuting, subject to a budget constraint. The budget constraint says that expenditures on housing, goods, and commuting must not exceed income. In this budget constraint, "income" must be interpreted as "potential income;" that is, it must include money income foregone as a result of commuting. Part of this potential income is "spent" on commuting. It is assumed that the household can buy as much of goods and housing services as it wants without affecting their prices. The price of goods is assumed not to vary with residential location, but the price of housing services depends on u, since the price depends on land rents, which in turn vary with u. In addition to subjective costs, commuting entails monetary costs in the form of fares or vehicle operating costs. The money cost per mile of commuting is assumed to be a constant, and commuting cost, like the cost of commodity shipment, is assumed to depend on the straight-line distance from the residence to the urban center. The coefficient of distance in the budget equation (t in Equation 5.4 below) includes both money and the subjective or time costs of commuting.

Wherever the household decides to live, it consumes the amount of housing services and goods that yields the greatest satisfaction at that location. Figure 5.2 illustrates the equilibrium choice for a household located u miles from the center. The term $x_1(u)$ is the consumption of goods, and $x_2(u)$ is the consumption of housing services. The straight line is the budget line for a household living u miles from the center. The term I is the highest indifference curve that can be reached, attained by con-

Figure 5.2

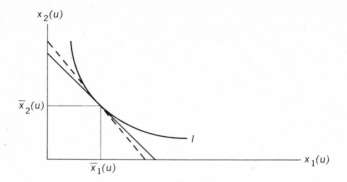

suming $\bar{x}_1(u)$ units of goods and $\bar{x}_2(u)$ units of housing services. The equilibrium condition is the familiar equation between the marginal rate of substitution, or the slope of the indifference curve, and the ratio of the prices of the two consumer goods. If we write Δx_1 and Δx_2 for small changes in the consumption of x_1 and x_2 that keep the household on the indifference curve, the slope of the indifference curve is $\Delta x_2/\Delta x_1$; and equilibrium requires the consumption of amounts of x_1 and x_2 such that

$$\frac{\Delta x_2}{\Delta x_1} = -\frac{p_1}{p_2(u)} \tag{5.3}$$

The household must also decide how far from the urban center to live. If its residence is close to the center, housing services are expensive, but commuting is cheap. If its residence is far from the urban center, housing services are cheap, but commuting is expensive.

Now suppose that the workplaces in the urban center occupy a space small compared with the rest of the urban area, which is occupied by residences. Approximate the area occupied by workplaces with a point at the urban center. Suppose also that $(\phi/2)u^2$ square miles of land are available for housing within u miles of the urban center. Finally, suppose that all households have the same tastes or indifference curves and the same money income. Then an equilibrium location pattern requires that households achieve the same satisfaction level wherever they live. If they did not, some households would move, and the system would be out of equilibrium.

Suppose, for example, that households living five miles from the urban center could achieve a higher indifference level than those living ten miles from the center. By moving closer in, those living ten miles away could achieve the same satisfaction as those five miles away, since they have the same tastes and income and face the same market prices. Thus, some households at the more distant location would move in. This would in-crease land and housing prices at the closer location, and reduce them at the more distant location. Thus, satisfaction levels would fall at the closer location and rise at the more distant location. Movement ceases only when equal satisfaction levels are achieved at all distances from the center.

Implications of the Model

What land-rent function shape is implied by this model? It is an interesting and important fact that *the model has a land-rent function steeper close to the city center than in the suburbs,* as did the model in the previous section. This can be seen as follows: the household budget constraint can be written

$$p_1x_1(u) + p_2(u)x_2(u) + tu = w \tag{5.4}$$

Here p_1 is the price of goods, which does not depend on u, and $p_2(u)$ is the price of housing services, which does depend on u. The term t is the cost per two miles of commuting. A worker who lives u miles from his work must commute $2u$ miles per day. The term w is income. Now consider the effect on p_2, x_1, and x_2 of a small change Δu in u. Since the budget constraint must be satisfied at both values, Equation 5.4 implies that

$$p_1\Delta x_1(u) + \Delta p_2(u)x_2(u) + p_2(u)\Delta x_2(u) + t\Delta u = 0 \tag{5.5}$$

Here Δx_1, Δx_2, and Δp_2 are the resulting small changes in x_1, x_2, and p_2. If the Δ terms are sufficiently small, the cross-product $\Delta p_2\Delta x_2$ is nearly zero, so it has been ignored in Equation 5.5.

Now Equation 5.3 can be written

$$p_1\Delta x_1(u) + p_2(u)\Delta x_2(u) = 0$$

Subtracting it from both sides of Equation 5.5 yields

$$\Delta p_2(u)x_2(u) + t\Delta u = 0$$

Rearranging terms, this equation can be written as

$$\frac{\Delta p_2(u)}{\Delta u} = -\frac{t}{x_2(u)} \tag{5.6}$$

The left-hand side of Equation 5.6 is the slope of the housing price func-tion. The minus on the right-hand side shows that the slope is negative; that is, housing is more expensive close to the urban center than in the suburbs.

Equation 5.6 also implies that the housing price function is steep wherever x_2 is small. Therefore the housing price function is steeper close to the urban center than in the suburbs if suburban residents consume more housing than those living closer in. But suburban residents must consume more housing or they could not achieve the same utility level as those living closer in. Therefore, the budget line of a suburban resident must be steeper than that of a close-in resident in Figure 5.2, since the housing price is lower for the suburban resident. But the suburban resident also spends more on commuting. Since equilibrium requires that the suburban and close-in residents achieve the same indifference curve, the combined effect of increased commuting cost and lower housing prices must make the suburban resident's budget line tangent to the same indifference curve as is that of the close-in resident. Thus, the broken line in Figure 5.2 is the budget line of a suburban resident, and the solid line is that of a close-in resident. It is clear from Figure 5.2 that *the suburban resident consumes more housing than the close-in resident.*

The foregoing result can be stated in terms of income and substitution effects. As one moves farther from the urban center, the price of housing falls. But the increased commuting cost exactly offsets the income effect of the decline in housing price. Thus, the new budget line is tangent to the indifference curve achieved before the move. It follows that the only effect of the move on housing consumption is the substitution effect of the decrease in housing price. It is a basic theorem of consumer behavior analysis that the substitution effect on the consumption of a product whose price falls is to increase the consumption of the product.

It is easy to see that the assumption that u does not appear directly in the utility function is crucial in the foregoing demonstration. If u did appear in the utility function, a move away from the urban center would shift the indifference curve in Figure 5.2, and it would not be possible to predict the effect on housing demand.

It has now been shown that suburbanites consume more housing than close-in residents in equilibrium. It follows from Equation 5.6 that the housing price function must be steeper close to the urban center than in the suburbs. If nonland input prices do not vary with distance, housing price can be steep only where the land-rent function is steep. Thus, the land-rent function becomes steep close to the urban center in the consumer model, just as in the producer model.

The consumer model has two very realistic implications. First, suburbanites consume more housing than residents close to the urban center. Second, since land is cheaper relative to other housing inputs in the suburbs than it is close to the urban center, suburban housing uses lower capital/land ratios than downtown housing. These two implications entail lower suburban population densities than those near urban center. (None of the above implies that suburbanites are better off than those living close to the urban center. In this model, all households have the same income and all achieve the same satisfaction level. This assumption is dropped in the next section.)

The consumer model here can also provide insight into the process of suburbanization. Suppose that all incomes rise in the urban area. There is considerable evidence that housing demand rises rapidly with income, that is, that the income elasticity of demand for housing is near 1.0. Therefore we should expect housing demand to rise considerably. The increase in housing demand may cause the price of housing to rise, but it cannot rise enough to offset completely the effect of the increase in income on housing demand. Even if p_2 rises, Equation 5.6 shows that the housing price function becomes less steep as x_2 increases. Therefore, as income rises, housing prices vary less between downtown and suburb, as do the demand for housing and the land intensity of housing. Thus, population density varies less with u as incomes and the resulting housing demand rise. As can be seen from Equation 5.6, the effect also results from a decrease in t, which represents the cost of commuting. A reduction in t not only has a direct effect on flattening the housing price function, but may also increase the demand for housing, since more income is left after paying commuting costs. This, of course, further flattens the housing price function.

Reductions in the variability of population density with distance from the city center have been observed in U.S. and other urban areas for many decades. (Some of this evidence is reported in Chapter 12.) Consumer behavior theory provides an explanation of the observed trend. Real incomes have risen rapidly. In addition, although this is less well documented, it is likely that the money cost per mile of commuting has fallen relative to other prices. This is the probable result of a succession of urban transportation innovations, such as the mass production of automobiles and improved urban roads.

SEVERAL URBAN SECTORS

We have now considered two one-sector models in which the urban area contains only producers or only households, thus developing the basic location theory of firms and households. In this section, the theory is extended to explain the location pattern of several sectors in one urban area. A **sector** is defined as a set of institutions that have the same rent functions. Firms' rent functions are affected by their production functions, prices of nonland inputs, and product demand functions. Households' rent functions are affected by their incomes, their tastes for housing, commuting, and other goods and services, and by the prices of consumer goods other than housing. Thus, there are many distinguishable sectors in even

Figure 5.3

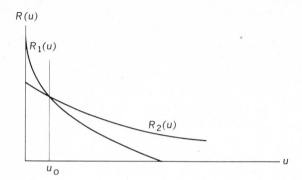

a fairly small urban area. For theoretical purposes, the number of sectors makes little difference, but for applied research and for ease of exposition, it is important to keep sectors to a manageable number. This necessitates the grouping of similar, but not identical, institutions as an approximation of a sector. In applied research, the way data are collected and published usually dictates the definition of sectors.

The key to understanding the location pattern of several sectors in an urban area is the notion, introduced in Chapter 4, that land owners want the largest return possible from their asset and hence allocate their land to the institution that offers the highest rent.

Two Industries

Suppose that two industries bid for land in an urban area. The rent that firms in each industry can offer for land at each distance from the center is found in the way discussed at the beginning of the chapter. From here on, the rent that each industry can pay at each u will be referred to as the industry's **rent-offer function.**

Designate the industries as 1 and 2, and suppose that their rent-offer functions are as shown in Figure 5.3. At values of u less than u_o, industry 1 can offer higher rent than industry 2, and at values of u greater than u_o, the opposite is true. Land close to the urban center is used by industry 1, and land beyond u_o is used by industry 2. At each u, the rent actually paid is the higher of the two rent-offer functions. That is, the rent function is the **envelope** of the rent-offer functions.

Why should firms in industry 1 pay much more for land than $R_2(u)$ at small values of u? After all, industry 1 firms can rent the land if they offer just a little more than industry 2 firms. The answer is that industry 1 firms are competing not only with industry 2 firms but also with each other. Remember that the entire analysis here rests on the assumption that firms enter each industry until profit is just zero. Thus, the complete set of equilibrium conditions for our two-industry urban area is as follows:

1. Wherever firms in each industry locate, they must make zero profit.
2. Each plot of land goes to the highest bidder.
3. Supply and demand for land must be equal.
4. Supply and demand for the product of each indusry must be equal.

There is a very simple rule for the urban location pattern of industries with linear rent-offer functions. Imagine an arbitrarily large set of industries, each of which is able to bid successfully for land somewhere in the urban area, and each of which has a linear rent-offer function. The industries are ranked by distance from the urban center in the order in which they are ranked by the steepness of their rent-offer functions. The industry with the steepest rent-offer function is closest to the urban center, followed by the industry with the next steepest function, and so on. This is illustrated in Figure 5.4. The heavy line is the rent function, constructed as the envelope of the industries' rent-offer functions. It is easy to see that in an urban area with a large number of sectors, the rent function would be nearly smooth, and would become flatter the greater distance from the center, even if each industry had a linear rent-offer function.

Although Figure 5.4 shows the shape of the rent function, it does not indicate which industries will locate in the urban area. It is not necessarily

Figure 5.4

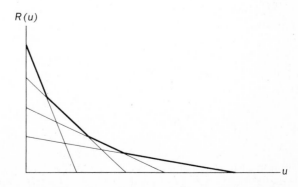

Figure 5.5

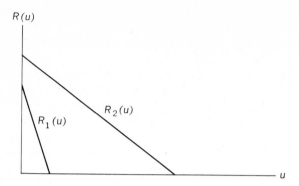

true that industry 1 will locate in the urban area at all. This possibility is illustrated in Figure 5.5. Here, $R_1(u)$ is steeper than $R_2(u)$, but $R_1(u)$ is nowhere above $R_2(u)$, so industry 1 therefore does not locate in the urban area.

As we have seen, inputs and product substitution mean that industry and household rent-offer functions are typically not straight lines. In that case, no simple rule indicates the locational pattern to be expected in the urban area. But the locational pattern must satisfy the four equilibrium conditions listed above.

Figure 5.6 illustrates a realistic possibility. Here, the industry 1 rent-offer function is steep at the beginning and flattens as it moves out, whereas the industry 2 function is more nearly linear. The result is that industry 1 locates at values of u less than u_o and at values of u greater than u_1, whereas industry 2 locates at distances between u_o and u_1. There are, however, some reasonable sets of assumptions that preclude multiple intersections. Suppose that each industry has a Cobb-Douglas production function (discussed in detail in the Appendix). Suppose further that the two industries differ only in that their production functions have different land intensities. Then their rent-offer functions cannot intersect twice. Alternatively, if the industries differ only in the demand elasticity for their products, their rent-offer functions cannot intersect twice. But there are situations in which multiple intersections can occur.

Households and Industries

An industry's rent-offer function is unique because zero profit is a well-defined notion. But in considering the rent-offer functions of households, zero **utility** is not a sensible notion. In fact, in modern ordinal utility theory, any "bundle" of goods and services whatever can be assigned zero utility. All that matters is whether one bundle yields more or less utility than another. For a sector of households with given tastes, income, and prices for nonhousing goods and services, a rent-offer function exists for each utility level. The lower the rent-offer function, the higher is the utility level, since paying less land rent leaves more money to spend on housing and other goods and services. This is illustrated in Figure 5.7, where $R_1(u)$ is the rent-offer function corresponding to a low utility level for the set of households, and $R_2(u)$ corresponds to a high utility level.

Which rent-offer function is relevant? The relevant rent-offer function is the one that equates supply and demand for labor provided by these households. Figure 5.8 illustrates this notion. Here $R_1(u)$ is the rent-offer function of an industry that employs labor. $R_2(u)$ is a rent-offer function for the households that supply labor to the industry; it represents a high utility level and a small supply of labor. $R_3(u)$ is another household rent-offer function representing a low utility level and a large supply of labor. If labor demand and supply are equal when the household rent-offer function is $R_2(u)$, it is relevant. But if labor demand exceeds supply, and if the wage rate is high enough to attract more workers to the urban area from elsewhere, the household rent-offer function rises to one like $R_3(u)$, the labor supply expands, and utility falls. Thus, the equilibrium conditions for households' location are similar to those for industrial location:

1. Wherever households with given tastes and income reside, they must achieve the same utility levels.

2. Each plot of land goes to the highest bidder.

Figure 5.6

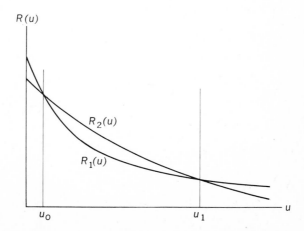

3. Supply and demand for land must be equal.

4. Supply and demand for labor provided by the households must be equal.

Condition 4 implies that household utility levels in this urban area must be equal to those that can be achieved elsewhere. For some kinds of labor, the lowest rent-offer function that commands land anywhere in the urban area may be so high that the households to which the labor belongs achieve lower utility levels than those that can be achieved elsewhere. Households of this type simply do not locate in this urban area. Farmers rarely reside in large urban areas, and highly specialized labor, such as an eye surgeon, is rarely found in small towns.

As was shown in Figure 5.6, not all the firms in an industry necessarily locate in a contiguous area. The same is true of households. In Figure 5.6, $R_2(u)$ might be the rent-offer function of an industry employing labor, and $R_1(u)$ might be the household rent-offer function that produces equilibrium in the urban area's labor market. Then, some households would live downtown and some in distant suburbs. The two residential areas would be separated by an industrial area. The two groups of households would, however, be equally well off, and neither would benefit from a move.

We can now use the analysis to understand one of the most interesting of urban phenomena, namely the location effects of differences among households. Some differences are easy to dispose of. Households with unusually strong preferences for housing tend to live far out because housing is relatively cheap there. Likewise, workers who attach relatively little disutility to commuting, perhaps because it enables them to escape

Figure 5.7

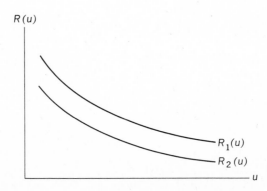

noisy telephones at the office and noisy children at home, also live in distant suburbs.

The most interesting issue has to do with the effects of income differences on location. Suppose there are two household sectors with identical tastes but with different incomes. Does the high- or low-income group live closer in? Other things being equal, the high-income group demands more housing than the low-income group, which encourages the high-income group to move out where housing is cheap. But the marginal disutility of commuting also depends on income, and it may (theoretically) rise so fast with income that the high-income group stays put and spends its money on other things. A remarkably simple and realistic result (proved in the Appendix) can be stated:[3] Suppose that the disutility of a mile of commuting is proportionate to the wage rate, and that the factor of proportionality is no greater for high- than for low-income workers. Then, if the income elasticity of demand for housing exceeds 1.0, high-income workers live further from the urban center than do low-income workers. If the income elasticity is less than 1.0, high-income workers nevertheless live farther out, provided the demand for housing is not too inelastic with respect to its price.

The result does not, of course, depend on the existence of only two income groups. Even if there is an arbitrarily large number of income groups, if all satisfy the conditions of the theorem, their residences will be ranked by distance from the urban center inversely to their rank by in-

Figure 5.8

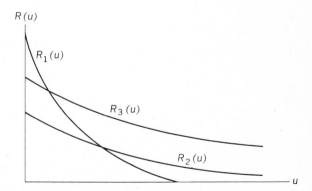

---

3.   This result had been seen intuitively, but the first satisfactory proof was by Muth, pp. 29 *et seq.*

come; that is, the lowest income group will be closest in, the next lowest will be next closest, and so on. This is a remarkably realistic result, and it mirrors closely the predominant pattern in U.S. urban areas.

The result does not rest on coercion. In the model, the poor live close to the urban center because it is the best place for them to live. But in no sense is it a justification for coercion. First, it is not best for all low-income people to live near urban centers. As has been indicated, not everyone has the same tastes for housing, commuting, and other things. Realistically, at least some low-income people want to live in suburbs and commute long distances, and at least some high-income people want to live close in and commute short distances, as a matter of taste.

REALISTIC URBAN LOCATION PATTERNS AND URBAN SIMULATION MODELS

The model of urban land use developed in previous sections is important. It and many generalizations of it have been developed by many scholars during a decade or so. It provides valuable insights. It shows how and why land is used more intensively near urban centers than in suburbs. It shows why virtually all land very close to urban centers is used for employment instead of for housing. It shows how and why population density falls as one moves away from urban centers. It provides one strong reason that high-income people live further from urban centers than low-income people. And it provides a basic explanation for the urban decentralization that was shown in Chapter 3 to have been occurring for several decades.

Yet the model has severe limitations as a description of reality. Some of the limitations can and will be removed by further research, but some are inherent in the model. Most important is the fact that all employment is assumed to be concentrated in the urban center. As has been seen in Chapter 3, that is far from the truth and becomes less accurate every decade. In principle, employment can be introduced at suburban locations in the model. But most suburban employment is not located uniformly at all locations a particular distance from the urban center. And the model contains only a one-dimensional description of location; that is, it contains distance, but not direction from the urban center. It might be possible to introduce a two-dimensional description of location into the model, but it would make the model extremely complex.

Such complex models yield few analytical results. It generally is necessary to estimate or assume numerical values for the elasticities and other parameters of the model and to solve them on a computer. The idea of using large, modern computers to solve or simulate[4] urban models has opened up a large area of research since the 1960s. Computers have an enormous capacity to solve large systems of equations and inequalities. Since the late 1960s, several urban models have been published that make use of this capacity and are closely related to the urban models discussed in this chapter.[5]

All computer simulation models start with a discrete description of locations in the urban areas. A set of locations is defined (each might be a census tract) and the computer keeps track of where each location is in relation to all the others. Typically, the computer records a great deal of information about housing and employment at each location. Important characteristics of the existing housing stock might include the numbers, kinds, and ages of dwellings at each location. Employment information might include numbers, industries, and occupational descriptions of jobs. Housing demand equations relate residents to desired housing, making use of such information as family size, income, race, and education. Account is taken of considerations that induce people to move: their present dwelling is unsatisfactory, employment changes, or there is a change in family status. New construction is brought into the picture via a supply curve of new housing. Then the movers are matched up with the available housing supply according to a market-clearing equation.

The great advantage of computer simulation models is the detail they can employ regarding housing demand and supply in relation to locations of housing and workplaces. A major purpose of such models is to analyze effects of alternative national housing policies. Suppose, for example, that a national program is proposed to subsidize housing of low-income people in a specific way. What will be the effect of the program on the amounts and qualities of housing they inhabit? What will be the effect on housing inhabited by those with incomes too high to be eligible for the program? Existing simulation models are designed to answer such hypothetical questions.

The most important limitation of existing simulation models is their limited success in making amounts and locations of employment endogenous to the model. Usually, the models' solutions are conditional, depending on forecasts of exogenous amounts and locations of employment.[6] Simulation models have thus not yet succeeded in incorporating one of the

---

4. **Simulation** means repeated solution of the model with different parameter values to test the effects of parameter changes on the solution of the model.

5. See Ingram, et. al.; deLeeuw and Struyk; and Birch, et. al. For a different approach, see Mills.

6. Birch and Mills are partial exceptions to this conclusion. An "endogenous" variable is determined within a theoretical model, whereas an "exogenous" variable is determined outside the model.

important determinants of the speed and direction of urban growth or decline.

Urban simulation models are expensive. It requires a small team of experts and at least two years to formulate the model, collect the data, estimate the parameters in the model, program a computer to solve it, and simulate alternative government programs. Gradually, however, available models become more sophisticated so that they can analyze not only housing programs, but also transportation investments; local government taxation, spending, and regulatory programs; national environmental protection programs; and so forth.

SUMMARY

This chapter has shown how to extend theories of consumer and producer behavior to an urban spatial context. The result is an urban land-use model that provides important insights into urban spatial characteristics.

Most analytical models assume that everything produced in an urban area must be shipped to the urban center for sale inside or outside the urban area. Spatial production theory then shows how production is distributed around the urban center. Spatial consumer theory shows how employees and their families distribute their residences around the employment locations. Such models can provide results that show how land values, land uses, input ratios, and population density vary with distance from the urban center.

Such analytical models are simplified and long-run in character. Computer simulation models have been formulated to analyze in detail the way households distribute themselves among the available housing stock in an urban area. Simulation models can incorporate much locational detail, many demand determinants, and many characteristics of the housing stock.

QUESTIONS AND PROBLEMS

1. How would you introduce real-estate taxes into an urban land-use model?

2. Is it possible in equilibrium that land rent might increase with distance from the urban center?

3. Evaluate the argument that employment has moved to suburbs because

central business district land values have gone so high that employers can no longer afford to locate there.

4. Consider the model in the Appendix, with one household sector. What does your intuition tell you should happen to $\bar{u}$, the radius of the urban area, if t falls? Can you check your intuition mathematically?

REFERENCES AND FURTHER READING

David Birch and others, *The Community Analysis Model*. Washington: U.S. Government Printing Office, 1979 (Document No. 023–00–00497). *A complex urban simulation model in which not only housing location and consumption, but also employment location, are determined.*

Frank deLeeuw and Raymond Struyk, *The Web of Urban Housing*, 1975. *A computer simulation model designed to investigate alternative national policies to subsidize housing for the poor.*

Gregory Ingram and others, *The Detroit Prototype of the NBER Urban Simulation Model*, 1972. *A large computer simulation model designed to investigate a variety of national and local government housing policies.*

Edwin S. Mills, *Studies in the Structure of the Urban Economy*, 1972. *A research monograph in which congestion is introduced into an urban land-use model.*

Edwin S. Mills, "Planning and Market Processes in Urban Models," in *Public and Urban Economics* (Ronald Grieson, editor), 1976. *An urban simulation model based on linear and nonlinear programming.*

Richard Muth, *Cities and Housing*, 1969. *A modern classic in urban economics.*

THE PRECEDING CHAPTERS HAVE BUILT A THEORETICAL AND empirical framework within which to analyze urban processes and trends. In Part Three, attention is focused on the analysis of urban problems and of alternatives open to society to solve them. Welfare economics is the link between the positive analyses and the normative or policy analyses. A brief presentation is included here to emphasize certain topics that are important in urban policy analysis. Fuller treatment can be found in a good intermediate price-theory text.

6
Welfare Economics and Urban Problems

WHAT IS WELFARE ECONOMICS?

Welfare economics is a branch of economic theory concerned with evaluating the performance of the economic system. In order to decide whether the system is performing well, and whether a change in government policy would improve its performance, a yardstick is needed by which to measure performance. Such a yardstick is called a **value judgment.** Some people feel that economics becomes unscientific, or at least less scientific, when value judgments are introduced into analysis, but the feeling is misplaced. Economic theory is the deduction of implications from assumptions or axioms. There is no reason for economists not to include value judgments among their assumptions, and hence judgments about the performance of the economy among their conclusions. It is important that economists make their value judgments as clear and explicit as possible, so that others can decide whether to accept the value judgments and hence the concluding evaluation of performance. A major element of progress in welfare economics during recent decades has been to make value judgments explicit rather than implicit in the analysis. This has been part of an important trend in economics to make all assumptions as explicit as possible.

The other side of the coin is that it is not possible to judge the performance of the economy without value judgments. Whenever someone judges that an economy is performing well or badly, that person is explicitly or implicitly using a value judgment as to what constitutes good or bad performance. The implication is that if economics did not involve value judgments it would be an entirely academic discipline, incapable of advising society on solutions to economic problems.

What value judgments should economists use in evaluating the economy's performance? In a free society, people can make whatever value judgments they wish. Economists have spent enormous amounts of time and effort discussing and clarifying value judgments that would be interesting and acceptable to many people, or at least to many thoughtful people. The value judgments underlying modern welfare economics are the result of decades of thought and analysis. Nevertheless, they *are* value judgments, and the conclusions of analysis can be no more persuasive than the value judgments and other assumptions from which they follow.

Welfare economics begins with the idea that the purpose of economic activity is to produce goods and services for people to use. It leads to the broad judgment that *the economic system should be evaluated by the efficiency with which it produces goods and services, and by the efficiency and equity with which it distributes them for people's use.* For many purposes, goods and services can be defined narrowly as inputs and outputs traded on markets. But for some purposes it is desirable to broaden the definition. To take the most important example, suppose that the production and consumption of traded goods and services affect the environment in undesirable ways. Then one can broaden the definition of goods and services to include the quality of the environment, and include it in the analysis. Of course, the broader definition may require somewhat different and more complex analysis than the narrow definition.

The foregoing value judgment is not sufficiently precise for purposes of analysis. A crucial step toward precision is the assumption that each individual has a set of preferences for goods and services that lead to indifference curves which have the properties postulated in consumer behavior theory, and that a person's welfare is measured by the indifference or utility level attained. This value judgment is usually expressed by the assumption that each individual is the best judge of his or her welfare. Nobody accepts that value judgment without qualification. We all make mistakes, and a few people are persistently incapable of judging their self-interest. But for many people, the attractiveness of this value judgment as a broad guide to public policy is clinched by the following consideration. People make mistakes in choosing cars to buy, plays to see, and someone to marry. But who among humanity is qualified to make such decisions for us? *The value judgment that each person is the best judge of his or her welfare underlies all the subsequent analysis in this book.*

CRITERIA OF ECONOMIC PERFORMANCE

The foregoing consideration leads economists to two specific criteria for evaluating the performance of an economy. The economy is said to perform well if, given the productive resources and technology available to it, (1) no reallocation of inputs and outputs can improve the welfare of some without worsening the welfare of others, and (2) income and wealth are equitably distributed. Criterion 1 is known as the efficiency criterion, or sometimes the **Pareto efficiency criterion,** after the economist who first proposed it; and criterion 2 is known as the **equity criterion.**

Most people find these criteria easy to accept. Objections come from the fact that 2 does not specify what distribution of income and wealth is equitable. Utilitarian economists of the nineteenth century believed that a society's welfare was the sum of the utilities of its members. Add the assumptions that all people have the same utility functions and that marginal utility decreases with income, and it is easy to derive the utilitarian conclusion that social welfare is maximized if income is equally distributed. But modern theory of consumer behavior does not attach any meaning to the sum of people's utilities. Specifically, if a utility function can be found that represents a person's preferences, any utility function that is an increasing function of the first one will represent that person's preferences equally well. In particular, one can make the sum of all people's utilities any number one likes by choosing appropriate individual utility functions.

Despite this, all of us have strong feelings about the distribution of income. But at the present, economics is able to provide very little help in forming or evaluating such feelings. About all that can be said is that each person's evaluation of public policy proposals should depend on the effect of the proposals on income distribution. Of course, a citizen can unhesitatingly support a policy proposal that improves the economy's efficiency without worsening its income distribution, given the citizen's feelings about income distribution. Likewise, he or she can support a proposal that improves the income distribution without worsening efficiency. The difficult choices involve proposals that would improve efficiency at the expense of equity, or vice versa.

But disagreement about equity issues should not be exaggerated. Nearly all Americans agree that government should raise living standards of society's neediest people by taxing those with substantial incomes for the purpose. And nearly all Americans agree that high-income people should pay a larger percentage of their income in taxes to support government than should middle-income people. There is a great deal of disagreement on the specifics of these matters, but it occurs mainly within a broad consensus on basic issues.

The assumption that each person is the best judge of his or her welfare has an important and controversial implication: *government programs to improve equity by raising living standards of the poor should provide them money, not commodities or services.* You cannot make a person worse off by providing him or her the money value of commodities or services instead of the commodities or services. Most people probably accept this general principle. Yet the political process continues to provide or subsidize food, health care, housing, and other things for the poor, instead of providing them with money. Direct provisions of commodities and services for the poor is justified only if there is **market failure** in private provision of the commodities or services. An important task of this and subsequent chapters will be to analyze arguments for direct provision of commodities and services to the poor.

The first task is to lay out criteria for market efficiency.

CONDITIONS FOR ECONOMIC EFFICIENCY

The efficiency criterion has implications for the allocation of both outputs and inputs. The basic ideas are most easily understood by considering the simplest situation in which a problem of resource allocation can be posed, a model of pure consumption.

A Pure Consumption Model

Suppose a society must allocate fixed amounts of two consumption goods per unit of time between two members. Shortly, it will be assumed that the commodities are produced with scarce inputs, but for the moment it is assumed that they simply appear in fixed amounts. X units of one good are available and Y units of the other. Designate the two people A and B, and the amounts of the two goods allocated to each by X_A, X_B, Y_A, and Y_B. The allocation of the goods must satisfy the conditions

$$X_A + X_B = X \qquad Y_A + Y_B = Y$$

and all of the allocations must be non-negative.

Individuals A and B have indifference maps representing their tastes for the two goods, as shown in Figure 6.1. Society's allocation problem is usually represented as in Figure 6.2. The horizontal and vertical axes of the indifference diagrams in Figure 6.1 have been extended to lengths X and

Figure 6.1

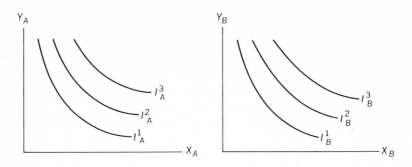

Y, and the indifference diagram for B has been rotated so that its origin is in the upper right-hand corner of the rectangle. Each point in Figure 6.2 corresponds exactly to one of the possible allocations of X and Y between A and B. Society's problem is therefore to choose a point in the rectangle which satisfies the efficiency criterion.

Unless the tastes of A and B differ greatly, there will be some allocations at which the indifference curves for A and B have the same slope. Assume that such allocations exist and can be represented by a continuous curve, designated *cc* in Figure 6.2. The *cc* curve represents all of the allocations such that

$$MRS_A(X_A, Y_A) = MRS_B(X_B, Y_B) \qquad (6.1)$$

where *MRS* stands for one person's marginal rate of substitution between the two goods. The **basic welfare theorem** in the pure consumption model is that the set of allocations that satisfies the efficiency criterion is precisely the set that satisfies Equation 6.1.

To prove the theorem, consider an allocation P_1, not on *cc* in Figure 6.2. There must be exactly one of the indifference curves for A and one for B passing through P_1, but they cannot be tangent. Then any reallocation from P_1 to a point like P_2, which lies between the indifference curves passing through P_1, must place each individual on a higher indifference curve than he or she was on at P_1. Thus, each person is better off at P_2 than at P_1. Repeating the argument shows that reallocation from P_2 to a point between the two indifference curves passing through P_2 makes both individuals still better off. The argument can be repeated until an allocation is reached on *cc*. This proves the theorem.

Note that nothing in the argument rests on the assumptions that there are only two people and only two goods in the society. If it consists of any finite number of people, and the problem is to allocate among them fixed amounts of any finite number of goods, an efficient allocation must satisfy Equation 6.1 for every pair of goods and every pair of people.

All of the points on *cc* are efficient, but they are by no means all equitable. At allocation P_4, *A* has practically all of both goods and *B* has almost nothing, whereas at P_3 the opposite is true. Thus, a person who felt that *A* was relatively deserving would prefer P_4 to P_3, whereas a person who felt that *B* was relatively deserving would prefer P_3 to P_4. The efficiency criterion narrows society's choice from the set of points in the rectangle in Figure 6.2 to the set of points on *cc*. The equity criterion narrows the choice from the set of points on *cc* to one or a few of those points.

What kinds of institutions might society develop to solve its allocation problem? If someone knew each person's indifference map, that person could compute the set of efficient allocations. But of course no one has the required information. Recall from price theory that if goods are allocated on markets, and if the price each person pays for each good is independent of the amount bought, each individual maximizes his or her welfare by buying amounts of goods that equate his or her marginal rates of substitution to the price ratios of pairs of goods. Thus all buyers who face the same prices choose amounts of goods that equate to each other every person's *MRS* for a particular pair of goods. Competitive markets, in particular, will allocate goods to satisfy Equation 6.1 and hence allocate efficiently. In the pure consumption model, monopoly is also efficient, but it will be shown that only competitive markets, among all market allocations, satisfy the efficiency conditions when input allocations are included in the model.

Are competitive markets equitable as well as efficient? Not necessarily, since competitive markets ensure only that the allocation will be on

Figure 6.2

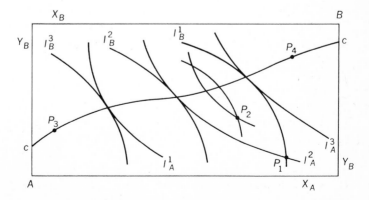

Figure 6.3

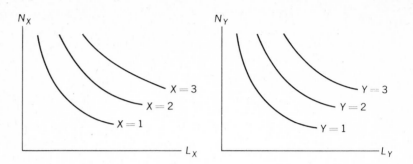

cc, and not that it will be at any particular point on *cc.* Equity depends on how much purchasing power or income *A* and *B* bring to the market. Suppose, for example, that *A* and *B* each inherit amounts of the two commodities. Their inheritances put them at a point like P_1, and they then trade the commodities on competitive markets and end up on *cc* between I_A^2 and I_B^1. The point P_1 is entirely determined by the legacies, and the amounts *A* and *B* inherit determine where on *cc* they end up after trading. Thus, competitive markets can guarantee only to get the society to *cc,* not to an equitable point on *cc.* In this simple example, society could insure equity as well as efficiency by enacting inheritance laws that reallocated purchasing power in an equitable way and then letting individuals trade on competitive markets.

A Production-Consumption Model

The model can now be enriched by recognizing that *X* and *Y* are produced with scarce inputs. Suppose there are two inputs, labor and land, with fixed amounts of each available to society. There are *N* units of labor and *L* units of land. Both inputs are needed to produce each output. The amounts of the goods produced are related to the amounts of the inputs used by two production functions

$$X = F(N_X, L_X) \qquad Y = G(N_Y, L_Y)$$

Subscripts indicate the amounts of the inputs used to produce the commodity indicated, so the use of inputs is limited by

$$L_X + L_Y = L \qquad N_X + N_Y = N$$

Society now has two problems. First, it must allocate the inputs to production of the two commodities. Second, it must allocate the commodities to the two individuals. The production functions can be represented by their **isoquants,** as shown in Figure 6.3. A representation of the input allocation problem can be formed from Figure 6.3 in precisely the same way that Figure 6.2 was formed from Figure 6.1. The result is Figure 6.4, where the horizontal sides of the rectangle have length L and the vertical sides have length N. The origin for the production of Y is at the upper right-hand corner of the rectangle.

Given an understanding of the proof of the theorem in the pure consumption model, it is easy to see how inputs must be allocated in the production-consumption model to satisfy the efficiency criterion. Any allocation of the two inputs between X and Y corresponds to a point in Figure 6.4. The curve **dd** connects all the points of tangency between pairs of isoquants. It is shown in price-theory texts that the slope of an isoquant is the ratio of the marginal products of the two inputs. Thus, **dd** is the set of input allocations such that the ratio of the marginal products of the two inputs is the same for the production of both commodities at a given point; that is, **dd** is the set of input allocations such that

$$\frac{MP_{LX}}{MP_{NX}} = \frac{MP_{LY}}{MP_{NY}} \tag{6.2}$$

The basic efficiency theorem in the production-consumption model is that the set of input and output allocations that satisfies the efficiency criterion is precisely the set that satisfies Equations 6.1 and 6.2. The theorem and its proof are analogous to those in the pure consumption model. Suppose that the input allocation is at a point like P_1 in Figure 6.4, not on **dd**. Then the same amounts of the two inputs can be reallocated so as to produce more of both X and Y by moving from P_1 to a point like P_2, which

Figure 6.4

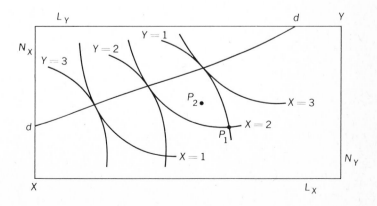

is between the isoquants passing through P_1, since P_2 is on higher isoquants for both X and Y than is P_1. Clearly, P_2 represents more output of both X and Y than P_1 does. Thus, it is possible to improve the welfare of both individuals (A and B) by moving from P_1 to P_2, since each can receive more of both goods. Repeating the argument shows that reallocations of inputs can improve the welfare of both individuals as long as the input allocation is not on dd.

The set of efficient input allocations is the set on dd. But given the total outputs of X and Y, efficiency also requires that the outputs be allocated efficiently between A and B. Thus, Equation 6.1 is also a condition for efficiency, just as in the pure consumption model. Therefore, input and output allocations are efficient only if Equations 6.1 and 6.2 are both satisfied. Once again, it is easy to see that the argument applies if there are more than two inputs or outputs. If more than two inputs are used to produce X and Y, Equation 6.2 must hold for each pair of inputs taken separately. There would then be many equations like Equation 6.2. If there are more than two outputs, input allocations must satisfy Equation 6.2 for those outputs as well as for X and Y.

The conditions for efficient allocation of inputs and outputs have been derived without reference to social institutions that might undertake production and distribution. It can now be shown that allocations of inputs and outputs by competitive markets do satisfy the efficiency conditions. It is shown in price-theory textbooks and in Chapter 5 that the necessary conditions for profit maximization for producers who deal in competitive input and output markets are

$$MP_{L_X} \cdot p_X = R \qquad MP_{N_X} \cdot p_X = w \qquad (6.3)$$

for an X producer, and

$$MP_{L_Y} \cdot p_Y = R \qquad MP_{N_Y} \cdot p_Y = w \qquad (6.4)$$

for a Y producer. MP is the marginal product of each of the two inputs in producing the two outputs; p_X and p_Y are the prices of X and Y; R is the rental rate of land; and w is the wage rate.

It only remains now to show that Equations 6.3 and 6.4 imply Equation 6.2. Divide the first equation by the second in Equations 6.3 and 6.4. The result is

$$\frac{MP_{L_X}}{MP_{N_X}} = \frac{R}{w} \qquad \frac{MP_{L_Y}}{MP_{N_Y}} = \frac{R}{w}$$

Thus, the two ratios of marginal products are equal to the same input price ratio, and hence to each other. This shows that competitive profit-maximizing firms employ inputs in amounts that satisfy the efficiency criterion of Equation 6.2. It was shown in the pure consumption model that competitive output markets satisfy Equation 6.1. Thus, competitive input and output markets satisfy both sets of efficiency conditions.

A corollary to the foregoing discussion is that efficiency requires outputs of X and Y to be such that their marginal costs are equal to their respective prices. This condition is of course satisfied by competitive (but not by monopoly) markets.

The efficiency criterion tells society that, among all the points in Figures 6.2 and 6.4, it should choose input and output allocations on cc and dd. As in the pure consumption model, there are many efficient input and output allocations, but not all of them are equitable. Suppose (to stay within the two-input model) that every worker is equally productive, and thus in competitive markets receives the same earned income. Suppose further that ownership of land is determined by inheritance. Then each unit of land receives the same rental rate, but the overall distribution of income or purchasing power is affected by the distribution of land ownership. In this model, society can obtain efficient and equitable input and output allocations by using an inheritance tax to produce an equitable distribution of land ownership, and by permitting competitive markets to allocate inputs and outputs. The inheritance tax might, for example, tax those whose incomes exceed the average and distribute the proceeds to others.

A Variable Input/Output Model

The pure consumption model assumed that the amounts of the two consumer goods available to society were fixed. The assumption was relaxed in the consumption-production model, and replaced by the assumption that the amounts of inputs were fixed. In the model here, the assumption of fixed input quantities is relaxed. It is replaced by the assumption that workers can vary their supplies of labor freely, at least within limits.

This assumption is of course an approximation, since many jobs require more or less rigid hours of work. But hours of work are more flexible than is sometimes realized. Over a period of a decade or two, hours of work change substantially, falling as incomes rise. But even within short periods of time, there are many ways to vary hours of work. Moonlighting, overtime, and part-time jobs are available. Many professional and self-employed workers have flexible hours of work. So, to some extent, do many commission and piece-rate workers.

Leisure, a catchall for whatever is done during nonwork hours, is valuable, just as consumer goods are valuable. Assume that each individual has a set of indifference curves between leisure and each commodity, as illustrated in Figure 6.5. $\bar{N}_A$ represents hours of leisure for A per unit of time, just as X_A represents the amount of X consumed by A per unit time. If N_A is hours of work for A, $N_T = N_A + \bar{N}_A$ is the total hours

Figure 6.5

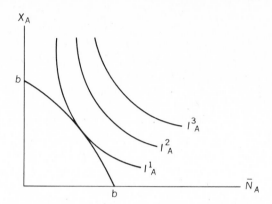

available to A for work and leisure. The indifference curves in Figure 6.5 depend only on the tastes of individual A. Now introduce the production side by supposing that A produces X at work. The output of X depends on A's hours of work, and therefore varies inversely with the amount of leisure he or she takes. The relationship is shown by *bb* in Figure 6.5. Since *bb* shows how production of X by A varies with his or her hours of leisure, its slope is minus the marginal product of an extra hour of work by A in producing X. If *bb* is concave, as shown in Figure 6.5, it means that the marginal product of A falls as he or she works more hours producing X.

The final criterion for efficient resource allocation can now be derived. It says that the hours of work by A should equate his or her marginal rate of substitution between X and leisure to his or her marginal product in producing X; that is,

$$MRS_A(X_A, \bar{N}_A) = MP_{AX} \qquad (6.5)$$

The curve *bb* is like a budget constraint for A, showing the combinations of leisure and X available to him or her. A achieves the highest possible indifference curve by choosing a combination of X and leisure that places him or her at the point of tangency between *bb* and an indifference curve. Since the movement of A to the point of tangency from another point on *bb* does not affect the welfare of other members of society, the move satisfies the efficiency criterion; that is, it makes him or her better off without making anyone else worse off. Going up *bb* means working more hours, and concavity implies that each additional hour results in a smaller increase in production of X.

It only remains to show that competitive markets satisfy this efficiency criterion, as well as those already discussed. If A sells his or her labor and buys X and Y on markets, the budget constraint is

$$p_X X_A + p_Y Y_A = w(N_T - \bar{N}_A) \tag{6.6}$$

where $N_T - \bar{N}_A$ is the number of hours A chooses to work, and w is the hourly wage rate. If the labor market is competitive,

$$w = MP_{AX} \cdot p_X$$

Substituting for w in Equation 6.6 and rearranging terms, the budget constraint can be written as

$$X_A = \left(MP_{AX} N_T - \frac{p_Y}{p_X} Y_A \right) - MP_{AX} \bar{N}_A \tag{6.7}$$

Thus, in a competitive labor market, the slope of the budget constraint of A is MP_{AX}, the same as that of bb. It follows that the market choice by A will lead him or her to the tangency point in Figure 6.5 that has been shown to satisfy the efficiency criterion.

In the consumption-production model, it was shown that society could obtain an efficient and equitable resource allocation by choosing an appropriate initial distribution of input ownership and permitting exchange of inputs and outputs on competitive markets. In the model, input supplies were fixed and therefore redistribution of their ownership did not affect resource allocation decisions. But matters are more complicated in the model with variable inputs. In this model, only a wage rate equal to the value of the worker's marginal product results in an efficient allocation of labor resources. If there are many workers, with a variety of skills and abilities, the wage of each must be equal to the value of the worker's marginal product. Thus, in the variable input model, the efficiency conditions imply a distribution of earned income, which will be referred to as an efficient distribution of income.

Is an efficient distribution of income also equitable? The competitive market values of worker skills vary enormously. Many people have no saleable skills at all because of physical or mental disabilities, whereas some have skills worth hundreds of thousands of dollars per year. Most people's sense of equity requires an income distribution less unequal than the efficient distribution. As a result, societies have long had policies of reducing income inequality through government tax-transfer systems. In every society, resolution of the conflict between efficiency and equity and between the various income groups is one of the most important and controversial tasks of government.

SOME CAUSES OF RESOURCE MISALLOCATION

The discussion of the social efficiency of competitive markets is now complete. There are several reasons to believe that markets are less efficient than the preceding discussion has indicated. This chapter concludes with a general classification and analysis of reasons for resource misallocation. Succeeding chapters will analyze specific problems of efficiency and equity in the urban economy. Each problem requires facts and analysis specific to that problem, and they are presented in the appropriate chapters.

Monopoly and Monopsony

It is easy to show that *monopolists and monopsonists misallocate resources.* A monopolist maximizes profits by employing input quantities that satisfy equations similar to 6.3 and 6.4, but with product prices replaced by marginal revenues. Since a monopolist's marginal revenue is less than price, profit maximization requires that marginal products be greater for the monopolist than for the competitive firm for given input prices, and the monopolist therefore employs smaller input quantities and produces less output than is efficient from society's point of view. Similar reasoning shows that Equation 6.7 is also violated if the employer is a monopoly, and therefore inefficient amounts of labor are supplied. (As an exercise, it should be possible to show that monopsony power also leads to inefficient resource allocation.)

The quantitative importance of resource misallocation from monopoly and monopsony is a subject of debate among specialists in industrial organization economics. If misallocation is substantial, it must be substantial in urban areas, since most economic activity occurs there. But it is claimed in following chapters that monopoly is unimportant in understanding most serious urban problems; poverty, poor housing, congestion, pollution, and inadequate public services result only to a minor extent from monopoly power. They would be serious problems even if all markets were perfectly competitive. Many people resist this conclusion, in part because they use the term "monopoly" more broadly than economists do, and in part because of the human tendency to search for villains to blame for problems.

External Economies and Diseconomies

For decades, economists have analyzed a closely related set of considerations that entail resource misallocation, even in competitive markets. Despite important recent progress in clarifying the concept, there is still considerable disagreement among economists about the causes and effects of **externalities.** The result is that the term tends to be used somewhat loosely in applied studies. Especially in urban economics, the term is badly overused and abused.

The basic idea behind the notion of an **external effect** is that *the actions of one person or institution may affect the welfare of another in ways that cannot be regulated by private agreements among the affected parties.* As has been discussed, if a firm buys and sells on competitive markets in certain assumed circumstances, market prices and profit maximization induce the firm to behave efficiently from society's point of view. It employs just the inputs and produces just the output that are in society's interest. Now suppose that one of the firm's activities affects people's welfare in a way not based on agreement or market transaction. The classic example, used by generations of writers, is smoke emission. Suppose that a certain fuel is among the firm's inputs, and that burning the fuel creates smoke which spreads over the neighborhood and reduces residents' welfare. If the fuel is an important input, and its smoke is not too harmful, some smoke may be worth its cost to the firm and to the public. But there is no market on which to register the advantages of smoke production to the firm and its disadvantages to the neighbors. If the firm maximizes profits, it fails to take into account the cost that its smoke imposes on others. Even though some smoke may be worth the cost, too much is produced. The smoke is then said to be an **external diseconomy.** The resulting resource misallocation, too much smoke, is no less serious just because the firm buys inputs and sells outputs in competitive markets.

In fact, smoke is a less serious problem than it used to be, but nearly all economists agree that air pollution is a serious public problem because of its external effects. In a general way, almost everyone would agree on the underlying explanation that private agreements cannot allocate resources to abate air pollution efficiently. Disagreement comes when we try to establish exactly why private agreements do not work.

The basic reason that private agreements do not work is that *private transaction costs sometimes exceed the potential gain from the agreement.* The reason is not hard to understand in the smoke example. Many people suffer more or less harm from the smoke, and many sources may be more or less responsible for the smoke damage to each person and to each person's property. Thus, a private agreement to abate smoke discharges would require negotiations among large numbers of people and factories, and the public would have complex and poorly understood interests in abatement by particular sources. Obviously, a private agreement on such an issue would be extremely difficult and costly to specify and negotiate. That is the meaning of the statement that the transaction costs of such an agreement are high.

Exactly what circumstances entail transaction costs so high as to prevent otherwise desirable agreements? There is no satisfactory answer at present, and the result is that many studies of externalities are merely anecdotal. About all that can be said is that transaction costs may be high regarding agreement about an activity if the activity affects large numbers of people in complex ways. But any study of an apparent externality should include a careful investigation of the kinds and amounts of transaction costs that prevent agreement.

Once an important externality has been identified, the next question is what to do about it. The usual answer is that the government should tax or subsidize so as to create an appropriate market, or it should regulate so that private activity approximates the missing market. In the smoke example, the government can tax emissions, subsidize abatement, or regulate emissions. But the first question that needs to be asked is whether transaction costs will be lower if the government intervenes than if private parties try to reach agreement. If not, the transaction costs are unavoidable and the agreement is not worth having. In the smoke example, the disadvantage of the smoke may be smaller than the cost of doing something about it. In many cases, however, the government can adopt policies that at least approximate the results of private agreements, and with relatively small transaction costs. But in each case, the facts must decide the issue. Sometimes government programs become cumbersome because the government must bear exactly the transaction costs that prevented the private sector from undertaking the transactions in the first place.

If transaction costs are low enough that government intervention is justified, the appropriate policy is easy to specify in principle. In the smoke example, the efficient amount of smoke is the amount such that the cost to the neighbors of a little more smoke equals the cost to the factory of a little more abatement. Another way to put it is to say that the amount of smoke should be such that marginal costs and marginal benefits of abatement are equal. The goal might be achieved by an appropriate tax on smoke, or by regulation of smoke discharges. Which policy should be chosen depends on the transaction costs of the policies and on the extent to which they approximate efficient resource allocation. Of course, in practice, the benefits of abatement may be difficult to estimate.

Externalities in an Urban Context

What are the important externalities in urban areas? There is no agreement on this matter in the relevant economics literature. Environmental pollution commands the greatest agreement. Almost all economists agree that polluting discharges to air and water result in resource misallocation and that government should tax or regulate such discharges. Consensus could probably also be reached on housing. Most people's welfare is affected by the quality of housing in the neighborhood where they live. And most economists would probably agree that government interference in housing markets is justified. But there is little agreement as to the best kind of government interference. In fact, we have a panoply of taxes, subsidies, codes, and controls on housing markets.

What about urban transportation? Most economists would agree that a street or subway system must be planned as an integrated whole in an entire urban area. This justifies government ownership or regulation of the basic infrastructure. But how should the use of the streets or tracks by vehicles be controlled? It will be shown in Chapter 9 that congestion is an external diseconomy that might justify government intervention in use of rights-of-way by vehicles.

These and other resource allocation problems raise complex issues about whether and how government should intervene. Many of the issues will be discussed in subsequent chapters. The logical sequence of the argument is the same with every issue. What is the justification for government intervention? And what is the best kind of intervention? Both questions are important.

Taxes

Governments must raise large amounts of money by taxes on citizens to finance the public services and transfers demanded of them. In fact, total tax payments to all levels of government are almost one third of GNP in the U.S. An important goal of tax policy should be to employ taxes that cause as little resource misallocation as possible.

Price-theory texts show that a change in the price of a consumer good has an income effect and a substitution effect. Almost all taxes are directly or indirectly taxes on particular kinds of goods and services. They therefore alter the prices of the taxed items relative to untaxed items. The income effect is the desired effect of the tax, and represents no misallocation of resources. The purpose of a tax is to transfer resources from the private to the public sector, and the income effect measures the value of the resources transferred. If the resources are less valuable in the public sector than in the private sector, there should be no tax and no transfer. But if the resources are more valuable in the public sector, the transfer should be made, and the income effect of the tax is the desired reduction of private purchasing power. The income effect may reduce demands for private goods and services by varying amounts, but it represents the least costly way of transferring the purchasing power represented by the tax.

The substitution effect of a tax on the demand for the taxed goods and services represents a loss of welfare to consumers beyond that which is necessary to transfer purchasing power. The substitution effect leads to what is called the **excess burden** of the tax, that is, the excess welfare loss over that necessary to transfer the purchasing power to the public sector.

Figure 6.6

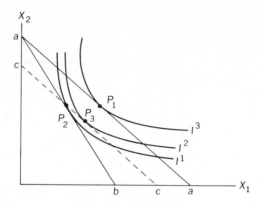

Among all the taxes that have a given income effect in transferring given resources to the public sector, the best is the one with the smallest excess burden, or substitution effect.[1]

These ideas can be illustrated with the property tax (discussed in detail in Chapters 8 and 10). Here it is necessary to note only that the property tax is a high sales tax on housing services. Figure 6.6 shows a household's set of indifference curves between housing services x_1 and another commodity x_2 for a given amount of a public service provided by the government. Suppose that x_1 and x_2 are produced by competitive firms, and that *aa* would be the household's budget line in the absence of any tax. Then P_1 would be the household's equilibrium, and it would be efficient. But P_1 is not available because it does not provide resources to the government necessary to produce the public service. Suppose then that the government finances the public service with a property tax, and that the entire tax is paid by the consumer of housing services. The household's budget line is shifted to *ab*. Its new equilibrium is P_2. Budget line *cc* is drawn parallel to *aa* and passes through P_2. P_3 is the household's equilibrium position for budget line *cc*. The movement from P_1 to P_3 is the income effect of the tax; that is, it represents the household's loss of welfare if the government had taken the resources it needs without affecting the relative prices of x_1 and x_2. The movement from P_3 to P_2 represents the substitution effect of the tax. The fact that the property tax has a substitution effect causes an excess burden of the tax on the household that reduces its welfare from I^2 to I^1.

What kinds of taxes would have no excess burdens? In principle, the answer is that the only taxes with no excess burdens are those that do not affect relative prices. *A "head" tax, which simply charges the same amount*

1.   See Scitovsky for a complete discussion of the issue in this and the preceding paragraph.

of tax to each person, is probably the only tax that has no excess burden. The property tax is presumed to have a large excess burden, since it is a high tax on a narrow range of activities, namely, housing consumption. A broadly based sales tax is probably somewhat better. A sales tax that taxed all consumer goods and services at the same rate would be a flat-rate consumption tax. It would leave unaffected the relative prices of goods and services. But most sales taxes fall far short of this ideal. Most are levied on a narrow set of consumer goods, excluding almost all services and some commodities. Some are also levied on a few intermediate goods, which entails double taxation of the final goods they are used to produce.

An income tax, like a broadly based sales tax, leaves relative prices of goods and services unchanged, which accounts in part for the strong preference of most economists for income taxes over other taxes. But an income tax and a broadly based sales tax do have an excess burden. An income tax is a tax on the result of hours spent working, but not on hours of leisure. In Figure 6.5, an income tax changes the relative prices of goods and leisure, and therefore, the slope of the budget line *bb.* The substitution effect of an income tax is an inefficiently large amount of leisure. The total effect that an income tax has on hours of work and leisure depends on the relative sizes of the income and substitution effects.

Is the excess burden of an income tax large? The best study on the subject, by Harberger, concludes that it is substantial, but probably small relative to the excess burdens of existing sales and property taxes. Sales and property taxes, like income taxes, affect the relative prices of goods and leisure. But, unlike income taxes, they also affect the relative prices of goods and services.

It should be emphasized that the entire discussion here has been about the efficiency aspects of taxes. Taxes, like other public policies, also have important equity effects. A major goal of government tax policy is to redistribute income, specifically to reduce income inequality. That goal requires progressive taxes or transfer payments, and the income tax is almost the only tax that can be made to be progressive. Thus, *if equity considerations require progressive taxes, they are an important reason for the use of income rather than other taxes.* It is also possible that equity considerations indicate the desirability of one kind of tax, and efficiency considerations indicate the desirability of another. In such cases, a compromise between equity and efficiency is necessary.

SUMMARY

Welfare economics is a branch of economic theory concerned with evaluating the performance of the economic system. Economists evaluate the system's performance by its efficiency and equity in meeting people's economic wants.

An elaborate system of conditions for economic efficiency has been worked out by economists during recent decades. A major result obtained in welfare economics is that competitive markets allocate resources so as to satisfy the efficiency conditions, if strong assumptions are made. But competitive markets may not produce distributions of income and wealth that meet people's senses of equity.

Monopolies and monopsonies misallocate resources, although neither is likely to be an important source of urban problems. External economies and diseconomies imply that even competitive markets misallocate resources. Pollution and congestion are examples of external diseconomies in urban areas.

Governments raise large sums of money by taxes to finance public services and transfer payments. Taxes should be equitable and should cause as little resource misallocation as possible. Most economists believe that sales and property taxes are both less efficient and less equitable than income taxes. But there may well be conflict between efficiency and equity in the tax policy.

QUESTIONS AND PROBLEMS

1. Show that price discrimination violates the requirements for efficient resource allocation.

2. Economists tend to argue that activities causing external diseconomies be taxed, whereas government officials tend to regulate such activities. Which strategy is better on equity and efficiency grounds?

3. The do-it-yourself movement, in which homeowners repair and maintain their houses instead of hiring craftsmen, has blossomed since World War II. Do-it-yourself labor is not subject to income tax, whereas a craftsman's wages are. Do you think the do-it-yourself movement is a distortion in resource allocation resulting from high income-tax rates?

4. Governments tend to provide or subsidize goods and services to the poor, despite economists' advice that money transfers are preferable. One possibility is that taxpayers prefer to provide goods and services instead of money. Another possibility is that interest groups determine the form of transfers. For example, farmers like food stamps and builders like housing subsidies. What do you think the correct reason is?

REFERENCES AND FURTHER READING

Francis Bator, "The Simple Analytics of Welfare Maximization," *American Economic Review*, Vol. 47, March 1957, 22–59. *A fine presentation of modern welfare economics.*

Arnold Harberger, "Taxation, Resource Allocation, and Welfare," in *The Role of Direct and Indirect Taxes in the Federal System*, 1964. *A thorough study of distorting effects of taxes.*

E. J. Mishan, *Cost-Benefit Analysis*, 1976. *A classic study of the use of welfare economics to analyze benefits and costs of proposed government projects.*

Tibor Scitovsky, *Welfare and Competition*, 1971. *A microeconomics text with a strong welfare-economics orientation.*

HOUSING, LIKE FOOD, SATISFIES A FUNDAMENTAL HUMAN need. Except for food, no commodity is more important than dwelling place in determining standard and style of living. Indeed, if housing costs are taken to include the cost of operating as well as of owning or renting a dwelling, the average American spends about the same part (20 percent) of his disposable income on housing as on food. In poor countries, larger parts of income are spent on both commodities. On the supply side, the two industries are similar in that, in contrast with manufactured goods, food and housing are produced by small, competitive firms. A further similarity is that housing and food production are among the most land-intensive of industries. About half the land in urban areas is devoted to housing. But a crucial difference between the two industries is that housing is the most durable of capital goods, whereas food is the least durable of commodities.

8

Housing, Slums, and Race

Housing, especially in urban areas, is the subject of controversy, and of public policies of great variety and complexity. Slums are rightly at the head of the list of controversial housing topics, and rank just behind poverty as the most serious contemporary urban problem. Americans are now clearly aware that many people, especially blacks, live in poor housing in metropolitan central cities. A great deal of public effort has been devoted to the design of programs to improve or eliminate slums. And a great deal of public and private controversy has been devoted to the merits of alternative slum improvement proposals.

The literature on urban housing and slums is enormous. As with poverty, the study of housing and slums is by no means the exclusive preserve of economists. Yet housing and real estate has been a recognized specialty among economists for decades. During the 1970s, there was an outpouring of high quality economic research on housing demand and supply. Understanding of housing markets is much better than it was in the 1960s.

Housing is a complex and diverse commodity. It would be hard to find two dwellings that did not differ in some way that was important to consumers. First, dwellings differ in their physical characteristics, such as the numbers, sizes, and arrangements of rooms; the kinds and conditions of materials in the structure; and the conditions of utilities, style, and decoration. Second, dwellings differ in their location relative to work places, shopping facilities, and recreational opportunities. Third, dwellings differ as to neighborhood characteristics, such as the density and condition of nearby dwellings. Fourth, dwellings differ in the local government services provided and the taxes levied in the jurisdiction in which the dwelling is located.

The stock of housing is a **capital asset.** In fact, it is society's most valuable asset. The market value of dwellings in the United States is about 1.4 times annual GNP, much more than the value of all manufacturing assets. The housing stock, like other products, is produced with a variety of land, labor, capital, and raw-material inputs. Housing is more durable than most assets. Whereas manufacturing equipment may have a life of 10 years, an average dwelling has a life of 40 or 50 years. Housing services are provided to residents by the housing stock, fuel, labor, and material inputs. Whereas the price of a house is the price of the asset, the rent of the house is the value of the flow of housing services. Asset values and rents are observed on markets because dwellings are sold and rented. But many dwellings are owner-occupied, in which case the rental value must be imputed from market data on similar dwellings. As a rule of thumb, a dwelling may generate a monthly rent of about one percent of the asset value.

Both asset and rental values have the dimension of price times quantity. Some dwellings obviously embody much larger quantities of housing than others. Because of the diversity of dwelling types, estimating the quantity of housing in a dwelling is difficult. But the attempt must be made or important questions cannot be addressed. For example, ascertaining whether blacks are discriminated against in housing markets requires separate data on housing price and quantity.

THE HOUSING STOCK

Americans are well housed, almost certainly better than ever in their history and probably as well as any nation in the world. People accustomed to reading about soaring housing costs find this hard to believe.

Table 8.1.   THE U.S. HOUSING STOCK

	1960	1970	1977
Number of dwellings (million)	58.3	68.7	80.9
Persons per dwelling	3.1	3.0	2.7
Market value (billions of dollars)	717	1,233	2,646
Average age (years)	27.9	25.8	25.0
Median rooms per dwelling	4.9	5.0	5.1
Percent owner-occupied	61.9	62.9	64.7[a]

[a]1976 figure

Source: U.S. Bureau of the Census, *Statistical Abstract of the United States*, 1978.

Some recent data are in Table 8.1. The first two lines show that the housing stock grew considerably faster than the population between 1960 and 1977. The number of people per dwelling fell from 3.1 to 2.7 during the period. The third line shows estimates of the market value of the housing stock; it was about 1.4 times GNP in both 1960 and 1977. The next two lines show that the average age of the housing stock decreased, and the average number of rooms per dwelling increased, during the period. Finally, the percentage of dwellings that are owner-occupied has increased steadily. Thus, during the 17-year period, the average dwelling became newer and larger and housed fewer people. It is not a bad record.

In 1978, Americans spent 14.3 percent of their disposable income on housing, up from 13.8 percent in 1960. This reflects the fact that housing prices have risen slightly faster than other prices during the 1970s. But these figures from the national income accounts ignore capital gains in housing. As with other assets, dwelling owners make capital gains or losses on their asset as its price goes up or down. Rapidly rising house prices during the late 1970s made dwellings an excellent investment, much better than the stock market. An owner-occupier with a mortgage equal to 50 percent of the value of the house makes a 20 percent return on the equity when the house price increases 10 percent per year.

Housing construction fluctuates widely during the course of a business cycle. Housing starts fell from 2.4 million units in the boom year 1972 to 1.2 million units in the deep recession year 1975. By 1977, they were 2.0 million units. Housing construction is as unstable as any large industry. As a rough approximation, if the average dwelling lasts 50 years, and the age distribution is about even, then two percent, or 1.6 million dwellings, must be replaced annually. Another 0.6 million units are needed to house the 0.8 percent annual population growth. Thus, upwards of two million units must be constructed annually to maintain the housing stock per capita constant. Housing improvement results from construction in excess of this number and from increases in the size and quality of housing.

HOUSING DEMAND

Much high quality statistical research on housing demand has been published during the 1970s. Economists have focused their efforts on attempts to estimate price and income elasticities of demand. The work of Muth, deLeeuw, Kain and Quigley, and Polinsky is especially important.

Demand equations specify quantity demanded as a function of product price, consumer income, and prices of related commodities and services. The first problem facing those who try to estimate housing demand is the absence of a set of units in which to measure housing quantity. Much ingenuity has been applied to the problem, but the fact is that *no single number can measure housing quantity.* The second problem is measurement of housing expenditure. For renters, the solution is easy: **contract rent** measures housing expenditure. For owner-occupiers, asset prices can be used, but ownership costs are what is wanted. **Ownership costs** consist of mortgage interest, foregone interest on the owner's equity in the house, maintenance and repair costs, insurance costs, real-estate taxes, and depreciation less capital gains. The problem is complicated by the fact that two costs, mortgage interest and real-estate taxes, are deductible on federal income tax returns. Thus, the cost to the owner is the sum of mortgage interest and real-estate taxes times one minus the owner-occupier's marginal federal tax rate. Data on these variables are rarely available. The asset value is most commonly used as an approximation to ownership costs, but ownership costs increase more slowly than asset values.

More and better estimates of the income elasticity of demand are available than of the price elasticity. It is reasonable to assume that the price per unit of housing is equalized by competitive forces within a local housing market. Employing such data, regression of housing expenditures on income provides estimates of the responsiveness of housing consumption to income. Careful studies during the 1970s placed the income elasticity in the range 0.5–1.5. It is a wide range, but correcting estimates for biases identified by Polinsky narrows it to about 0.75–1.20. There is of course no guarantee that the income elasticity is the same for all people and income levels, but the best guess is that income elasticities are clustered in a narrow interval around one, probably averaging somewhat less than one.

There are fewer estimates of the price elasticity of demand, but several excellent studies are referred to by Polinsky. Polinsky also concludes that the best estimates of the price elasticity of housing demand are somewhat less than one, perhaps clustering around 0.75.

Among the most interesting housing demand studies are those that employ the **hedonic price** approach. The approach recognizes that housing is a collection of characteristics, such as number of rooms, age, lot size, garage space, heating and cooling systems, and so forth, that have distinguishable values to consumers. The hedonic approach consists of regressing the asset price or contract rent on a function of such characteristics. The result is an estimate of the values that housing markets place on each house characteristic and of how the characteristics interact. Neighborhood characteristics, such as air quality, racial mix, and so forth, can also be valued. A good example of a hedonic price study is Grether and Mieszkowski.

A difficult issue with hedonic price studies is the interpretation to be placed on the hedonic equation. Under certain circumstances, it can be interpreted as a demand equation, but usually it is a set of demand and supply intersections. Further analysis is then needed to estimate separate supply and demand equations. These difficult theoretical issues are discussed by Rosen.

HOUSING SUPPLY

Careful housing supply studies are rarer than housing demand studies. If housing supply is interpreted to mean new housing supply, then construction firms and developers are the suppliers. It is a fragmented industry. Most houses are built by tiny firms, with only a few employees. There are more than 100,000 homebuilders in the country, mostly doing business in only one or two local government jurisdictions. Many construction firms are formed during good times and disappear during bad times. There is rapid movement of firms and workers between house construction, repair, maintenance, expansion, and rehabilitation.

If housing supply is interpreted to mean dwellings put on the market for rent or sale, then construction is only a small part of supply. It has been seen that construction provides only about two million units per year. But the average American moves about once in five years. Thus, about 20 percent of the 80 million dwellings in the housing stock come on the market annually. These figures imply that about one-ninth of the homes put on the market are newly constructed.

Finally, not all changes in the housing stock entail moves. Frequently, owners expand or improve dwellings while they or their tenants occupy the dwelling. Such activities constitute changes in supply from the existing stock.

Thus, the concept of housing supply depends greatly on whether one refers to supply from the existing stock or to changes in the stock by construction and demolition. Closely related is the distinction between long-run and short-run supply. During a short time, the supply of housing services is inelastic with respect to house prices, just because the stock cannot be expanded quickly and because there is a limit to the housing services that can be provided by the existing stock. But the stock can be expanded or contracted during a longer period. Building a house usually requires only a few months from start to finish. But assembling the land and obtaining necessary approvals from government agencies may require years. Thus, housing supply is much more elastic in the long than the short run.

The U.S. housing construction industry is extremely flexible. Starting from a recession year, it can double output within two years. Resources move freely into and out of the industry. Limits to the supply of new dwellings come mostly from limitations on supplies of inputs such as land or from limitations on government permission to build, not from limitations on the construction industry.

Because housing supply is such a complex concept, some economists start by estimating the housing production function. New houses are produced with materials, labor, land, and construction machinery, all of which can be substituted for each other. Such substitution can be estimated by statistical techniques. Furthermore, use of inputs to alter the supply of housing services from the existing stock can also be estimated. Having made these estimations, one can calculate the responsiveness of the supply of housing services to housing-price changes on the assumption that certain inputs are constant and others can be varied. The more inputs one permits to vary, the closer one comes to a notion of long-run supply.[1]

THE FILTER-DOWN CONCEPT

It has been seen that annual housing construction is about 2.5 percent of the housing stock and that the average dwelling is about 25 years old. As a house ages, it yields less housing service per year; thus, ignoring inflation, the annual rental falls as the house ages. The most important reason for the decline in services is that materials deteriorate with age and use. A secondary reason is that new houses embody the most recent technology, and old houses are, in part, technologically obsolete. Deterioration and obsolescence can be slowed, but not halted, by expenditures on repairs and maintenance.

For these reasons, new housing is always built for relatively high-income people, unless it is subsidized by governments. New housing comes in a variety of qualities; it is by no means true that only the richest 2.5 percent of the people live in the 2.5 percent of the stock that is newly constructed. But it is rare for a new house to be inhabited by residents below the top quarter of the income distribution. As the dwelling ages, it

---

1.   See Struyk and Ozanne.

deteriorates and gradually filters down to residents lower in the income distribution.

The filter-down process is sometimes misunderstood. People frequently bemoan the fact that only a quarter of the population can afford a new house. But there is no reason for sadness. The construction industry could build houses for the poorest people. In many poor countries, the poorest people build their own housing. But *the filter-down process provides higher quality housing for the poor than can be provided by construction of new houses for them.* A better view of the situation is that we are fortunate that housing is so durable that the filter-down process can provide such high quality housing at a price the poor can provide.

Filtering is partly a function of time and use and partly a function of demand. During the 1950s and 1960s, it was common for low-income blacks to migrate to central cities and occupy old dwellings formerly occupied by high-income whites. At such times, townhouses were divided into apartments and maintenance was reduced to a level that could be afforded by the new residents. The filter-down process accelerated. More recently, the reverse process has occurred as middle-class residents have bought old centrally located residences and renovated them. The result is a temporary reversal of the filter-down process. In both cases, the speed and direction of filtering were affected by demand shifts.

The filter-down process complicates analysis of housing markets as they affect low-income residents. How quickly and completely does the process respond to demand shifts? Does it respond as well in reverse as incomes of poor residents rise, or do their attempts to improve their housing require moves? A beginning at answering such questions has been provided in papers by Sweeney and others.

HOUSING ADEQUACY AND RACE

Slums, like poverty, are a matter of degree. Housing of given quality is better for people than housing of lower quality. The housing quality and quantity to which a nation or a family aspires should depend on its income and on the costs of housing and of other things it wants. The fact that many residents of poor countries live in housing of worse quality than that of almost any Americans is hardly grounds for complacency. With housing quality, as with incomes, the entire distribution would ideally be available and each person could choose his or her estimate as to where slums or poverty begin. But housing quality is much harder to measure than income, and only fragmentary data are available. In addition, slum housing, like poverty, is by no means restricted to urban areas. Some of our worst housing is in rural areas. Attention is focused on urban slums mainly because they are much more visible than rural slums in Appalachia or elsewhere.

Table 8.2.   INCIDENCE OF HOUSING WITHOUT COMPLETE PLUMBING FACILITIES

	1960		1970		1975	
	Nonwhite	White	Nonwhite	White	Nonwhite	White
U.S.	40.7	11.9	16.9	4.8	8.7	3.0
SMSAs	24.1	6.3	7.2	2.4	3.4	1.6
Central cities	20.7	6.7	4.8	2.6	2.4	1.9
Suburbs	39.5	5.9	17.2	2.3	7.0	1.4

Source: U.S. Bureau of the Census, *Statistical Abstract of the United States*, and *Annual Housing Survey*, for years shown.

That some Americans live in terrible housing cannot be doubted by anyone who has visited the worst neighborhood in almost any city. But measurement is another matter. Poor housing is a matter of both quality and quantity. The only measure of housing quality available on a comprehensive basis in the U.S. concerns plumbing. A dwelling is said by the Census Bureau to have adequate plumbing if it has hot running water, a flush toilet, and a bathtub or shower. Plumbing is said to be inadequate if it lacks one or more of these items. Adequate plumbing is a minimal criterion for adequate housing. Housing may be inadequate for many reasons other than plumbing. But it is an objective criterion and is probably correlated with other characteristics of minimally adequate housing. During the late 1970s, the federal government attempted to collect new data on housing adequacy.

Data on the incidence of inadequate plumbing are presented in Table 8.2. The data show remarkable progress in eliminating housing without adequate plumbing. In 1960, no less than 40.7 percent of nonwhites and 11.9 percent of whites lacked adequate plumbing. By 1975, the percentages were 8.7 and 3.0. Fragmentary evidence suggests similarly rapid progress in eliminating other characteristics of inadequate housing. Many Americans fail to realize how much our worst housing has improved during the postwar period. The table also shows that nonwhites' housing has been much less adequate than whites'. Perhaps surprisingly, the table shows the least inadequate housing of nonwhites to be in metropolitan central cities. The incidence of inadequate plumbing among nonwhites in central cities was less than one-third the national average in 1975. The high incidence of inadequate plumbing among nonwhites in metropolitan suburbs is also surprising. It is likely that, especially in 1960, most of the nonwhites recorded in Table 8.2 as living in the suburbs actually lived in the rural parts of SMSAs.

The best single measure of housing quantity is the number of rooms per person. Census data are presented in Table 8.3. Once again, the most important characteristic of the data is the record of improvement. Rooms per capita increased 11 percent during the decade, 18 percent for nonwhites. In both census years, whites' housing was substantially more adequate than nonwhites', both nationally and in SMSAs. It is interesting to note that SMSA housing was more adequate than that elsewhere in 1960, but by 1970 the difference had disappeared. This trend reflects in part growing prosperity outside SMSAs, and in part the fact that urban migration has left large amounts of housing per capita in rural areas.

The data in Tables 8.2 and 8.3 hardly present a complete picture of housing adequacy. But they are the only national data available that cover a long time period. Studies of particular slums, books of photographs, and personal visits are valuable sources of supplementary information. But none of them convey an adequate sense of the progress that has been made in improving both the worst and average housing during the period since World War II.

CAUSES OF INADEQUATE HOUSING

Social reformers have long speculated about the causes of slums. Many people have been blamed for them, from greedy landlords to city officials to white suburbanites who exclude the poor and black from suburban housing. Many causes do contribute to the creation of slum housing, but it is certain that by far the most important proximate cause of slums is poverty. Many residents in the late 1970s had incomes equivalent to no more than about $5,000 per year for a family of four. That was below the poverty line and simply did not permit purchase or rental of adequate housing at market prices, even in the absence of discrimination or any other interference with housing choices by the poor. Food and other necessities permit even the poorest people to spend no more than about a third of their incomes on housing. One third of a $5,000 annual income amounts to only $32 per week. Even the best-functioning housing market could not provide much housing for that expenditure. The contribution of discrimination and other factors to slums will be examined in this section.

The most subtle hypothesis is that causation runs not only from poverty to slums but also from slums to poverty. The notion that slums cause

Table 8.3.   ROOMS PER CAPITA, U.S. AND SMSAs

	1960		1970	
	Total	Nonwhite	Total	Nonwhite
U.S.	1.63	1.31	1.81	1.55
SMSAs	1.65	1.36	1.80	1.48
Central cities	NA	NA	1.85	1.58
Suburbs	NA	NA	1.74	1.46

Source: U.S. Bureau of the Census, *Census of Housing*, 1960 and 1970.

alienation and perpetuate poverty is a favorite among anthropologists. A varient of this hypothesis is that *poverty* causes poverty, in the sense that poverty itself causes alienation and other personality characteristics, and that *these* cause poverty to be passed from one generation to another. But we have seen throughout American history that poor immigrants escape poverty after a generation or so as opportunities are presented to them. The reason blacks have found escape from poverty so difficult is that discriminatory barriers erected against them have been higher and more durable than those erected against other groups. This leads to the hypothesis that the important causal chain is from discrimination to poverty to slums, at least among blacks. Here, discrimination refers not only to housing markets but also to employment markets, public and private education, and other areas of life.

Racial discrimination and segregation.[2]   The two notions are related, but distinct. Suppose that whites have an aversion to living near blacks but not vice versa. The situation has been analyzed using the urban land-use model presented in Chapter 5.[3] Whites' aversion to blacks leads them to pay more for housing that is far from black neighborhoods. The result is a segregated residential pattern. Since blacks' incomes are lower than whites', the analysis in Chapter 5 predicts that the pattern of segregation would be one in which blacks locate closer to the urban center than whites. This is the pattern observed in most American urban areas. Whites' aversion to living near blacks reduces the housing prices and population density along the white side of the border between black and white neighborhoods. The surprising result is that blacks' housing prices are lower and their welfare greater than if whites had no aversion to living near them.

In this model whites' aversion to blacks leads to segregation and to an increase in blacks' welfare. Such analysis of segregation can be embedded in models with a variety of spatial details, but the conclusion that blacks benefit from whites' aversion to them is invariant. But this model misses an important component of reality. Suppose, as before, that blacks are segregated close to the urban center because of whites' aversion to living near them and because of their low incomes. Suppose, in addition, that blacks' housing demand is expanding because of black immigration from outside the urban area and because of rising incomes of black residents. The result is pressure by blacks to shift the black-white border outward. Now suppose that whites are averse not only to living near blacks but also to selling or renting housing to them. In this model, two opposing forces are at work on whites. On the one hand, they are tempted to flee

2.   The classic analysis of these issues is in Becker.
3.   See Courant and Yinger.

and permit the border to move outward because of their aversion to living near blacks; on the other hand, they resist because of their aversion to selling or renting to blacks.

The foregoing was a typical urban situation in the 1950s and 1960s, when black migration to cities was rapid and blacks' incomes were rising. Trauma and tension were produced as whites organized to resist intrusion by blacks; suddenly, the dam would burst and a neighborhood would quickly become black. The theoretical model leaves unclear whether the result would be higher or lower average urban housing prices for blacks than for whites. Many hedonic housing price studies were undertaken to estimate the extent to which race affected housing prices.[4] *Most careful studies conclude that blacks paid 5 to 15 percent more than whites for housing of given physical characteristics and location relative to the urban center.*

Interestingly, the most recent hedonic studies, such as Berry's, used data from the late 1960s or early 1970s and found little or no price discrimination against blacks. By that time, migration of blacks to cities had slowed, housing discrimination had been made illegal, and white aversion to dealing with blacks had perhaps slackened. It is tempting to conclude that the period of discrimination against blacks in housing was ending. But the conclusion may be optimistic.

Neighborhood effect.   Some writers have long identified high densities as a cause of slums. It is certain, however, that high population density is not a major cause of slums. Many high-density urban neighborhoods, such as Park Avenue in New York or the Lakefront in Chicago, have very high quality housing. And much low quality housing is found in low-density rural areas. But high density may contribute to problems of inadequate housing.

Most people prefer to live in neighborhoods where the houses are attractive and well maintained. Thus, people are willing to pay more for a dwelling of given characteristics when the quality of neighboring dwellings is higher. That in turn implies that part of the total return to investment in constructing and maintaining dwellings accrues to owners or residents of neighboring dwellings. The result is an external economy in housing investment, of the type discussed in Chapter 6. Suppose a resident can obtain a 10 percent annual return by investing his money in a financial asset. Then he invests money in painting his house if the return, in increased value or utility, exceeds 10 percent. Suppose that leads to a paint job every five years. If he took account of the benefit of his paint job to his neighbors, he might paint the house every four years. The example implies underinvestment by 20 percent per year because of the external

4.   See Grether and Mieszkowski and references therein.

economy, or **neighborhood effect.** Similar analysis applies to any housing investment.

How large is the neighborhood effect? Nobody knows, but fragmentary evidence suggests that 10 or 15 percent of the returns to housing investment accrues to neighbors in a typical urban setting. For example, low-density suburban zoning is frequently justified by the neighborhood effect, but most suburbs do permit density increases if land values become very high. It is clear that the neighborhood effect is more important when the density is higher. Thus, it is more important in an urban slum than in a suburb. Yet, if it were very large, there would be more common ownership of neighboring slum properties than there appears to be.[5] If the neighborhood effect is 10 or 15 percent of the return to housing investment in urban slums, it could result in substantial underinvestment in slum housing.

GOVERNMENT HOUSING PROGRAMS

Many government activities affect housing. In fact, housing construction and use is probably the most heavily regulated of major economic activities. That is ironic given the competitive nature of urban housing markets. But government activities that affect housing markets have many purposes. Some are intended to correct real or imagined deficiencies in housing markets. Some are intended to protect particular groups from the normal implications of competitive markets. Some have non-housing goals, and affect housing in indirect and unforeseen ways. And some have no rational basis.

Real-Estate Taxation

The purpose of real-estate taxation is to finance local governments, a role discussed in Chapter 10. But it inevitably affects resource allocation in housing. Annual urban real-estate taxes are generally 2 or 3 percent of the asset value of land and structures. Annual market or imputed rents of dwellings are about 10 or 15 percent of asset values, about one percent per month. Thus, urban real-estate taxes probably average about 20 or 25 percent of rental values. It is ironic indeed that society levies the equivalent of a 20 percent sales tax on a commodity whose underconsumption is of such great public concern.

The only other commodities taxed so heavily are alcoholic beverages,

---

5. See Sternlieb.

cigarettes, and motor fuel. Consumption of the first two is discouraged by high taxes because they can be harmful to health. As will be shown in Chapter 9, motor-fuel taxes are best regarded as road-use fees, in that they are paid proportionately to road use. To the extent that they are fees for the use of expensive facilities, they do not have the distorting effect of the taxes discussed in Chapter 6. Real-estate taxes finance local government services, especially education, and might be regarded as "prices" for such services. The subject is discussed more fully in Chapter 10. There it will be shown that the key issue is whether consumers have enough options in choosing among local government jurisdictions so that they can match their tastes and incomes with menus of services and taxes offered by local governments. The conclusion will be that the view of local real-estate taxes as prices of local government services is a good approximation in metropolitan suburbs, but not in central cities. And so, real-estate taxes are likely to cause greater resource misallocation in central cities than in suburbs. Thus, the irony of real-estate taxation is compounded by the fact that it has great distorting effects where the poor are concentrated. The final irony, also to be shown in Chapter 10, is that real-estate taxes are higher, relative to asset values, in central cities than they are in suburbs.

Income-Tax Treatment of Owner-Occupied Housing

Federal income-tax provisions for owner-occupied housing are different from those for rental housing. Few owner-occupiers understand the tax break they receive, but an example will make it clear. Suppose that two next-door neighbors have identical incomes, and that they are owner-occupiers of identical homes. Suppose both itemize deductions on the federal personal income-tax return and are in the same marginal tax bracket T. Both pay the same interest rate r on their mortgages, which, in turn, is the rate they could make if they invested the equities in their homes in interest-earning assets, such as savings accounts. Then, to each, the opportunity cost of home ownership is R_1, where

$$R_1 = t(1 - T)A + r(1 - T)A + dA$$

Here A is the market value of the house, t is annual real-estate taxes as a fraction of the house's market value, and d is the annual depreciation and maintenance cost, also as a fraction of market value. The cost of tA dollars of real-estate taxes to the owner-occupier is $t(1 - T)A$ dollars, because real-estate taxes are deductible, which means that *Uncle Sam pays a percentage T of the real-estate tax in the form of reduced income tax.* Each owner pays rM dollars of annual interest on a mortgage of M dollars, which is also deductible. Each forgoes $r(1 - T)(A - M)$ dollars of after-tax income on an equity of $A - M$ dollars. The sum $r(1 - T)M + r(1 - T)(A - M)$ is the term $r(1 - T)A$ in R_1. If the house yields R_1 dollars worth of housing services, the owner receives the opportunity cost of his or her equity from ownership.

Now suppose each neighbor moves into the other's house and agrees to pay rent to the other. What rent must they pay to yield the same after-tax return on equity? The rent must be

$$R_2 = dA + tA + rA$$

If the rent is R_2, each owner has a before-tax return on his equity of $r(A - M)$, or an after-tax return equal to the opportunity cost $r(1 - T)$ $(A - M)$. Of course the owner of the rental housing pays income tax only on the amount left over after subtracting his depreciation and maintenance, real-estate tax, and mortgage interest expenses from the rent he receives.

If we subtract R_1 from R_2, we get

$$R_2 - R_1 = (t + r)TA \tag{8.1}$$

which is the extra cost to each neighbor of renting rather than owning identical houses. The reason for the difference between R_2 and R_1 is that income on the owner's equity is taxed if the house is rented, but not if it is owner-occupied.

It can be seen in Equation 8.1 that the tax break for ownership is larger, the larger are t, r, T, and A. In particular, the higher the income, the higher is the marginal tax bracket, and the greater is the tax break for owner occupancy. Aaron estimates that the difference $R_2 - R_1$ in Equation 8.1 amounts to about 15 percent of housing cost for the average owner-occupant.

The tax break has two effects. First, it increases the demand for housing by those in a position to take advantage of it. Second, it changes the mix of rental and owner-occupied housing. The percentage of housing that was owner-occupied changed little from 1890 to 1940, when it was 43.6. Since then, federal income-tax rates have become high and the ownership percentage had risen steadily, to 64.7 in 1976.

Accelerated Depreciation

Under certain circumstances, federal income-tax provisions permit landlords to depreciate during the first few years of ownership more than $1 \, n$th of the fair market value of rental property with a life of n years. Later, they must deduct less, since only 100 percent can be deducted over the useful life of the structure. If the market value of the property decreases less rapidly than the allowable depreciation during the early years of ownership, it pays to sell the property after only a few years of ownership. Thus, the tax provision encourages rapid turnover in the ownership of rental property.

Most writers believe that rapid turnover leads to poor maintenance since the owner has no long-term interest in the property. But the reasoning is faulty. The rent that can be charged tenants, and therefore the market value of the property, depends on its maintenance. Accelerated depreciation probably has little effect on maintenance.

Accelerated depreciation lowers the cost of rental dwellings and competition forces owners to pass a large part of the saving on to residents. But Aaron concludes that the saving is small relative to the saving provided owner-occupiers by the income-tax provision. In addition, the saving depends on sale of the property every few years. Thus, the saving is greater for high quality rental properties for which there is a ready market than for slum rental properties, for which there is sometimes hardly any market.

Land-Use Controls

In the United States, local governments have been given remarkably broad powers to control land use to protect the health and welfare of residents. One category of controls is intended to segregate industrial and commercial from residential uses. But the category of concern here is intended to control uses of land for residential purposes. The simplest such control is **zoning,** which stipulates the density and kinds of dwellings permitted. For example, a suburban community might be zoned for single family detached homes on no less than two acres of land each. Or it might be zoned for multifamily dwellings with no more than eight dwellings per acre.

There are many kinds of land-use controls other than conventional zoning. For example, **subdivision controls** might compel a developer to donate land for roads and other public uses, to install water mains and sewers, to build no more than a certain fraction of multifamily units, to build swimming pools, or not to build at all on some land for a stipulated number of years.

Some land-use controls are intended to protect health in straightforward ways. But many are intended to exclude low-income people, people with many children to be educated, or people who are thought undesirable for other reasons. Some land-use controls are even intended to prevent or delay construction of any kind. Many suburban communities use land-use controls to exclude all housing except that which is desired by upper-middle-class people. The result is to raise housing prices and restrict the housing choices of low-income people.

Mortgage Guarantees

The Federal Housing Administration and the Veterans' Administration insure or guarantee home mortgages in urban areas. There are several programs, but the most important pertain to owner-occupied homes. The programs reduce the risk of loss to the lender from default, and thus make him willing to lend at lower rates and for larger fractions of market value than otherwise. The volume of insurance and guarantees has been large, especially on new suburban housing, and some writers have been led to believe that the programs have been mainly responsible for postwar suburbanization of population in urban areas.

That claim greatly exaggerates the effects of the programs. It was seen in Chapter 3 that suburbanization long predates the federal programs. In addition, mortgage interest cost is usually less than one half of the cost of home ownership, and insured loans are no more than 0.5 to 1 percentage point cheaper than conventional loans. Thus, the federal programs reduce housing costs by no more than about 10 percent and probably by less. With a price elasticity of demand less than one, housing demand would be increased by less than 10 percent if all housing, rental and owner-occupied, were under the federal programs. But only part of owner-occupied housing, and little of rental housing, is. It follows that only a small part of the postwar growth of urban housing can be explained by federal programs.

Although federal mortgage-insurance programs can hardly have had a major effect on suburbanization, they have probably been worthwhile. They make use of the public sector to reduce the risk of important and relatively risky private transactions. The subsidy element of the programs is small. In the FHA program, administration costs are paid by a fee charged to the borrower.

Building Codes

Local governments in urban areas compile and enforce standards which housing must meet. Codes typically specify kinds, amounts, and conditions of materials in the structure and are often extremely detailed. Their purpose is to protect the buyer or renter from fraud and from shoddy workmanship. A house is a complex product, and laymen are often unable to appraise the adequacy of materials and workmanship. In addition, some flaws are difficult to detect once the structure is completed.

The rationale is unexceptionable. Many products in our complex economy are difficult for laymen to evaluate, and protection of consumers is a proper function of government. Nevertheless, almost every writer on housing problems is critical of housing codes. In connection with slums, the most common criticism is that codes are not enforced there. Although it is a fact, the observation is superficial. The reasons for poor enforcement reveal the basic issues.

Codes are drawn up in close consultation with the local construction industry. Since housing is built almost exclusively for middle- and upper-income residents, the construction industry naturally thinks in terms of code requirements appropriate to such housing. But we have seen that the basic characteristic of slums is that poor people cannot afford housing maintained at middle-income standards. Thus, the major problem with code enforcement in slums is that it forces owners to undertake more maintenance than the slum housing market can support. The result is flagrant violation, poor enforcement, corruption of public officials, and abandonment of structures on which codes have been enforced. The above is not to say that most standards required by codes are not desirable; they are. But it *is* to say that the poor are not helped by standards set so high that no one can meet them and still supply housing to poor people. *Codes raise the cost and quality of slum housing, but they do not increase the ability of poor residents to pay for it.*

Codes tend also to be poorly drawn. They stipulate kinds and amounts of materials in great detail. The result is that new and superior materials often cannot be used. Innovation is stifled in housing, an industry in which technical progress has been notoriously slow. Codes tend to exclude competition from construction firms or materials producers who do not have access to narrowly specified materials in the code. The remedy to the defect is to write codes that specify performance rather than materials. For example, flooring requirements should be in terms of load-carrying capacity and resistance to rot rather than of materials. However, a higher level of professional training is required to write performance codes than to write materials codes.

Almost all of the objections to building codes would be met if they emphasized disclosure rather than coercion. The government might inspect buildings and materials before, during, and after construction. It could then rate buildings in quality categories ranging from very high to very low, based more or less on technical considerations. Then it could require that the classification be shown to prospective buyers or renters. Buildings should be reinspected periodically so that classifications could be changed to reflect improved or worsened conditions. Low-income people could still occupy housing that was rated low if that was the best they could afford. And coercion regarding kinds and amounts of materials would be avoided.

Rent Control

Noneconomists often favor legal ceilings on rents that can be charged for housing in urban areas to protect renters, especially in low-income brackets, from price increases that would put decent housing beyond their means. Economists almost always oppose rent control except in wartime. Housing is a competitive industry, and the classical analysis of the effects of price control applies. If the controlled price is at least as high as the equilibrium price, controls have no effect. If it is below the equilibrium price, supply is less and demand more than in equilibrium. Thus, *controls keep the price down, but at the cost of reduced housing supply,* manifested by a low rate of construction of new housing and by reduced maintenance of old housing. In low-income areas, rent control means that housing is of poorer quality than it would have been without controls.

New York, the only large city in which rent control has been important throughout the post-World War II period, displays all the manifestations of such control. There is practically no private housing construction except for very high-income families, there is excess demand for housing, and the city has fallen far behind the rest of the country in reducing the amount of substandard housing.

In the 1970s, a small wave of state and local government rent-control laws swept the nation. They were inspired by rapidly rising rents. But the causes of rent inflation are the overall inflation rate in the economy, resulting high mortgage interest rates, the severe recession of 1974 and 1975, and suburban land-use controls that decrease supplies and increase prices of new housing. In most communities, the greatest effect of rent controls is to induce landlords to sell rental dwellings to owner-occupants. That avoids the harmful effect of rent controls on housing supply, but it hardly helps low-income residents who cannot make down payments and may not be able to obtain mortgages.

The basic point is simple. Not only do rent controls violate economists' dictum that the best way to help the poor is to provide them money, not commodities; but also, *forcing down the price of a commodity is of little help to the poor unless someone undertakes to guarantee the commodity's supply.*

Federal Subsidy Programs

The federal government has long had programs to subsidize housing for the poor. Some programs were begun in the 1930s, but most were begun by the Johnson administration in the 1960s. In 1974 the Housing and Community Development Act abolished some programs and reformed others, consolidating them under one act.

Most of the $3.1 billion of federal housing assistance recorded in Table 7.6 for 1977 is spent under the Housing Assistance Program, frequently referred to as "Section 8" housing. Its provisions differ little from those of programs started in the 1960s. It subsidizes those who build or renovate housing for the poor. To qualify, all residents of the housing must have incomes no more than 80 percent of the median in the community, and at least 30 percent of the residents must have incomes no more than 15 percent of the median. Eligible housing must be built or renovated to federal government standards and at costs not regarded as excessive by the government. The government subsidizes the housing by paying the owner the difference between the cost of the housing and the 25 percent of their incomes tenants are required to pay in rent.

The 1974 act is a major improvement over previous federal programs. It reduced the number and complexity of programs. It provides subsidies carefully focused on groups whose need characteristics are controlled by the law. Furthermore, its emphasis on rehabilitation is desirable. Housing newly constructed to meet standards acceptable to the American political process is an expensive kind of housing for the poor. Recent federal housing programs have settled, not unreasonably, on 25 percent of incomes as the maximum that poor people should be required to pay in rent for federally subsidized housing. But such rents cover no more than half the cost of newly built housing for the poor people. Thus, a large subsidy is required. Given the inevitable limitation on the amount of money society is willing to appropriate for low-income housing subsidies, a small and rather arbitrarily selected group of low-income people is given a large subsidy. This is probably not an equitable way to provide housing subsidies. It is also inefficient, because such large subsidies induce the poor to consume more housing than they would if they were given equivalent money payments. Thus, the housing provided is worth less to recipients than its cost to taxpayers, as was shown in Chapter 6.

Section 8 permits subsidies to be spent on rehabilitation, thus providing a more modest subsidy per unit and permitting more low-income residents to be helped. This is probably better from both the equity and efficiency points of view. The problem is that it is more difficult for the government to set standards for adequate rehabilitation than for adequate new housing. It remains to be seen how well this part of the program will work.

HOUSING ALLOWANCES

The most prominent proposal for reform of federal housing programs is to substitute a housing allowance for existing federal subsidy programs. The basic idea of a housing allowance is very simple: the federal government would pay each family the difference between the cost of adequate housing and a percentage of its income. Under most proposals, a condition of eligibility would be that the family live in adequate housing.

Three decisions must be made to implement a housing allowance program. First, the cost of adequate housing must be estimated. It depends on the housing standard deemed adequate and would need to vary by family composition and perhaps by community. Second, the percentage of income deemed reasonable for a poor family to spend on housing would have to be chosen. Any percentage could be chosen, but 25 is by now deeply entrenched in housing programs. Third, the standard of housing adequacy in the eligibility requirement must be chosen.

In the absence of a requirement that the recipient live in adequate housing, a housing allowance would not differ in concept from a negative income tax. The cost of adequate housing is analogous to the intercept in the negative income tax formula, the subsidy payment if the family has no income. The percentage of income deemed reasonable to spend on housing is analogous to the marginal tax rate in the negative income tax; each dollar of additional income reduces the subsidy by that amount.

Starting in the early 1970s, a ten-year housing allowance experiment was conducted by the federal government. The purpose of the experiment was to study effects of housing allowances on housing demand, on supply responsiveness, and on housing conditions for nonparticipants in each housing market. By 1979, most of the data from the experiment were in.

The crucial difference between existing programs and housing allowances is that *housing allowances place money in the hands of the poor, whereas existing programs place money in the hands of builders, landlords, or rehabilitators.* Thus, existing programs provide subsidized housing in places and of types chosen by a political process. Housing allowances would permit recipients to live where they wished and in housing of their choice, subject only to the requirement that the dwelling chosen be deemed adequate. Thus, housing allowances would provide an important degree of freedom to recipients. Equally important, housing allowances encourage recipients to make the best bargain with a landlord possible. Under existing programs, the beneficiary pays 25 percent of income in rent, and the market rent, and hence the subsidy, is negotiated between the landlord and the government. Thus, the recipient has no incentive to obtain an approved dwelling at the least total cost. Under a housing allowance, the rent paid would be entirely between the landlord and tenant. In principle, landlords need not even know that tenants receive benefits under the program. Of course, occasional inspection by government officials would be necessary to ensure that the dwelling met standards of adequacy.

Housing allowances would be an important step in providing consumer sovereignty to recipients of federal housing subsidies. For that reason, they are opposed by spokesmen for builders, banks, and local governments, all of whom now share in government programs to subsidize low-income housing. Housing allowances would circumvent such groups, placing money directly in the hands of intended beneficiaries and encouraging them to spend the money to their best advantage, subject only to the restriction that they inhabit housing deemed adequate. Since only the poor would benefit, the proposal is opposed by groups that are traditional lobbyists for government housing programs!

SUMMARY

Americans are well housed, in comparison with their own history or with the current housing of any other country in the world. Housing, of the poor and of others, has improved greatly during the postwar period. Housing is a complex commodity for which quantity and quality are difficult to measure. The housing industry is competitive, yet housing is taxed and regulated more than other commodities.

Poor housing is still found among the urban and rural poor. The federal government has many programs intended to increase housing supply or demand: income-tax treatment of owner-occupied housing, mortgage guarantees, and subsidy programs for low-income groups. Many local government actions inhibit the provision of housing: real-estate taxation, land-use controls, rent controls, and building codes.

Many economists favor substitution of a housing allowance for housing subsidy programs.

QUESTIONS AND PROBLEMS

1. On which of the following programs do you think a billion dollars of government expenditures would have the greatest effect in reducing crime and drug abuse by slum dwellers: money transfers to the poor, improved housing, or dispersal of slum residents around metropolitan areas?

2. Calculate the probable cost of a reasonable housing allowance program and compare it with current federal housing expenditures and with Aaron's estimate of the "tax subsidy" to owner-occupiers.

3. In the worst parts of some metropolitan areas such as the South Bronx in New York and the near South Side of Chicago, there are large tracts of land that have been abandoned or burned out and are unused. How do you explain this phenomenon? What, if anything, should government do about it?

4. Try to ascertain and explain how groups who speak for the urban poor, such as the Urban League and the NAACP, feel about housing allowances.

REFERENCES AND FURTHER READING

Henry Aaron, *Shelter and Subsidies,* 1972. *A fine study of federal housing programs.*

Gary Becker, *The Economics of Discrimination,* 1971. *A classic analysis of discrimination.*

Brian Berry, "Ghetto Expansion and Racial Residential Segregation in an Urban Model," *Journal of Urban Economics,* Vol. 3, No. 4, October 1976, 397–423. *A statistical study of blacks' and whites' housing costs in Chicago.*

Paul Courant and John Yinger, "On Models of Racial Prejudice and Urban Residential Structure," *Journal of Urban Economics,* Vol. 4, No. 3, July 1977, 272–291. *A survey of theoretical models of racial discrimination and segregation.*

Frank deLeeuw, "Demand for Housing," *Review of Economics and Statistics,* Vol. 53, No. 1, February 1971, 1–10. *A careful survey of housing demand studies.*

D. M. Grether and Peter Mieszkowski, "Determinants of Real Estate Values," *Journal of Urban Economics,* Vol. 1, No. 2, April 1974, 127–146. *A high quality hedonic price study of housing.*

John Kain and John Quigley, *Housing Markets and Racial Discrimination,* 1975. *A thorough analysis of effects of racial discrimination on blacks' housing.*

Richard Muth, *Cities and Housing,* 1969. *A definitive study of urban housing.*

Mitchell Polinsky, "The Demand for Housing: A Study in Specification and Grouping," *Econometrica,* Vol. 45, No. 2, March 1977, 447–462. *An abstract conceptual analysis of housing demand. Requires considerable knowledge of econometrics.*

Sherwin Rosen, "Hedonic Prices and Implicit Markets," *Journal of Political Economy,* Vol. 82, No. 1, January/February 1974, 34–55. *A fundamental theoretical contribution to hedonic price analysis. Requires advanced economics.*

George Sternlieb, *The Tenement Landlord,* 1969. *A study of slum landlords in Newark, New Jersey.*

Raymond Struyk and Larry Ozanne, *The Price Elasticity of Supply of Housing Services,* 1977. *A careful study of housing supply.*

James Sweeney, "A Commodity Hierarchy Model of the Rental Housing Market," *Journal of Urban Economics,* Vol. 1, No. 3, July 1974, 288–323. *A study of the filter-down concept.*

THE THEORETICAL ANALYSIS IN PART TWO SHOWED THAT THE function of an urban area is to facilitate exchange of goods and services by proximate locations of diverse economic activities. Firms whose products are exported from the urban area have an incentive to locate near ports, railheads, highway interchanges, or other places from which intercity trade can be conducted economically. So do households that provide the work force in export industries or consume goods imported into the urban area. Finally, so do firms that produce inputs for the export industries or consumer goods for local residents. Thus, an urban area consists of large numbers of specialized economic institutions that produce goods and services with large ratios of other inputs to land, and that locate close to each other in order to facilitate exchange.

9

Urban Transportation

Exchange of goods and services entails movement of goods and people. Thus, the size, structure, and efficiency of an urban area are influenced by the transportation system on which goods and people are moved. **Commuting**—that is, transportation of people for the exchange of labor services—is the single most important kind of urban transportation, and by far the most studied. Households also use the urban transportation system for noncommuting trips for shopping, recreation, and social activities. The movement of goods, or freight, within urban areas has been much less studied than the movement of people. Many writers assume explicitly or implicitly that an urban transportation system adequate for commuting is also adequate for all other demands made upon it. Although the assumption may be justified for analysis of an overall urban transportation system, it is not necessarily valid with respect to all the details of the system. Since little is known about the subject, practically nothing will be said in this chapter about the movement of freight in urban transportation systems.

Urban transportation is one of the most interesting examples of a mixed public-private sector in the U.S. economy. The supply side is clearly a public-sector responsibility. Streets and highways are constructed, maintained, and owned by governments. Public transit facilities such as buses, subways, and commuter trains are either owned or regulated by governments.

The demand side is more complex. Trucks and cars are privately owned, and pay to use the public streets with user fees, such as taxes on motor-vehicle fuel and tires, and vehicle registration fees. Public transit riders pay fares. To the extent that both are available, urban residents choose without coercion between private cars and public transit, depending on the combination of fares or fees and service they prefer. In contrast, public education (for example) is supplied with an important element of coercion. Children are forced to go to school, and public schools are financed by tax revenues. Thus, parents cannot avoid paying for the public service, even if they refuse to consume it and instead send their children to private schools.

The difference is important. However bad public education is, large numbers of people consume it just because they cannot afford to pay for both the public and the private service. But the use of private cars is almost always a viable alternative to the use of public transit systems. If the combination of fares and service is sufficiently bad in public transit systems, people simply refrain from buying the service and use their cars instead. Of course, governments can greatly influence the attractiveness of alternative modes of urban travel by the policies they follow. For example, public transit in the form of a subway system is relatively attractive if it provides frequent, economical service. Likewise, automobile travel is attractive if a system of urban expressways and adequate parking are available.

Thus, the basic decisions about the supply of urban transportation modes are the responsibility of the public sector. But consumers choose among available modes according to the terms on which modes are made available and according to their needs and tastes. The public sector's task is to provide the urban transportation system that best serves the community. An important and beneficial constraint on the public sector is that transportation services are bought by the public, and they can register dissatisfaction with one mode by purchasing the services of another.

A Great Debate has been underway regarding urban transportation since the 1960s. The issue is whether public policy should encourage the use of automobiles or public transit for urban commuting. One school of thought believes that only large public investment in mass-transit facilities can save central cities from strangulation by congestion and pollution. Rapid inflation of fuel prices has provided ammunition for transit advocates since the early 1970s. Another school of thought believes that the advantages of the automobile to relatively high-income commuters are so great that no viable alternative exists to investment in urban expressways. A third school of thought advocates a balanced urban transportation system, normally interpreted to mean substantial investment in both public transit and urban expressways.

The issues are complex, and careful measurement of the benefits and costs of alternative urban transportation systems is an underdeveloped speciality. In part, complexity results from the availability of several related alternatives. Streets and highways must be available in urban areas because there is no feasible alternative to the movement by motor vehicles of practically all intraurban freight and at least some intraurban passengers. To some extent, automobile commuters can share these facilities. So can at least one major form of public transit, buses. The other important kinds of public transit, subways and commuter railroads, require their own right-of-way, which is practically unusable for intraurban freight movement. General railroad rights-of-way, however, can be shared among commuters, interurban freight, and interurban passengers.

The details of urban transportation investments must be tailored to the size, structure, and existing transportation facilities of each urban area. Transportation investments that are optimum for the Philadelphia metropolitan area may not be appropriate for Los Angeles or Albuquerque. This chapter therefore explores the implications for transportation policy of pervasive characteristics of U.S. urban areas, and surveys systematic procedures for evaluating the benefits and costs of alternative transportation systems.

TRENDS IN URBAN TRANSPORTATION

There can be no doubt that overall travel in U.S. urban areas has increased rapidly since World War II. Rapid increases in urban population, incomes, auto ownership, and suburbanization have inevitably led to rapid growth of both passenger and freight transportation in urban areas. But by far the most dramatic change in urban travel has been the changing mix of modes.

Table 9.1 summarizes data on urban travel modes since 1940. However, public transit and passenger-car figures cannot be added. The transit data refer to total passengers, whereas the automobile data refer to vehicle miles. The ideal figures to have would be passenger-miles, but they are not available. Trip length per transit passenger and passengers per car have probably changed relatively little, so passenger-miles are about proportionate to the figures shown. But the factors of proportionality differ among modes. A second caution is that the 1945 figures are badly distorted by the effects of World War II. Suspension of auto production and gasoline

Table 9.1.   URBAN TRAVEL, 1940–1975

Public Transit Passengers (millions)

Year	Railways[a]	Subways[b]	Trolleys	Buses	Total	Passenger Car[c] (billions of vehicle miles)
1940	5,943	2,382	534	4,239	13,098	129.1
1945	9,426	2,698	1,244	9,886	23,254	109.5
1950	3,904	2,264	1,658	9,420	17,246	182.5
1955	1,207	1,870	1,202	7,240	11,529	224.5
1960	463	1,850	657	6,425	9,395	284.8
1965	276	1,858	305	5,814	8,253	278.2
1970	235	1,881	182	5,034	7,332	494.5
1975	1,810		78	5,084	6,972	609.6

[a]Data for 1970 refer to reclassification as "light rail."
[b]Includes elevated railways. Data for 1975 refer to reclassification as "heavy rail."
[c]Includes taxicabs and motorcycles.
Source: *Statistical Abstract of the United States*, 1969 and 1977.

rationing caused many travelers to use public transit during the war. The 1940 figures are therefore a better base for postwar comparisons.

The stark message of Table 9.1 is that urban auto travel in 1975 was 4.7 times its 1940 level, but public transit travel had fallen to little more than half its 1940 level. Thus, *the postwar growth of urban travel has been accompanied by a massive shift from public transit to private cars.* Data from metropolitan transportation studies suggest that there are about 1.5 passengers per car on an average urban passenger-car trip and that the average transit trip is about five miles. If those averages are applied to the 1975 data in Table 9.1, they indicate that more than 95 percent of passenger-miles traveled were by car. Thus, popular writers do not exaggerate when they emphasize the dominance of the automobile as the mode of U.S. urban travel.

The postwar decline of public transit travel has been accompanied by shifts in the vehicle mix. Railroads and trolleys have nearly disappeared as modes of urban travel. Subway travel declined only moderately from 1940 to 1960, and increased somewhat during the 1960s. Bus travel has been greater since the war than in 1940. Although still far below its early postwar level, it increased slightly in the first half of the 1970s.

Much of the urban transportation problem is a peak-load problem, resulting from concentration of travel at morning and evening rush hours. Most rush-hour travelers are on their way to or from work, and much concern with urban transportation is therefore focused on work trips. In Chapter 3 it was shown that rapid suburbanization of both employment and residences has occurred in the postwar period. Considerable diversity should therefore be expected in origins and destinations of work trips. Comprehensive data are presented in Table 9.2 for SMSAs of at least 100,000 population.

Despite suburbanization, the largest group in Table 9.2 is people who both live and work in central cities, amounting to more than one third of all SMSA workers. Less than one third of those who work in central cities commute in from suburbs. And twice as many suburban residents work in suburbs as work in central cities. Indeed, nearly half as many workers commute out of central cities to suburbs on the way to work as commute from suburbs to central cities. These reverse commuters have grown rapidly as a percentage of all SMSA workers. Many who live and work in suburbs, and some of those who live and work in central cities, commute crosstown (e.g., around a circumferential highway) instead of toward or away from a central business district. Beyond a doubt, the growth of automobile ownership and greatly improved urban expressways have contributed greatly to the diversity of origins and destinations since World War II. Not only are U.S. suburbs low density compared with metropolitan areas in other countries, but workplace destinations are also more diverse here than elsewhere. All discussions of public transit must take account of that fact.

Modal choices for work trips are somewhat different from modal choices for other kinds of urban travel. Some data are in Table 9.3. It was calculated from data in Table 9.1 that 95 percent of urban travel is by auto; but Table 9.3 shows that 88 percent of work trips are by auto. Within metropolitan areas, the largest group of public transit users is those who live and work in central cities. Suburban residents commute by public transit much less than do central-city residents. But suburban residents who work in central cities are much more inclined to use public transit than are those who also work in suburbs. Thus, auto travel dominates metropolitan commuting, but less than it dominates other urban travel. Within metropolitan areas, the vast majority of those who commute by public transit either live or work, or both live and work, in central cities.

Data presented in this section imply that the most drastic decline in public transit use has been for off-peak travel. It is not difficult to guess the reasons. Destinations of nonwork trips are probably even more diverse than of work trips, making auto travel relatively convenient. Also, several

Table 9.2.   PLACES OF WORK AND RESIDENCE IN SMSAs WITH AT LEAST 100,000 POPULATION, 1970

	Live in Central City			Live in Suburban Ring			
	Work in Central City	Work in Suburban Ring	Work Outside SMSA	Work in Central City	Work in Suburban Ring	Work Outside SMSA	Totals
Number (thousands)	17,843	3,456	882	8,626	16,238	2,101	49,146
Percent	36.3	7.0	1.8	17.6	33.0	4.3	100.0

Source: United States Census of Population, 1970.

Table 9.3.   PERCENT USING PUBLIC TRANSPORTATION FOR WORK TRIPS IN SMSAs WITH AT LEAST 100,000 POPULATION, 1970

Live in Central City				Live in Suburban Ring				
Work in Central City	Work in Suburban Ring	Work Outside SMSA	Subtotal	Work in Central City	Work in Suburban Ring	Work Outside SMSA	Subtotal	Total
21.8	9.1	15.1	19.5	9.6	2.7	8.1	5.3	11.8

Source: United States Census of Population, 1970.

people may travel together on nonwork trips, which adds almost nothing to the cost of auto travel but increases transit fares proportionately. Finally, many nonwork trips are for shopping, and autos are more convenient than public transit vehicles for transporting purchases. Large drops in off-peak transit use have made the financial position of transit companies even worse than is indicated by the overall decline in transit use. Vehicles and many employees and other facilities can be reduced proportionately only to peak use, but revenues fall proportionately to overall use.

In most metropolitan areas, the worst road congestion is in central cities. Table 3.4 showed that central-city employment has increased only slightly in the postwar period. Yet congestion has become worse, at least according to popular accounts. It seems paradoxical that central-city congestion should worsen during a period when its employment has hardly changed.

The resolution of the paradox is in the data in Table 9.1. To the extent that congestion has worsened, the cause has been the massive switch from public transit to automobile travel in urban areas. Trains and subways do not use streets and highways, and trolleys and buses use them much more passenger-intensively than do cars. Thus, the switch from public transit to cars increases travel on urban roads, and changes use to a mode that generates more congestion. Urban road capacity has increased since the early 1950s, mainly as a result of construction of urban parts of the interstate highway system. But increased capacity has not kept pace with the rapid increase in urban automobile travel.

The same data in Table 9.1 suggest that, even in the absence of shifts in government policy, urban road congestion may have passed its peak. With 95 percent of urban passenger travel already by car, it is unlikely that the percentage will increase much in coming years. If, in addition, central-city employment continues to grow only slightly, it seems likely that demands placed on central-city streets and highways will grow little. If public transit use increases even moderately, congestion may decrease.

DEMAND FOR URBAN TRANSPORTATION

Concern about energy and environmental problems has increased the intensity of the debate about urban transportation during the 1970s. Many people believe that high prices and unreliable supplies of gasoline, as well as pollution problems resulting from urban automobile driving, imply that more use should be made of public transit and less of autos in urban transportation. This is a complex matter that cannot be settled in this chapter. But it is possible to indicate what is known and what needs to be studied to obtain answers.

As with the market for any commodity or service, there is a demand side and a supply or production side to the market for urban transportation services. Basic transportation facilities are typically constructed and owned by governments, and cost data are made available by engineering studies undertaken to plan new facilities. The demand side, however, is subtle, because of the complex interaction between government and private decision making. Only in the 1970s have high quality demand studies been undertaken by economists.[1] The analysis will be couched in terms of **work trips,** since that is the subject of most available studies and is the most important kind of urban travel. But nonwork trips are a majority of all urban trips, and the analysis that follows applies equally to them.

It is useful to divide work trips into three parts, referred to as suburban collection, line haul, and downtown distribution. **Suburban collection** refers to the trip from the residence to the vehicle on which the longest part of the trip is made, regardless where the worker lives. If the trip is by car, suburban collection entails no more than a walk to the garage or street. If the trip is by bus, suburban collection refers to the walk to the bus stop. If the trip is by rail, suburban collection may consist of a walk or a car or bus ride to the station at which the worker boards the train or subway. **Line haul** refers to the trip by car, bus, subway, or train from the suburban collection point to the downtown distribution point. **Downtown distribution** refers to the part of the trip after the line-haul vehicle has been left. It is most commonly done on foot, but may entail a bus or taxi ride for some workers.[2]

Modal choice refers to choice of line-haul vehicle. In contemporary U.S. urban areas, the realistic choices are between car, bus, and subway. But *the mode chosen by a worker depends on characteristics of all three parts*

---

1.   Good references are the books by Mohring and by Domencich and McFadden, on which much of this section is based.

2.   A few commuting trips do not fit easily into this classification. Some workers walk or ride bicycles from their residences to their work places. Readers can make the necessary changes in the text to cover these possibilities.

of the trip. Ignoring this fact is the cause of much confusion in thinking about urban transportation. People sometimes conclude that subways are better modal choices than cars because subways are both faster and cheaper than cars. Whether they are faster and cheaper will be analyzed below. But the point to be made here is that subway commuting entails suburban collection and downtown distribution trips that may be much longer than those entailed by automobile commuting. If so, it will affect the modal choice of a rational commuter.

Trip characteristics that appear to have the greatest influence on modal choice are the time and money costs of each part of the trip. Certain modal characteristics, such as privacy and comfort, may also affect modal choice. In many studies, such data are either unavailable or indicate little effect on modal choice. They will be ignored here, but they can easily be included in Equation 9.1 below. In addition, certain characteristics of the worker, such as age, sex, and income, may affect modal choice. Once again, other variables can be included; but income has been shown to be important, and only it will be included here.

What variable should be used to represent modal choice? There are advantages to the use of q_{ij}, the probability that person i chooses commuting mode j. Then, the modal choice equation can be written

$$q_{ij} = f(p_{S_{ij}}, p_{H_{ij}}, p_{D_{ij}}, t_{S_{ij}}, t_{H_{ij}}, t_{D_{ij}}, y_i) \tag{9.1}$$

Here, S refers to the suburban collection part of the trip, H to the line haul, and D to the downtown distribution. The symbol p refers to the money cost of the part of the trip indicated by the subscript, and t refers to the time cost. p_S might be bus fare for getting to the suburban rail or subway stop. The symbol p_H is the fare on a line-haul public transit vehicle or the cost of operating a car. Transit fares are set by transit companies. Operating costs of cars are the sum of depreciation, fuel, and other costs, and might be fifteen cents per mile in the late 1970s. Of course, a unique suburban-collection or downtown-distribution mode does not correspond to a line-haul mode. For example, it might be possible to drive a car to a suburban railway station and leave it there or to take a bus there. For simplicity, such choices are ignored in Equation 9.1.

Each p and t depends on both i and j. They depend on the person, i, because commuters have different origins and destinations, so the money and time cost of the trip varies from person to person as well as by mode. Income y depends only on the person.

Domemcich and McFadden have shown how Equation 9.1 can be used to analyze modal choices. In a large sample, q_{ij} can be replaced by N_{ij}/N_i, where N_i is the number of people in group i (they live and work in similar areas and have similar incomes) and N_{ij} is the number of them who choose mode j. Thus, N_{ij}/N_i is the fraction of the people in group i who choose mode j.

Estimates of equations similar to Equation 9.1 have taught economists important lessons about modal choice. Most important is that people make substitutions between fares and travel time. Suppose, for example, that commuters who earn $6.00 per hour are observed to switch from bus to car if the time saving is 10 minutes even though the car trip costs $0.33 more than the bus trip. Then the commuters are observed to value travel time at about $0.03 per minute, or at $2.00 per hour. In fact, this result is typical. Commuters typically value travel time in line-haul vehicles at between one third and one half their wage rates. But several studies have shown that time spent walking to or waiting at transit stops is valued at two to four times the value placed on line-haul travel time. Exposure to weather and noise, and fatigue probably account for the high value placed on such suburban-collection times. Presumably, the same is true of downtown-distribution times, although evidence is lacking.

It is now possible to place the modal-choice problem in perspective with some realistic data. Consider a group of commuters who earn $6.00 per hour and who value line-haul travel time at $2.00 per hour and walking and waiting time at $6.00 per hour. The commuters live 5 miles from work and each drives a car. Suppose that getting to the car from home and from the car to the office takes 5 minutes of walking time. The roads are congested, so the 5-mile trip is made at an average speed of 20 mph, and takes 15 minutes. Car ownership costs are $0.15 per mile. The local government wants to relieve congestion and pollution, so they propose an express bus service for the commuters. The bus trip will require 10 minutes and, with federal subsidy, can be financed with a $0.50 fare. The local government calculates that the commuters' car travel costs are $0.75 (=5 × $0.15) per trip. Thus, it claims, the express bus will be both cheaper ($0.50 fare compared with $0.75 of driving costs) and faster (10 minutes by bus, 15 by car). Thus, they expect commuters to flock to the bus and they are disappointed that nobody uses it.

The correct cost comparison is as follows:

Express Bus		*Car*	
Walking and waiting time		Walking time	
(10 minutes @ $6.00)	$1.00	(5 minutes @ $6.00)	$0.50
Line-haul time		Line-haul time	
(10 minutes @ $2.00)	0.33	(15 minutes @ $2.00)	0.50
Fare	0.50	Vehicle ownership costs	
Total	$1.83	(5 × $.15)	0.75
		Total	$1.75

The government's calculation ignored the 10-minute walking and waiting time for the bus and the fact that commuters place a high value on such time. Even though total commuting time is the same for the two modes (20 minutes), the mix of high- and low-value time is different.

The point of this example is that transportation planners pay attention to line-haul travel (by express bus or subway), but they pay too little attention to suburban-collection and downtown-distribution problems. A well-designed line-haul transit system provides travel that is attractive compared with car travel, but if service is infrequent or the transit system is far from residences of potential customers, commuters will not use it. In estimating public transit demand, careful attention must be paid to time costs. In the example, time costs were more than half the total for auto commuters, and almost three quarters of the total for bus commuters.

The example is relevant to proposals for high quality express bus or subway transit systems. In fact, in most U.S. cities, travel by bus is slower than by car. One therefore finds that most bus commuters are low-income workers, whose time value makes bus travel economical compared with car travel.

Congestion and Pricing

Controversy surrounds the pricing of both automobile and transit use in urban areas. Most controversy pertains to whether one mode or another is or should be subsidized. To understand these issues, it is necessary to investigate the effect of congestion on optimum pricing policy.

It has already been noted that congestion slows travel. The theoretical analysis is the same for all modes. There are many cities in the world in which buses congest streets, but in the United States emphasis is properly placed on congestion from cars.

The basic theoretical issue can be posed in a simple example. Consider a road stretch with no access or exits between points A and B. Suppose cars enter the road at A at a uniform rate per hour. Even if the rate is small, a maximum travel speed is imposed by legal speed limits and safety considerations. Associated with the maximum speed is a cost per vehicle mile of travel. It includes both time and operating cost, and depends on the maximum travel speed and on the characteristics of the vehicle. Now suppose there is an increase in the rate at which vehicles enter at A. When the number of vehicles entering per hour becomes great enough, congestion occurs and travel speed falls.

The critical rate of entry at which congestion begins depends on characteristics of the road such as width, grade, curves, and surface. But on any road stretch, congestion occurs if the number of vehicles is great enough, because there are too many cars to permit the headway necessary for safety at high speeds, and cars must slow to a speed consistent with the available headway. Automobile operating costs are relatively insensitive to speed, but time costs are inversely proportional to speed. Thus, slow travel caused by large numbers of cars entering at A increases the cost per vehicle-mile of travel from A to B.

Figure 9.1

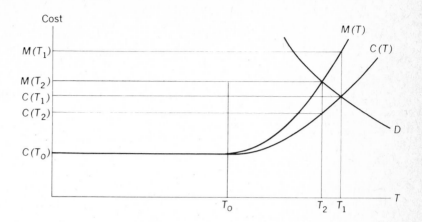

The foregoing ideas are illustrated in Figure 9.1. T is the number of vehicles entering per hour at A, and $C(T)$ is the cost per vehicle-mile of travel between A and B. $C(T)$ is constant for values of T up to T_0, which can be called the design capacity of the road. Beyond T_0, $C(T)$ rises rapidly with T. Several specific forms of $C(T)$ have been estimated by economists.

Now suppose, in the spirit of Equation 9.1, that the number of users of the road from A and B depends on the cost of travel. If travel is costly, people use a different route or mode, or alter their places of work or residence to avoid the trip. The number of people who make the trip as a function of the travel cost is the demand curve for travel on the road from A to B, designated D in Figure 9.1. The equilibrium travel on the road is then T_1 vehicles per hour, the number of travelers willing to pay the cost of the trip. The equilibrium cost per vehicle is $C(T_1)$. $C(T_0)$ is the cost per vehicle in absence of congestion, and $C(T_1) - C(T_0)$ is congestion cost per vehicle.

With a constant rate of entry at A, all vehicles travel at the same speed, and incur the same cost $C(T_1)$. Thus, $C(T_1)$ is the total cost of travel for those making the trip divided by the number of travelers, or average cost per traveler. Elementary price-theory texts show that if an average cost curve is rising, the corresponding marginal cost curve must be above it. In the present context, marginal cost means the increase in travel cost to all travelers resulting from an increase in the number of vehicles using the road. In Figure 9.1, marginal cost is the curve designated $M(T)$. It is important to understand exactly why $M(T)$ is above $C(T)$. If T exceeds T_0, speed decreases with increases in T and $C(T)$ therefore exceeds

$C(T - 1)$. But, since everybody travels at the same speed, everybody goes slower if T cars enter per hour than if $T - 1$ enter. Thus, *the addition of a Tth user imposes costs on all T users because of the reduced speed.* $M(T)$ exceeds $C(T)$ by the amount of the increased costs imposed on other travelers by the Tth entrant.

The excess of $M(T)$ over $C(T)$ is an external diseconomy of the type defined in Chapter 6. Each traveler perceives and bears the average cost $C(T)$. No traveler has any way of perceiving the cost his travel imposes on others. Therefore, the equilibrium number of travelers T_1 equates average cost to the price of the trip. As was shown in Chapter 6, the situation represents an inefficient allocation of resources in that too many people use the road and there is too much congestion. T_2 entrants per hour, which equates marginal cost to price, represents efficient road use. Of course, if D intersects $C(T)$ to the left of T_0 in Figure 9.1, there is no congestion and no misallocation of resources.

The analysis above implies that a special method of rationing the use of the road is needed. How can it be done? If congestion were the same at all times and places, a gasoline tax would be an efficient congestion toll. The tax should be $M(T_2) - C(T_2)$ per vehicle-mile in Figure 9.1. The appropriate tax equals the excess of social marginal cost over the cost perceived by the traveler, at the optimum use T_2. But congestion is not the same at all times and places. The worst congestion is restricted to rush-hour travel on radial routes, in most urban areas.

Some economists and engineers believe it would be technically feasible and economical to meter use of urban streets and highways by electronic means and to charge congestion tolls appropriate to time and place. But neither technical nor economic feasibility has been demonstrated. In the absence of metering, planners are tempted to use nonprice rationing schemes: controls or prices on downtown parking, carpool requirements, and banning cars from certain areas are examples. All such proposals entail arbitrary rationing, in which users are selected without regard to the value of the arrangement to them. The value of **price rationing** is that it permits people to decide whether the trip's value to them exceeds its social cost.

How much would optimum congestion tolls be? Studies by Mohring and others indicate that two or three cents per vehicle-mile of rush-hour travel would not be unusual. Peak tolls would be much greater. Such numbers are large relative to present gasoline taxes, which are generally no more than one cent per vehicle-mile.

Most countries in which auto transportation is important have opted for much higher gasoline taxes than U.S. levels. It is a crude congestion toll, but is probably better than alternative ways of rationing use of congested roads. It has the great advantage that it leaves travel decisions in the hands of the traveler. In most urban areas, a state gasoline tax at least twice the present level would be justified. Then rural residents, who could demonstrate that they did not use cars in congested urban areas, could apply for refunds. It would be far from a perfect congestion toll, but it would be much better than the present situation.

In fact, U.S. governments have moved in the opposite direction. Underpricing of automobile-caused congestion leads to excessive auto commuting and too little use of public transit. Buses economize on road space compared with cars, and subways travel under roadways. Believing that adequate congestion tolls cannot be levied, governments have subsidized public transit systems on the theory that correct relative prices of auto and public transit use are thereby established. The federal government has paid the large capital costs of recently constructed subway systems (e.g., in Washington), and fares have, at most, covered the relatively small operating costs. Bus subsidies are smaller, but they are growing.

This policy may establish the correct relative prices of the two modes, if the subsidy level is appropriate, but it means that urban transportation is underpriced relative to other commodities and services. The result is that *urban Americans simply travel too much.* It would be better to have much higher gasoline taxes and insist that public transit come closer to paying its way.

Public transit fares should not necessarily cover the full costs of a public transit system. The analysis in Chapter 6 implies that the optimum price of such a service equals its long-run marginal cost. Transit systems are probably **decreasing-cost activities,** which implies that marginal cost is below average cost. If so, optimum fares do not cover total costs. It is frequently proposed that gasoline taxes be used to subsidize public transit. But there is no relationship between receipts from optimum congestion tolls and optimum subsidies for transit systems. If congestion tolls exceed public transit subsidies, then toll revenues can be used to reduce other, distorting, taxes. If congestion tolls are less than transit subsidies, then the remaining subsidy must be paid from government general revenues, unless it is decided that the distorting effects of the taxes needed to raise subsidy revenues exceeds the distorting effect of excessively high transit fares. That might be the case if local real-estate taxes are the source of the extra tax revenues. In that case, transit fares should be set to cover costs without subsidy.

Costs and Supply of Urban Transportation

Line-haul public transit systems are subject to decreasing costs. Cost per passenger-mile of travel falls as the number of passengers using an uncongested right-of-way increases, because indivisible capital and land costs are significant parts of the total. The same is true of car travel, but scale economies are exhausted at much lower service levels than on public transit systems. A subway or express bus lane on an expressway can easily carry 10,000 or 15,000 passengers per hour in one direction, whereas an urban expressway with two lanes in each direction can carry only about 3,000 cars per hour in one direction of uncongested travel.

Especially for subway systems, capital costs are very great. Subways require large numbers of riders to spread capital costs over enough riders so that cost per ride is down to a level competitive with car travel, even if the subway is subsidized. Capital costs of bus systems are much more moderate than those for subway systems. In addition, bus systems have the important advantage that they can share rights-of-way with cars and trucks. Other vehicles can use the roads at peak and off-peak hours; and if costs or demand shift so that there is more car and less bus travel, the roadway continues to be utilized. If travel shifts away from a subway system, the capital is left idle.

An important element of increasing returns has to do with **service frequencies.** Unless there is car pooling, cars are self-scheduled. If public transit times are known and frequent, customers can arrive at stops and board vehicles without delay or inconvenience. But in the United States, the usual procedure is for riders' arrival times to be random in comparison with the transit vehicle's arrival time. Thus, average waiting time is half the transit vehicles' **headway** (time between arrivals of vehicles). Each 10 percent increase in the number of transit vehicles means a 10 percent decrease in average waiting time. According to Mohring, this results in a substantial decrease in cost per ride. But the saving is realized by riders, not by transit companies. Thus, subsidization may be justified to obtain optimum service frequencies. In addition, vehicle speed may increase if service frequency increases, because fewer—or less time-consuming— stops may be needed per vehicle. Finally, if increasing service frequency induces some people to switch from car to public transit vehicles, road congestion may decrease. The resulting reduction in travel time for auto-mobile commuters is an additional benefit of improved service by the public transit system.

Public transit investments should be made on the basis of costs and benefits of the entire system. Scale economies mean that public transit systems, especially subways, cannot succeed on a small scale. If a worker can take a subway only part way to work and then has to switch to a bus or has a long walk, he or she is likely to commute by car. Likewise, if the worker has a long trip by car, foot, or bus to get to a suburban stop, he or she is likely to commute by car. Finally, if the worker has a long wait for the transit vehicle, he or she is likely to commute by car. All these considerations mean that public transit systems must fail unless the system links many origins and destinations and provides fast, frequent service. The implication is that it is pointless to start with a small public transit system, with the idea of increasing it if it appears successful. To start with a small system is to guarantee failure. Only careful analyais of demands and costs can indicate what type and scale of system can be successful.

Of course, there is no guarantee that any type or scale of system can be successful. For many urban areas, an auto-based transportation system is best, and not even the best planned and operated public transit system can produce benefits that exceed its costs.

Some Examples

Each urban area has its peculiar size, structure, and inherited transportation system. Planning urban transportation investments must take account of many facts that are peculiar to each urban area. In this section, some general observations are made, but they may not apply to particular urban areas.

In the United States, nearly all large SMSAs already have subway systems. New York, Chicago, Philadelphia, and Boston have long had subway systems. The exceptions are Los Angeles and Detroit. Los Angeles has grown up around a freeway system. Studies have shown that its origin-destination pattern is so diverse that it cannot justify a subway system. In Detroit, the presumed reason is that it is the auto capital of the country. In the 1970s, subway systems were built in the two next-largest SMSAs, San Francisco and Washington. Small metropolitan areas cannot justify subway systems. Their optimum transportation systems are a mix of buses and cars. Thus, serious controversy centers around the roughly 10 SMSAs that are between about 2 and 3 million population. A few now have rudimentary subway systems, but none has an elaborate system. Included in this group are such SMSAs as Baltimore, Houston, Minneapolis, and Pittsburgh.

High fuel prices, congestion, and air pollution problems probably justify higher-quality public transit systems than are now available in at least several such SMSAs. What kind? To focus discussion, two possibilities will be considered. One is a subway system (which might be above ground in suburbs) with several radial lines from suburbs to the Central Business District (CBD). The other is an express bus service in which buses make frequent stops in specified origin areas and then, presumably full or nearly full, become express buses until they reach the CBD or other major employment area, where they provide local distribution service.

The bus system has important advantages over the subway system. Most importantly, one vehicle can be used for suburban collection and line haul, nevertheless picking commuters up near residences, whereas the subway requires a substantial trip from home to suburban stop for most commuters. A second advantage is that bus routes can be changed, established, or abandoned more easily than subway routes as suburbs grow and work places change, and if mistakes are made. A third advantage is that a high-quality bus service can be operated along a particular route with somewhat fewer passengers than are required for a subway line.

Consider a metropolitan area of about 2 million people with typical characteristics. One third of the population, say 650,000 people, work. As is indicated by Table 9.2, a little more than half, say 350,000 people, work in the central city. The urbanized part of the SMSA is semicircular, with one fourth of the circle unavailable because of a harbor or other topographical feature. The urbanized area has an area of 340 square miles, so it has a radius of about 12 miles and an average population of about 6,000 per square mile. Thus, worker density is about 2,000 per square mile, somewhat lower in distant suburbs and somewhat higher close to the CBD. As a good approximation, assume that only work trips are made by the transit system.

The subway can hardly be used by many who work outside the central city. Their origins and destinations are diverse, and most of their travel is circumferential, trips difficult to serve by transit systems. Thus, an upper limit to the number of transit riders is set by the 350,000 central-city workers. To be optimistic, suppose 200,000 workers per day ride the transit system. About 20,000 passengers each way per day (10,000 per hour during a two-hour peak period) are required to support a subway at a service frequency great enough to induce many workers to use it. Thus, the 200,000 riders could support 10 radial lines from suburbs to CBD. If the lines are spaced evenly around the semicircular metropolitan area, no resident would live more than three miles from a subway line, and most would live within two miles. Still, most of these commuters would be far enough from the nearest subway stop that they would commute by car rather than walk to the stop. But an express bus system could traverse most residential areas, passing within a short distance of most homes. Thus, *the low density of U.S. residential suburbs makes it extremely difficult for a subway system to compete with automobile commuting, and provides an important advantage to a bus system.*

If ridership was much less than 200,000, only few lines and infrequent service, or service which requires many stops to fill the bus, could be provided. In that case, even a bus system could not compete with automobile commuting. Thus, the key issue regarding public transit in middle-sized metropolitan areas is whether service can be provided that is frequent, fast, and pervasive among origins and destinations. If so, it can compete with autos at no more than modest subsidies. If not, people will not use it and they will refuse to pay taxes to provide the large subsidies required to preserve the system for the few who do use it.

THE EFFECTS OF TRANSPORTATION ON URBAN STRUCTURE

The foregoing analysis has taken as given the origins and destinations of work trips. In other words, it has assumed that the locations of residences and workplaces are unaffected by the urban transportation system. The assumption cannot literally be true. Indeed, the analysis in Chapter 5 showed that the residential density pattern is affected by the relationship between housing prices and transportation costs. Thus, it is inevitable that a major transportation investment such as the construction of a transit system would have at least some effect on the locations of residences and workplaces. Some writers take the view that the effect of transit systems on urban structure is profound. It is frequently maintained that a modern transit system would stop or reverse the alleged decay of downtown business areas, eliminate urban sprawl, and solve the unemployment problem among blacks in urban ghettos.

Effects of transit systems on urban structure depend on the system and metropolitan area in question. But it is easy to see that the strongest claims are exaggerated. Even the best designed and operated public transit system could have only a moderate effect in reducing the total of time and money costs of commuting. Although there has been underinvestment in public transit in U.S. urban areas, the existing, mainly auto-based, transportation system is simply not much more costly than one with a better mix of public transit and automobiles.

The purpose of a radial transit system is to make radial travel economical. People already employed in the CBD would find it advantageous to live farther out, on the average, to take advantage of low land (and therefore housing) prices. It was shown in Chapter 5 that a decrease in transportation cost would flatten the population density function of CBD workers.

The transit system would make the CBD more attractive for firms, because it would be more accessible to their employees. Thus, CBD employment would increase at the expense of suburban employment, making the employment density function steeper. It is also possible that the transit system would attract CBD employment that would not have located in the SMSA at all in the absence of the transit system. Construction of the subway system in San Francisco was accompanied by a surge of downtown skyscraper construction. But San Francisco was growing rapidly even before construction of the subway system. *It is unlikely that large transit investments would have a large effect on total employment and population in the SMSA.*

Furthermore, it is unlikely that transit improvements would have a large effect in creating CBD jobs for central-city unemployed. The main effect of the transit system is to increase accessibility to CBD from suburbs. Thus, most jobs created would probably be for predominantly well-educated and well-paid suburbanites. Central-city unemployed already have access to the CBD, and a transit system would hardly increase the attractiveness of the CBD as a place of employment for them.

The conclusion of this section is that *major transit improvements would slow, but probably not reverse, employment decentralization.* Nor would the effect on total SMSA employment be large. Transit investments would hasten the flattening of population density functions.

TRANSPORTATION AND URBAN POVERTY

There are two ways in which urban poverty enters into consideration of urban transportation. First, low-income housing is sometimes displaced by the construction of urban transportation facilities, especially expressways. In some ways, the problem is similar to the displacement of low-income housing by slum clearance projects. Unlike slum clearance, however, urban expressways are not restricted to poor parts of central cities. In fact, much of the postwar construction of urban highways has been of circumferential roads, which pass only through suburbs, and radial expressways, which pass through both low- and high-income areas.

The problem is similar to that of slum clearance, in that low-income people are affected differently by conventional compensation procedures than are high-income people. High-income residents tend to be owner-occupiers, and compensation of the property owner is therefore equivalent to compensation of the resident. Low-income residents, however, tend to be renters, and therefore do not benefit when property owners are compensated under condemnation proceedings. Moreover, renters may suffer, whether they are displaced by slum clearance or by highway construction, if their homes and neighborhoods are destroyed. It seems indisputable that renters should be compensated for such losses, be they financial or psychic. Determination of psychic losses is not easy, but it is done in other equity proceedings. The cost of such compensation is a cost of the facility constructed, and should be borne by those who benefit from the facility. Some federal programs now provide assistance to renters in finding places to live.

Second, and more complex: *an automobile-based urban transportation system has an* **income bias,** *in that the poorest people cannot afford cars.* The problem is especially acute among blacks confined to central-city ghettos because of racial discrimination in housing markets. Some people advocate construction of public transit systems in order to improve the access of ghetto residents to suburban employment centers.

It can hardly be doubted that the problem is real. Many labor specialists believe that ghetto unemployment rates are high partly because blacks who live there lack access to suburban jobs. Even if there were no effect of housing segregation on ghetto unemployment, segregation would nevertheless impose costs on blacks in the form of excessive commuting to suburban jobs.

The first thing to be said is that the problem is not basically one of transportation. If ghetto residents are deprived of access to suburban jobs because of housing segregation, the obvious answer is to open up suburban housing to blacks on the terms on which it is available to others. One might realistically view special provisions for transportation of ghetto residents to suburban jobs as a way of maintaining all-white suburbs.

The second point to be made is that little is known about what transportation system would be best for ghetto residents. It is clear that the mass-transit systems now being planned are designed to bring suburban residents to central cities rather than to bring central-city residents to the suburbs. This is at least suggested by the proposed locations of radial rights-of-way and of suburban line-haul stations. It is also clear that suburban bus systems are planned to bring suburban residents to line-haul stations and not to bring central-city residents from suburban line-haul stations to suburban employment centers.

It is possible that the diversity of origins and destinations of ghetto residents who would commute to suburban jobs is such that an automobile-based system would be better for them than a transit system. If so, that the poor cannot afford automobiles implies that they are even less able to afford transit transportation. But the foregoing comments are meant to raise questions rather than to provide answers. The special transportation needs of the urban poor are simply not known.

SUMMARY

The purpose of an urban transportation system is to facilitate the exchange of goods and services in the urban area. The optimum transportation system for an urban area depends on the area's size and structure as well as on the historical development in the area.

Since 1940, the volume of urban transportation has grown rapidly, and there has been a massive shift from public transit to private automobile transportation. Total commuting in an urban area depends on locations of employment and residences. Choice of mode depends on time and money costs of alternative modes. Among realistic alternatives in U.S. urban areas, time is likely to be the dominant consideration. Any mode becomes congested if used by enough passengers. Congestion costs are an important element in planning and pricing urban transportation systems. It is likely that both public transit and private automobile transportation are underpriced in U.S. metropolitan areas.

The major policy debate in urban transportation is the benefits and costs of public transit and automobile travel in medium-size metropolitan areas. The decision depends mainly on whether a combination of fares and conditions of service can be offered by public transit that will be attractive to enough commuters to make public transit economical. There is serious doubt whether subway systems can be economical for a large number of medium-size metropolitan areas.

There is considerable doubt about the effects of urban transportation systems on the structure of urban areas. Public transit systems would probably increase CBD employment, but it is unlikely that the effect would be large. Very little is known about the urban transportation needs of the poor, but it is unlikely that public transit systems being designed for many metropolitan areas will be valuable for low-income residents.

QUESTIONS AND PROBLEMS

1. It is frequently proposed that New York's subways and buses be free to all passengers. Evaluate the proposal on the grounds of efficiency and equity.

2. Suppose technical improvements made it possible for helicopter buses to carry 50 commuters each at 60 miles per hour and a fare of 20 cents per mile. What would be the effect on location of employment and housing in metropolitan areas during the remainder of the century?

3. Do you think it might be desirable to have one or more circumferential subway lines in large metropolitan areas at a future date?

4. Do you think that low-income workers spend more or less time commuting than do high-income workers in metropolitan areas? Which group do you think commutes longer distances? Can you reconcile your answers with the theoretical analysis in Chapter 5?

REFERENCES AND FURTHER READING

Thomas Domencich and Daniel McFadden, *Urban Travel Demand*, 1975. *A definitive technical study, using the probabilistic approach to travel demand.*

John Meyer, John Kain, and Martin Wobel, *The Urban Transportation Problem*, 1965. *A thorough analysis of benefits and costs of alternative transportation modes.*

Herbert Mohring, *Transportation Economics*, 1976. *A survey of transportation economics.*

Richard Quandt (editor), *The Demand for Travel: Theory and Measurement*, 1970. *Technical papers on travel demand.*

IN THE UNITED STATES, STATE AND LOCAL GOVERNMENTS PRO-
vide most of the government services that have a direct and immediate
impact on people's lives and welfare. A large part of the federal government's budget is devoted to national security and other activities that affect
the country's relationships with the rest of the world. Another part of the
federal budget finances programs, such as research and space explora-
tions, that affect the public only indirectly. A third use of federal funds is
to help finance programs that are the direct responsibility of state and local
governments. But state and local governments administer almost all government services provided directly to the people.

10

Financing
Local Government

Important examples are public education, public health and welfare
programs, police and fire protection, public transportation, and water
supply and sanitation. Most of these services have effects on people's lives
that are not only direct, but also important. Few things are more important
determinants of standard and style of living than the quantity and quality
of education received. Likewise, police protection involves the safeguard-
ing of life, property, and civil rights.

Almost no one is satisfied with the provision and financing of services
by state and local governments. Critics accuse these governments of timid-
ity in responding to social problems, of inadequate and burdensome methods of finance, of squandering taxpayers' money, of permitting the quality
of government services to deteriorate, and of other deficiencies. In fact,
it is striking how often complaints about the quality of urban life turn out,
on analysis, to be complaints about the provision of government services.
Many of these problems are beyond the economist's skills and tools. But
economics can shed light on important issues related to the provision and
financing of public services.

THE SYSTEM OF STATE AND LOCAL GOVERNMENTS

Under the U.S. Constitution, sovereignty is shared between federal and state governments. Local governments are the creations of state governments. A characteristic of our federal system is that state governments have created a bewildering variety of local governments. Although the subject is mainly the concern of political science rather than of economics, some understanding of the system of local government is prerequisite to understanding problems of local governments.

In 1977, there were nearly 80,000 local governments in the United States, almost all having limited power to levy taxes and spend the revenues collected. The best-known of these governments are the 3000 counties that nearly blanket the country and the 19,000 municipal governments. In addition, there are about 19,000 townships, 15,000 school districts, and 25,000 special districts. School districts are ordinarily empowered to levy property taxes to support public education. Special districts are established for specific purposes, most commonly water supply and waste disposal, and levy taxes to finance their activities.

The functions assigned to particular governments vary greatly from state to state. Some state governments perform functions that are performed by county or municipal governments in other states. In some states municipal governments provide public education, whereas school districts provide it in other states. Furthermore, there is little coincidence among boundaries of jurisdictions. School and special-district jurisdictions may overlap municipal and county boundaries. Thus, it is very difficult to obtain comparable data on state and local public finance. For example, the fact that one state government has a much smaller budget than another may simply mean that municipalities in the first state finance services financed by the state government in the other. Likewise, the central-city government in a particular SMSA may have an unusually small budget simply because it is in a state in which education is provided by county governments or by education districts.

As a result of the complexity of the system, many citizens are within the jurisdiction and taxing power not only of federal and state governments, but also of several local governments. Furthermore, an integrated economic area, such as an SMSA, may contain an extraordinarily large number of local governments. The Chicago SMSA has more than 1100 local governments, and the New York, Philadelphia, and Pittsburgh SMSAs have more than 500 local governments in each.

Political scientists tend to be critical of our complex system of local governments from the point of view of governmental operations. Although the issues go beyond the scope of economics, it is difficult not to conclude

Table 10.1.   PER CAPITA GOVERNMENT GENERAL EXPENDITURES, 1902–1975

Year	Federal	State and Local	Total	Federal as Percent of Total	Federal as Percent of GNP	Total as Percent of GNP
1902	7.14	12.80	19.93	35.8	2.3	6.4
1922	33.04	47.41	80.45	41.1	4.9	11.9
1940	67.33	69.85	137.18	49.1	9.2	18.7
1950	249.95	150.22	400.17	62.5	14.9	23.9
1960	426.26	288.21	714.48	59.7	17.9	30.0
1964–65	511.13	385.30	896.43	57.0	17.3	30.3
1969–70	706.99	646.20	1353.19	52.2	18.9	36.2
1975	1416.75	1075.93	2492.68	56.8	19.8	34.8

Source: (except for 1975) United States Census of Governments, Vol. 6, No. 4, 1972. 1975 data from the Survey of Current Business, 1977.

that the system is cumbersome and unwieldy. Some implications for government resource allocation are explored later in the chapter.

There has been a tendency to reduce the number of local governments during recent decades, although the reduction results entirely from school-district consolidation. In 1952, there were almost 117,000 local governments in the country, including 67,000 school districts. But the number of special districts has more than doubled since the early 1950s.

TRENDS IN STATE AND LOCAL GOVERNMENT FINANCE

Whatever disagreements there may be about the role of government, it must be agreed that it has been a growth sector in the U.S. economy during the twentieth century. Table 10.1 shows the trend of government general expenditure per capita since 1902. In 1902, governments spent only about $20 per capita. By 1975, 73 years later, it had risen to $2500. Since most government expenditure is financed by current taxes, taxes have risen at about the same rate. Of course, the private sector of the economy has also grown rapidly during the present century, and government expenditure has therefore risen less rapidly in relation to income or output than in relation to population. Between 1902 and 1942, per capita government expenditure approximately doubled each decade. This implies a 7 percent annual growth rate, considerably faster than the growth of the private sector. But since the adjustment following World War II, government expenditure has inched up only slightly in relation to total income. Government general expenditure was 23.9 percent of gross national product in 1950, and 34.8 percent in 1975.

There have been two major trends in the relative sizes of federal and state and local governments during the twentieth century. Until after World War II, the federal government grew much more rapidly than did state and local governments. Although the trend was apparent during earlier years, it clearly resulted mainly from the Depression of the 1930s and from World War II. But for most of the period since World War II the trend has been reversed, and state and local government expenditures have grown more rapidly than federal government expenditures. By 1970, state and local government expenditures were nearly as large as those of the federal government. During the 1970s, the earlier trend has been reasserted. In part, the rapid growth of state and local government expenditure since World War II has been financed through federal taxes. The federal government has always made grants to state and local governments to help finance specific programs. Since World War II, such grants have been a major source of increased state and local government revenue. Federal grants to state and local governments were $7.15 per capita in 1940 and $16.39 in 1950. By 1978 they had grown to $341.00. Since the early 1950s, about one third of the growth of state and local government expenditure has been financed by increased federal government grants.

It is sometimes claimed that state and local governments are inadequately financed because of the need to compete with each other for high-income population and employment, which makes it almost impossible for them to raise taxes. This claim is analyzed later in the chapter, but it should be noted here that the data in Table 10.1 do not lend it any support. Of course, no one knows how much state and local government expenditures would have grown if their taxation had not been affected by competition. However, the data in Table 10.1 make it clear that it is an exaggeration to say that state and local taxes are practically impossible to raise. Most state and local tax revenues grow less rapidly than personal incomes if rates are held constant. Yet state and local government expenditures grew from 11.6 percent of personal incomes in 1957 to 18.3 percent in 1975. That growth has necessitated frequent introduction of new taxes and increases in the rates of existing taxes.

Revenue

Table 10.2 presents a detailed picture of the sources of state and local government revenue. The percentages refer to amounts that the governments raise from their own sources. **Intergovernmental transfers** appear at the bottoms of the columns. Transfers to state governments are from the federal government. Transfers to local governments may come directly

Table 10.2   STATE AND LOCAL GOVERNMENT REVENUE, 1971–1972
(MILLIONS OF DOLLARS)

Source	State		Local		State and Local	
Property	1,257	1.5%	41,620	55.4%	42,877	27.0%
Sales and gross receipts taxes	33,250	39.4	4,268	5.7	37,518	23.5
Individual income taxes	12,996	15.4	2,230	3.0	15,227	9.5
Corporate income taxes	4,416	5.2	—	—	4,416	2.8
Other taxes, including licences	7,951	9.4	1,621	2.2	9,572	6.0
Charges and miscellaneous	10,780	12.8	15,810	21.1	26,590	16.7
Utility and liquor store revenue	1,905	2.3	7,924	10.6	9,829	6.2
Insurance trust revenue	11,806	14.0	1,622	2.2	13,428	8.4
Totals	84,362	100.0%	75,097	100.0%	159,456	100.0%
Intergovernmental transfers	27,981	—	39,694	—	—	—

Source: United States Census of Governments, Vol. 4, 1972.

from the federal government or indirectly through state governments, or they may come from funds raised by the state governments.

State governments raise almost 40 percent of their revenues from sales taxes. Almost all states levy sales taxes, although the rates and the transactions to which they apply vary greatly among states. Personal income taxes are the second-largest source of state government revenue, but they yield only 15.4 percent of total revenues. Of state government revenue, 15.1 percent comes from charges such as tuition at state universities, sales in state liquor stores, and license fees. The category "other taxes," which accounts for 9.4 percent of state government revenues, includes motor vehicle taxes, death and gift taxes, severance taxes, and several others.

Local governments receive about 55 percent of their revenue from property taxes. Many are also permitted to levy sales taxes, and a few have income or payroll taxes. But dependence of local governments on property taxes is great and of long duration. No other tax yields nearly as much revenue. Local governments also raise substantial amounts of revenue from such charges as water bills, tuition at community colleges, parking fees, transit fares, and license fees. Table 10.2 shows that nearly half of all taxes and charges collected by state and local governments are collected by local governments.

Expenditure

What do state and local governments do with the money they collect? Some comprehensive data appear in Table 10.3. Expenditures in the table refer to direct expenditures for the purposes indicated. For example, state

Table 10.3.   STATE AND LOCAL GOVERNMENT EXPENDITURES, 1971–1972
(MILLIONS OF DOLLARS)

Function	State		Local		State and Local	
Education	17,153	23.7%	48,661	41.2%	65,814	34.5%
Transportation	12,747	17.6	7,943	6.7	20,690	10.9
Public welfare	12,247	16.9	8,869	7.5	21,117	11.1
Health and hospitals	6,008	8.3	7,014	5.9	13,023	6.8
Police, fire, and correction	2,209	3.0	8,488	7.2	10,696	5.6
Parks and natural resources	2,470	3.4	2,971	2.5	5,440	2.9
Sanitation	—	—	4,846	4.1	4,846	2.5
Housing and urban renewal	—	—	2,700	2.3	2,700	1.4
Administration and interest	5,402	7.5	7,680	6.5	13,082	6.9
Utilities and liquor stores	1,495	2.1	9,903	8.4	11,398	6.0
Insurance trust	8,950	12.3	1,599	1.4	10,548	5.5
Other	3,816	5.3	7,327	6.2	11,143	5.8
Totals	72,496	100.0	118,001	100.0	190,496	100.0
Intergovernmental transfers	36,759	—	567	—	—	—

Source: United States Census of Governments, Vol. 4, 1972.

governments finance substantial parts of local government expenditures on public welfare. Such expenditures show up as a direct expenditure of local governments in the table, and as an intergovernmental grant of state governments at the bottom of the table.

Education takes nearly one fourth of state government expenditures. The figure is mostly expenditure on higher education in state colleges and universities, which has grown rapidly in recent years. Many state governments also finance substantial parts of the cost of local elementary and secondary education, but this is included in intergovernmental transfers in the state government column. Transportation occupies another 17.6 percent of state government budgets; it is mainly construction and maintenance of state highway systems. Public welfare and health expenditures together account for roughly 25 percent of state budgets, and grew very rapidly during the 1960s and 1970s.

Local governments spend more than 40 percent of their budgets on education. The 6.7 percent of expenditures for transportation is mostly for streets and highways. Health and welfare expenditures occupy only relatively small portions of local government budgets. Expenditures on utilities include publicly owned or subsidized water supply, gas, electricity, and transit systems.

Table 10.2 shows that state and local governments collect roughly equal amounts of taxes from their residents. But Table 10.3 shows that local governments spend almost two thirds more than state governments. The disparity between local government expenditures and tax collections is mainly financed by grants from federal and state governments.

Although total state and local government expenditures have grown rapidly since World War II, the proportions spent on important categories have changed relatively little. Contrary to much popular opinion, the proportion of state and local government expenditures used for health and welfare has changed little since the war. As was shown in Chapter 7, almost all income redistribution is carried out by the federal government. Among major expenditure categories, only education has increased substantially as a fraction of total state and local government expenditure since the war.

THE PLIGHT OF SMSA CENTRAL-CITY GOVERNMENTS

Much recent concern with local government finance has focused on the problems of central-city governments in metropolitan areas. Data presented in Chapter 7 showed that central cities contain a disproportionate share of the poor in metropolitan areas, and even the most cursory reading of daily newspapers indicates that central-city governments are financially pressed. But are they in worse financial straits than other local governments? If so, why? Is it because the central-city poor need more public services than do people elsewhere? Or is it because the poor are less able than others to pay taxes to finance local public services? And how do patterns of local government expenditures and tax receipts differ in central cities from those elsewhere?

Unfortunately, comprehensive data on local governments in central cities are not available. Many different local governments provide services and levy taxes in central cities, and many of their boundaries do not coincide with those of central cities. For example, most central cities are in counties that provide some government services to residents of the city. In a few cases, the county's boundaries coincide with those of the central city, but in most cases the county also includes some suburban areas. In such cases, it is difficult to estimate the services provided to central-city residents by the county government. It is also difficult to estimate the taxes paid by central-city residents to the county government. Similar problems arise concerning school districts and special districts.

Table 10.4 presents data on per capita revenues and expenditures for central cities and the entire SMSA for six SMSAs for which comprehensive data are available. The SMSAs were chosen partly because they are representative of conditions in older, predominantly eastern, SMSAs, but primarily because their local government structures are sufficiently simple to permit tabulation of data.

The top lines of the table show that central cities raise more revenue both from local taxes and charges and from intergovernmental transfers (provided by federal and state governments) than do suburbs in five of the six metropolitan areas. The only exception is New Orleans, where the

Table 10.4. LOCAL GOVERNMENT FINANCE IN SIX SMSAs, 1971–1972 (DOLLARS PER CAPITA)

	New York		Philadelphia		Baltimore		New Orleans		Richmond		Roanoke	
	Central City	SMSA	Central City	SMSA	Central City	SMSA	Central City	SMSA	Central City	SMSA	Central City	SMSA
Revenues												
Intergovernmental	518.10	451.38	216.35	165.79	464.56	312.93	148.99	146.48	253.53	182.66	180.92	159.93
From own sources	790.45	715.21	447.40	372.95	364.78	338.94	251.47	258.33	485.39	353.24	349.05	283.93
Total	1,308.55	1,166.58	663.75	538.75	829.34	651.88	400.46	404.81	738.92	535.90	529.97	443.86
Expenditures												
Education	289.88	340.41	223.74	243.67	244.11	277.66	142.78	159.28	196.54	217.43	188.25	193.86
Transportation	67.80	59.40	32.47	37.97	48.23	41.14	17.23	26.69	35.38	23.54	28.05	18.08
Public welfare	280.28	226.42	15.37	22.71	146.17	74.57	4.72	2.83	140.94	73.02	78.44	50.54
Health and hospitals	156.75	116.04	43.33	23.24	51.93	25.24	8.21	25.78	13.19	7.30	2.43	2.57
Police, fire, and correction	128.98	107.56	89.88	51.54	96.53	62.31	53.33	41.13	60.41	40.16	42.87	29.31
Parks and natural resources	15.86	20.58	19.86	11.11	22.03	13.56	18.52	17.66	23.76	12.82	33.19	19.71
Sanitation	44.53	46.21	27.72	30.38	37.18	35.05	26.13	20.57	79.42	46.40	27.01	24.92
Housing and urban renewal	61.49	43.54	46.34	22.13	72.73	34.59	1.90	1.61	24.76	11.92	5.37	2.73
Administration and interest	79.91	79.74	65.48	52.50	46.45	42.53	41.70	47.83	102.00	62.86	48.70	39.42
Utilities and liquor stores	141.11	101.33	72.70	36.07	19.26	18.30	12.35	15.75	81.21	49.18	29.82	41.87
Employee retirement expenditures	72.58	49.81	20.49	8.91	23.91	12.34	14.88	8.45	8.29	3.99	8.37	4.25
Other	90.49	77.54	70.60	38.77	34.03	26.72	44.49	30.39	39.58	26.50	29.25	21.72
Total	1,429.66	1,268.57	727.98	578.98	842.57	664.01	386.24	397.96	805.50	575.10	521.74	448.98
1970 population (in thousands)	7,895	11,572	1,949	4,818	906	2,071	593	1,046	250	518	92	181

Sources: United States Census of Governments, Vol. 5, 1972 and United States Census of Population, 1970.

central city raises slightly less revenue per capita from local sources than do suburban governments. On the average, the six central cities raise about 15 percent more from local sources and 25 percent more in transfers, on a per capita basis, than do all local governments in the SMSAs.

Everybody knows that per capita income is greater in metropolitan suburbs than in central cities. In fact, *suburban income per capita exceeds that in the central city by no more than 10 percent in most SMSAs,* less than many people think. That central cities receive more in intergovernmental transfers than do suburbs results from redistributive programs of federal and state governments. But why, given their lower incomes, do central-city residents vote to tax themselves more than do suburban residents? The answer must be that needs for government services and transfers are more pressing relative to needs for private consumption in central cities. On what programs do central cities spend more than suburbs? The answer is in the expenditure rows of Table 10.4. In each of the six SMSAs, per capita spending on public education is less in central cities than in the entire SMSA, and in each SMSA, total spending on transfers and other services is greater in central cities than in the entire SMSA. Total spending per capita by central cities exceeds that for the SMSA as a whole by about 22 percent for the six SMSAs. With a few minor exceptions, central cities spend more per capita on all programs other than education than do suburbs. For example, "police, fire, and correction" is a costly program in all SMSAs, and each central city spends more per capita on it than do its suburban governments. Public welfare is an expensive program in most SMSAs and central cities spend more per capita than do suburbs. An exception is Philadelphia, but in Pennsylvania, as in Louisiana, public welfare is financed mainly by the state (and federal) government. No single program accounts for a large share of the higher spending by central cities than by suburbs: *central cities spend more on everything except education.*

Incidentally, Table 10.4 shows how atypical New York City is. Both revenues and expenditures per capita are more than twice as great in New York City as in most other central cities in the table. New York City is not slighted by state and federal governments, since it also receives more than twice as much as most other cities in intergovernmental transfers. New York spends much more than other cities on almost every program, but its spending on welfare, health and hospitals, and employee pensions is especially great.

Why do central cities spend more than suburbs, despite lower incomes of residents? One answer is that it costs more to provide a given quantity and quality of government services in central cities. Unions of government employees are stronger in central cities, as are unions in private industries such as construction from which governments must buy products. But much of the higher expenditure in central cities is concentrated on programs and transfers provided for the poor: welfare, health and hospitals, and housing and urban renewal are the important examples. Higher expenditures by central cities in these areas are a direct reflection of the higher concentration of poor in central cities than in suburbs.

REASONS FOR FINANCIAL PROBLEMS OF STATE AND LOCAL GOVERNMENTS

The 1970s have frequently been referred to as a time of "fiscal crisis" for local governments. The term is more suitable for newspaper headlines than as a basis for serious analysis. However, there can be no doubt that important controversies surround the taxing and spending actions of local governments. The issues are complex and understanding them requires more review of the framework within which local governments operate.

It has been seen that local government taxes and expenditures have risen more rapidly than taxpayers' incomes since World War II, and that expenditures and taxes are higher, and taxpayers' incomes lower, in central cities than in suburbs. Why should local government spending rise so rapidly and why should local governments have such difficulty balancing their budgets? Some answers are easy to find, but others may be subtle or obscure.

Rising Relative Prices of Services

Most government expenditures are for services, and *service prices inevitably rise faster than those of commodities.* The phenomenon occurs in both the private and government sectors. Since World War II, the private service component of the consumer price index has risen almost twice as fast as the commodities component for the country as a whole. The trend has continued, at a slackened pace, even during the period of rapidly rising materials and fuel prices since the early 1970s. The main reason is that productivity rises much faster in commodity than in service production, mainly because of faster technological progress.

Increases in service prices relative to those of commodities are inevitable in a technologically progressive economy. It is unlikely that the trend will be reversed, in either the private or government sectors. In the private sector, the response has been to increase somewhat the fraction of income spent on services and to substitute commodities for services. Between 1950 and 1978, the percentage of private consumption expenditures that went to services rose from 32.8 to 46.0. An example of substitution of commodities for services has been the large-scale substitution of domestic appliances for domestic help during the same period, as the relative price of the latter has risen.

Much the same process has occurred in the government sector. As the relative price of services has risen, the share of total income devoted to government services has grown, as Table 10.1 showed. And computerized responses to inquiries made to government agencies are an example of the governments' attempts to substitute inexpensive computers for expensive civil servants. But, for both technical and political reasons, the possibilities of increasing productivity appear more limited with government than with private services. If so, the only options are to continue to increase the share of income going to governments, to place the services in the private sector, or to go without.

The best example of this dilemma is public education. Its cost has risen rapidly, and resistance to productivity increases has been powerful. Some of the most emotional battles concerning local governments are between those who want larger school budgets and those who want to keep real-estate taxes down.

Rapidly Rising Demand for Government Services

The demand for local government services has undoubtedly risen. One reason is that many government services, such as education and transportation, are superior goods whose demands rise rapidly with incomes. As income rises, people want more and higher-quality education for their children, and they are willing to increase the fraction of income devoted to the purpose. Likewise, it was seen in Chapter 9 that urban travel has increased more rapidly than incomes in the postwar period, and governments have been asked to devote increasing resources to transportation facilities. In sum, there is a high income elasticity of demand for public education and transportation.

It was shown in Chapter 7 that transfer payments to the poor have been a rapidly rising share of federal government expenditures. In addition, Table 10.3 shows that almost 20 percent of state and local government expenditures are for the three redistributive programs: public welfare, health and hospitals, and housing and urban renewal. (It must be remembered that most of the money for these programs comes from federal government grants.) Why is society willing to devote increasing shares of income to redistributive programs? The easy answer is that society has developed a growing sense of compassion for the needy. A different answer is that the poor have become politically more powerful, partly as a result of urbanization, and that they have been increasingly successful in demanding redistributive programs. Whatever the answer, society has revealed a high income elasticity of demand for transfers. Whether the pattern will continue is anybody's guess.

That there is a high income elasticity of demand for many services that government provides is certain. Why government is asked to provide them instead of the private sector is another question. Some services, such as police and correction, can be provided only by government. But many services can be and are provided by both government and private sectors. In Chapter 9, it was seen that transportation is provided partly by each sector. But the best example is education. At all levels, public education has grown most rapidly during the postwar period. Yet the private sector also provides education. The reason for the rapid growth of public education, despite widespread dissatisfaction with it, is the incentives provided to people. Unlike unsubsidized public transit systems, public education is paid for through taxes. *People must pay for it whether they consume it or not. And so, most people choose to consume it.* A **voucher system,** which has been extensively studied by economists and others, would provide parents vouchers that could be used to pay children's tuition at public or private schools. That system would make education like an unsubsidized transit system. If people did not like the government service, they would choose that provided by the private sector. Why the United States has moved increasingly in the direction of providing government monopoly control over services is a difficult question to answer.

The Nature of Local Government Revenue Systems

It was seen in Table 10.2 that local governments obtain the largest part of their revenue—55.4 percent of that raised from local sources—from property taxes. Federal and, to a lesser extent, state governments rely much more on progressive income taxes. In most communities, *property-tax receipts rise less rapidly than income, whereas receipts from a progressive income tax rise more rapidly than income.* The result is that as spending has risen at all levels of government, local governments have had to raise tax rates frequently, whereas federal and state governments can hold rates constant or raise them infrequently. From the point of view of the functioning of democracy, it is surely better that government be required to obtain approval of the voters, through their elected legislature, when it thinks spending should be increased. Thus, the local government system has much to be said for it. The difficulty is that the very characteristics that prevent tax receipts from increasing as rapidly as incomes tend to mean that high-income residents pay a smaller fraction of income in taxes than do low-income residents. That is, *local taxes are more regressive or less progressive than state and federal taxes.* This may have undesirable effects on income distribution.

Whatever one's view about the desirability of progressive local taxes, their regressiveness requires frequent rate increases, with the result that local governments are perpetually surrounded by political controversy. The need for frequent tax-rate increases provides an air of crisis around city halls. It gives citizens the impression that local government spending is rising more rapidly than the spending of state and federal governments, which are not raising tax rates.

Other characteristics of local government revenue systems contribute to the crisis atmosphere. One is their inability to run deficits. The federal government typically spends about 10 percent more than it raises in taxes. It finances the deficits by selling bonds and increasing the money supply. But local governments cannot print money and state governments place rigid constraints on their ability to go into debt. The result is that they must raise taxes enough to cover anticipated increases in spending. Breakdowns and gimmickry in their forecasting contribute to the sense of crisis.

Special Problems of Central Cities

The three reasons for local government financial problems just discussed apply as much to SMSA central-city governments as to other local governments. But central cities have other sources of financial difficulties. First, central-city property-tax yields are particularly unresponsive to economic growth. Neither the amount nor the value of central-city property increases quickly. The amount does not because most central cities have long been almost completely built up, and most new housing and employment are located in suburbs. The value of central-city property rises slowly because suburbanization, discussed in Chapters 3 and 5, means that most land-value growth occurs in suburbs.

Second, incomes are lower in central cities than in suburbs. Therefore, a given per capita tax burden is a greater percentage of incomes in central cities than in suburbs. Furthermore, central cities contain disproportionate shares of the poor, to whom society has committed itself to provide transfers and special services. Thus, *central cities have fewer taxable resources and more people who need help than do suburbs.*

Third, it is widely believed that central cities provide government services for the benefit of suburban residents who travel to central cities but pay no taxes there. The phenomenon is sometimes referred to as the exploitation of central cities by suburban residents.[1] Central-city services cited by those who believe the hypothesis include maintenance of the transportation system, libraries, zoos, museums, and other facilities used by suburbanites. In fact, there is little to the notion. Many of the services in question are financed by employment located in central cities. Commercial and industrial properties probably pay more real estate taxes than the value of local government services they receive, so they are not a net drain

---

1.   The best analysis is by Bradford and Oates.

on the local government. Whether such property taxes are imputed to employees who are suburban residents is immaterial. Zoos and museums are subject to user charges and such charges can be set so that suburban residents pay their share of the cost.

The most sophisticated form of the exploitation hypothesis is that suburban **land-use controls** condemn the poor to central-city residences, thus imposing the cost of the transfers and services they need on central-city governments. Land-use controls will be discussed in the next section, where it will be concluded that they cause more low-income people to live in central cities than would live there in the absence of land-use controls. But the cost of most of their transfers is not borne by other central-city residents. Most comes from the federal government, and programs are merely administered by local governments. But federal taxes are progressive and are paid in larger proportion by high-income suburban residents than by central-city residents.

THE TIEBOUT HYPOTHESIS

In 1956, Charles Tiebout put forward a provocative hypothesis about the interaction of government and private decision making in the context of the U.S. local-government system. Since then, dozens of books and papers have elaborated, criticized, and tested the theory. No one can understand local government in the United States without understanding the Tiebout hypothesis.

It was shown in Chapter 3 that U.S. metropolitan areas have been decentralizing for decades. In the nineteenth century, decentralization was typically accompanied by outward movement of central-city boundaries. Since World War II, decentralization has occurred on a massive scale, but movement of central-city boundaries has become the exception, instead of the rule.

It was shown in Chapter 5 that there is a tendency for high-income residents to live farther from metropolitan centers than low-income residents, even in the absence of local governments. Consider a typical postwar metropolitan area that is growing and decentralizing rapidly. People with average or above-average incomes are moving into areas outside the central city in large numbers. These residents must petition to be annexed to the central city; new local government jurisdictions must be formed; or rural governments must be made into suburban governments. The central city is being populated with low-income and black people, crime and tax rates are rising, and public schools are deteriorating. The new suburban residents perceive that they would be better off to have their own local government instead of being annexed to the central city. It will be most advantageous if a group of perhaps ten thousand to a hundred thousand people with similar incomes and demands for local public services form a new jurisdiction. There they can vote the bundle of local government services and real-estate taxes to pay for them that is best suited to their needs and tastes. In this way, several suburban governments are formed, within each of which live a few tens of thousands of people who are similar in income and family composition. Family composition is an important determinant of demand for the most expensive local government service, public schools. The advantage to groups of people with similar demands for local government services in locating in the same jurisdictions is the essence of the Tiebout hypothesis.

The American tradition of financing local governments by locally levied real-estate taxes complicates the analysis in the last paragraph. As was shown in Chapter 8, the income elasticity of housing demand is not far from one. Thus, the relatively high-income residents of a particular suburb own relatively expensive homes. The real-estate tax rate is set so that tax payments on the homes yield revenues needed to finance the chosen bundle of local government services. But a low-income family, with correspondingly modest housing demand, would be tempted to move to the community. Every resident pays the same tax rate, so total taxes on a modest home would be small. Thus, the low-income family could obtain the local government services at small cost. Such a family is referred to as a "free rider," in that their share of local taxes is smaller than the share of local government services they consume.

Communities have perceived that they can exclude free riders by land-use controls. The ostensible justification for land-use controls is to protect residents from nuisances such as noise, pollution, and congestion. But state governments and courts have given local governments wide latitude in choosing land-use controls. In the 1950s and 1960s, a common justification for land-use controls became "to protect the character of the community," which often means "to prevent free riders." Local land-use controls frequently specify minimum lot sizes, minimum square feet of floor space, no multifamily housing, etc. A long list of such requirements effectively excludes from a community those whose homes would not pay residents' shares of the cost of local government services. Land-use controls to exclude free riders were not emphasized by Tiebout, but have been emphasized by subsequent writers.

A large metropolitan area might have many suburban jurisdictions. Some might be inhabited by very high-income residents and have stringent land-use controls and very high quality government services. Others might be inhabited by people with more modest incomes and have correspondingly modest government services and land-use controls.

Realism of the Tiebout Hypothesis

Is the Tiebout hypothesis realistic? Its preconditions are that there be a substantial number of suburban governments in a metropolitan area, each with considerable local control over taxes, service provision, and land-use controls. Its implications are that such communities vary, but within a community there are people with similar incomes, houses, and demand for local government services.

No one can drive through typical metropolitan suburbs and believe there is no truth in the Tiebout hypothesis. Many observers have commented, sometimes sarcastically, about the homogeneity of suburban communities. In addition, statistical studies have shown that there is more homogeneity by income and house value within suburban than within central-city neighborhoods, and more than one would expect in the absence of the motivations in the Tiebout hypothesis.

Of course, there is variety within suburban communities. Choice of residential location depends on many things other than local taxes and government services provided. Suburbs are by no means as homogeneous as they would be if the Tiebout mechanism were the only force at work. But the Tiebout hypothesis contains important variables, without which the residential pattern of American suburbs cannot be understood.

Welfare Economics and the Tiebout Hypothesis

What about the normative characteristics of the Tiebout hypothesis? Do suburbs organized along Tiebout lines promote efficiency and equity in resource allocation? The question is important. Local government expenditures account for more than 10 percent of personal income in the United States. It is important that they satisfy the conditions for efficient and equitable resource allocation discussed in Chapter 6.

Many people are surprised to learn that a Tiebout-like world might be an efficient way to allocate resources to local governments. If there are enough local government jurisdictions, each person can live in a community that provides just the bundle of local government services—and corresponding taxes—that is optimum for that person. By choosing the right community, and voting for officials who favor the appropriate services and taxes, each person can consume the quantity and quality of local government services he or she would consume if the services were sold on competitive markets. The requirement is that there be enough communities to provide each desired bundle of local government services, houses of particular value, and location relative to work places. Of course, no metropolitan area has enough local government jurisdictions. However, the Tiebout hypothesis provides an approximation both to reality and to efficient resource allocation.

An important corollary to the efficiency characteristic of the Tiebout hypothesis is that there is no resource misallocation from local real-estate taxes. Shopping among different communities for the right bundle of local government services is just like shopping among car dealers for a car that combines the optimum combination of quantity, quality, and price for the customer. In both cases, the market satisfies the conditions for efficient resource allocation presented in Chapter 6.

Qualifications to this efficiency result are required. First, the limited number of metropolitan jurisdictions available means that the efficiency result is at best an approximation. Second, local governments must be free to choose their bundle of services and tax rates. In Europe, local governments are financed or tightly controlled by national governments. The Tiebout hypothesis cannot work there. It has been seen that in the United States local governments are increasingly financed by grants from state and federal governments. They prevent the Tiebout-like world from working efficiently. Third, some government services cannot be provided by fragmented local governments. Metropolitan area-wide public transit and water-supply systems are examples. Such services must be provided by state governments or by agreements among local governments.

The Tiebout hypothesis cannot ensure efficient resource allocation to local governments in metropolitan central cities. One reason is that most central cities were built before land-use controls became important. Therefore, land-use controls cannot perform their function of excluding free riders in central cities. Another reason is that central cities are too big. It is not possible, in most metropolitan areas, to find enough people with similar demands for local government services and location to populate a central city. The implication is that *real-estate taxes have much greater effect in distorting resource allocation in central cities than in suburbs.*

To be specific, consider the following example. Suppose a worker is promoted, raising his or her take-home pay 25 percent. As a result, the family wants a better house and better public education. If the family lives in a suburb, it can move to another suburb better suited to its higher economic status. If it moves from one house to another in the central city, it may obtain a better house, but the quality of public education is unlikely to be much better at one school than another within the central city. Thus, the higher taxes paid on the better house represent no higher quality local government services. Such taxes distort resource allocation.

If the family does not like the central-city schools and taxes, why doesn't it move to a suburb? One reason may be that the central city is a much better location for it, given the breadwinner's work place. Another reason may be that its income is not yet high enough to get the family over the barrier raised by exclusionary land-use controls in suburbs. A third reason may be that the family is black, and is excluded from or made unwelcome in suburban communities by racial prejudice.

It is unfortunate that the efficiency characteristics of the Tiebout hypothesis are unavailable precisely where residents can least afford the loss of welfare caused by distorting real-estate taxes. But that is not the end of the story. From an equity viewpoint, the basic purpose of "voting with your feet" is to avoid paying more in real-estate taxes than the local government services are worth to you. That is another way to say that, in a Tiebout world, local governments cannot redistribute income. If a suburban jurisdiction is homogeneous, there is nobody to redistribute income *to* within the jurisdiction. If the local government did levy significantly higher taxes on more valuable homes, the residents would move to a jurisdiction in which local taxes reflected their demand for local government services. Given the approximate nature of the Tiebout hypothesis, local governments can and do engage in some income redistribution, but it cannot be substantial.

The final aspect of the equity issue is that, in postwar United States, land-use controls that exclude low-income central-city residents from suburban residences by and large exclude blacks and other minorities. They therefore add the police power of suburban governments to other forms of discrimination against them in the United States.

One possible reaction to these equity issues is to decide that income redistribution should continue to be—as it has mostly been—left to the federal government. If one takes that view, and believes that enforcement of open housing laws makes the racial exclusion unimportant, one can approve of our Tiebout-like suburbs. The example is one in which, for many people, there is strong conflict between efficiency and equity considerations.

Federal and state legislatures have shown little hostility to exclusionary suburbs. But there have been strong and partially successful attacks in the courts. Some have contended that exclusionary zoning deprives central-city residents of access to government services, especially education, that are guaranteed by state or federal constitutions. Other attacks have been more broadly based, claiming that all residents have a right to live wherever they can bid successfully, and that land-use controls artificially raise housing costs beyond their reach.

Many attacks have not survived appeal. But some have, and courts are increasingly sympathetic to plaintiffs as their understanding of the implications of the Tiebout hypothesis improves. What influence the courts can have is another matter. Courts do not build houses. They can say that a certain pattern of controls is unconstitutional and must be redone within certain guidelines. Local planners then redo the controls and a new set of local procedures is required to test their constitutionality anew. The point is that the courts have permitted local governments to have a wide range of land-use controls. To distinguish between constitutional and unconstitutional uses of those controls is a difficult task.

SUMMARY

The United States has a complex and cumbersome system of local governments, consisting of counties, municipalities, school districts, and special districts. Since World War II, the state and local government sector has grown rapidly. Together, state and local governments spend more than 15 percent of GNP. Most government services provided directly to citizens are provided by local governments, although increasing percentages of their costs are financed by grants from federal and state governments. Forty percent of local government spending is for public education.

Local governments are in chronic financial difficulty. The costs of services they provide rise more rapidly than commodity costs; there is a high income elasticity of demand for them by constituents; and their tax receipts increase only slowly at fixed tax rates. Central-city governments are in especially severe straits because their tax receipts increase very slowly and they have large concentrations of citizens with special needs for government services and transfers.

Following the work of Tiebout, economists have become interested in the problem of **optimum jurisdiction** for local governments. The Tiebout hypothesis shows that our system of fragmented suburban governments has some of the desirable efficiency characteristics of competitive markets. But its equity properties worsen the lot of the poor and black residents of central cities.

QUESTIONS AND PROBLEMS

1. What would be the effect on central-city government finances of a negative income tax? Of a housing allowance?

2. The federal government can redistribute income by taxing high-income people and providing transfers either to low-income people or to local governments with large low-income populations. Which do you prefer?

3. What would be the effect of metropolitan area-wide local government on local taxes paid and government services received by poor central-city residents?

4. The tax revolt of the late 1970s was a revolt of middle-class suburban residents against local governments. Transfers to the poor appeared to be the object of their hostility, yet suburban governments transfer little money to the poor. How do you explain this?

REFERENCES AND FURTHER READING

William Baumol, "Macroeconomics of Unbalanced Growth: The Anatomy of Urban Crisis," *American Economic Review,* Vol. 57 (1967), 414–426. *A study of long-run implications of low productivity growth in the government sector.*

David Bradford and Wallace Oates, "Suburban Exploitation of Central Cities and Government Structure," in *Redistribution Through Public Choice* (Harold Hochman and George Peterson, editors), 1974. *The most thorough analysis of the suburban exploitation hypothesis available.*

Robert Inman, "The Fiscal Performance of Local Governments: An Interpretative Review," *Current Issues in Urban Economics* (Peter Mieszkowski and Mahlon Straszheim, editors), 1979. *A survey of research on determinants of local government spending.*

Edwin Mills, "Economic Analysis of Urban Land-Use Controls," in *Current Issues in Urban Economics* (Peter Mieszkowski and Mahlon Straszheim, editors), 1979. *A survey of research on the legal and economic status of land-use controls.*

William Oakland, "Central Cities: Fiscal Plight and Prospects for Reform," *Current Issues in Urban Economics* (Peter Mieszkowski and Mahlon Straszheim, editors), 1979. *An essay on fiscal problems of metropolitan central cities.*

Charles Tiebout, "A Pure Theory of Local Expenditures," *Journal of Political Economy,* Vol. 64 (1956), 416–424. *A pathbreaking analysis of the political economy of U.S. local governments.*

PUBLIC AND PRIVATE CONCERN WITH POLLUTION HAS IN- creased enormously since World War II. Before the war, concern with pollution was mostly restricted to small groups of conservationists, who sometimes appeared to be urging on society the irrational policy of not using depletable natural resources.

11

Pollution and Environment Quality

All that has now changed. Opinion polls show environmental problems to be high on the list of public concerns. Articles on the despoilation of the environment fill newspapers and magazines. Officials pollute the media with statements on pollution. Dozens of laws have been passed by federal, state, and local governments with the purpose of abating pollution.

The reasons for increased concern are not hard to find, although no one can work long with environmental problems and not realize the inadequacies of the data base. First, there can be no doubt that the volume of wastes discharged into the environment has increased in recent decades. At a given state of technology, and with a given mix of inputs and outputs, waste generation is about proportionate to the production of goods or to the level of real income. In 1978, real income and output were more than four times their 1940 levels. Improvements in technology and public policy undoubtedly mean that waste generation increased by less than output during this interval, but it cannot be doubted that the increase was substantial. And modern technology produces some particularly persistent and harmful wastes that were unknown a few decades ago. Atomic radiation and pesticides are good examples.

Second, pollution is more bothersome than it used to be. Popular writers refer to the revolution of rising expectations regarding the environment. It is a short step from that view to the position that worsening of pollution is partly a matter of perception. Widespread prosperity has provided the income and leisure necessary to enjoy the environment through boating, camping, swimming, hiking, and skiing. Income elasticities of demand are high for such activities. Somewhat more subtle, but closely related, is the fact that people become much more concerned with effects of pollution on health and mortality when urgent problems of massive unemployment and poverty have been solved. Such concerns are neither irrational nor frivolous.

Third, rapid urbanization of the country makes pollution worse than it used to be. Despite some views to the contrary, *waste discharges per capita are not greater in urban than in rural areas.* The opposite is true, since some large waste-producing activities such as agriculture and mining occur predominantly in rural areas, and more resources are devoted to waste disposal in urban than in rural areas. The environment has the capacity to assimilate wastes. If that capacity is not exceeded, environmental quality remains intact. But large concentrations of people and economic activity place great stress on the environment. Thus, the most serious deterioration in air and water quality has occurred in large metropolitan areas such as New York, Chicago, and Los Angeles.

It has been shown that poverty, poor housing, and inadequate finance of local public services are by no means exclusively urban problems. Pollution is no exception. Some of the worst open dumps and littering of landscapes are in rural areas. Rural lakes and streams are frequently polluted. Even though urban areas have more than their share of air and water pollution, rural pollution is of concern to urban residents.

WHAT IS POLLUTION?

Although illustrations have been given, no limits have yet been placed on the concept of pollution. As pollution abatement has become an accepted goal, the tendency has been to include a variety of odious activities under the rubric of pollution. Air and water pollution are familiar concepts. Most people are used to describing as pollution the littering of the landscape with solid wastes. Some people would include excessive noise under the pollution heading. Others would include a range of issues that relate to the beauty of urban and rural areas, social tensions, and other problems.

Here, the term will be used narrowly. Economic activity requires the withdrawal of materials from the environment. Most materials are eventually returned to the environment in ways more or less harmful to use of the environment. The term **pollution** will be used to describe the impairment of the environment by the return or discharge of materials to it. The definition includes the usual categories of air, water, and solid-waste pollution. But it excludes a broad range of social and aesthetic issues sometimes classified as environmental. The reason for limiting the subject is not that the included problems are necessarily more important than the excluded ones, but that waste disposal problems have important elements in common that are not shared by the excluded issues, and that can be analyzed in certain ways. Air, water, and solid-waste pollution result from waste disposal, and mostly involve materials that have potential economic value. These characteristics are not shared by an inadequate architectural environment, for example.

MATERIALS BALANCE

The first step in thinking systematically about environmental problems is to place them in the context of the materials balance. This leads to some of the fundamental insights regarding environmental problems.

All commodity production consists of the application of other inputs —labor, capital, etc.—to materials extracted from the environment, to transform them from their natural state into useful products. As materials are extracted and processed, large amounts of unwanted materials are separated and returned to the environment. Once the completed commodities lose their economic value, they too must be returned to the environment or be recycled back into the productive process. The **materials balance** is an identity that equates exhaustive lists of sources and dispositions of materials. In its simplest form, it can be stated: *All the materials in the economic system at the beginning of a year, plus those extracted from the environment during the year, must equal those in the system at the end of the year, plus those returned to the environment during the year.* Additions to the stock of materials in the economic system are **capital accumulation.** Thus, the materials balance can also be stated: *In any year, material extractions from the environment equal discharges to the environment plus capital accumulation.*

The materials balance bears the same relationship to the national materials accounts that the identity between sources and dispositions of income bears to the national income accounts. Unfortunately, only fragmentary data are available concerning components of the materials accounts. Capital accumulation is 10 to 15 percent of total production and is probably about the same proportion of materials output. Thus, returns to the environment equal about 85 to 90 percent of withdrawals from the environment in the United States.

Table 11.1 shows some private estimates of materials extraction plus net imports in the U.S. for 1965. The volume of extraction is enormous. The total in Table 11.1 comes to about 70 pounds of materials extracted

Table 11.1.   WEIGHT OF BASIC MATERIALS PRODUCTION IN THE UNITED STATES PLUS NET IMPORTS, 1965 (MILLIONS OF TONS)

Material	Weight (millions of tons)
Agricultural	
Crops	364
Livestock	23.5
Fisheries	2
Subtotal	389.5
Forestry products	
Sawlogs	120
Pulpwood	56
Other	42
Subtotal	218
Mineral fuels	1,448
Other minerals	
Iron ore	245
Other metal ore	191
Other nonmetals	149
Subtotal	585
Total	2,640.5

Source: Allen Kneese, Robert Ayres, and Ralph D'Arge, p. 10.

from the environment per person per day! And that excludes masses of construction material that are moved from one place to another without being processed. Of the total in the table, more than half is fuels. The remainder is divided about equally between nonfuel minerals and agricultural, forestry, and fishery products. Unfortunately, the numbers in the table are dated. For 1980, 100 pounds per person per day is probably a good estimate of total withdrawals. The relationships among the numbers are probably as accurate as they were in 1965.

Form of Discharges

The materials balance tells us that 85 percent or so of the roughly 100 pounds per person per day of materials withdrawals is returned to the environment. What happens to this enormous volume of discharges? Of the large volume of withdrawals in agriculture and minerals-extraction industries, much is returned to the environment on the site from which it was extracted. Some such returns do no harm to the environment, but most extractive industries do great environmental damage unless materials are returned with care. Strip mining of coal is a currently controversial example in this category.

    Smaller, but still large, parts of withdrawals are processed and incorporated in products. All such materials are eventually returned to the environment as discharges into air, water, or land. Which of these media wastes are discharged depends on the technical characteristics of products and production processes and on economic variables. For example, fuels are burned, discharging some materials to the air and leaving some as solid waste. The energy released is converted to heat, which is eventually discharged to the air. Solid waste from fuel results in part from impurities, but also in part from incomplete combustion. The amount of such waste to be disposed of depends in part on the relative prices of fuels and high quality combustion systems.

Most liquid waste, both in industry and in households, is really solid waste which is either dissolved or conveniently floated away in water. For example, kitchen garbage appears as solid waste if it is put in the garbage can and as liquid waste if it is ground in the disposal and washed down the drain.

Thus, many wastes can be discharged as liquid, airborne, or solid wastes, depending on the products produced, production processes, and on the treatment processes employed to convert wastes from one form to another. *The effects of waste discharges on people and on the environment depend crucially on the form in which they are discharged.* The materials balance tells us that most materials withdrawn must be returned to the environment, but it does not tell us the form in which they are returned or the medium to which they are returned. Those depend on technical, economic, and government policy variables.

Amount of Discharges

The materials balance tells us that, except for capital accumulation, materials discharges equal materials withdrawals. If production of commodities and services were proportionate to material inputs, then the only way to reduce withdrawals and discharges would be to reduce production, and therefore living standards. Some environmentalists have indeed urged governments to reduce living standards systematically in order to preserve environmental quality. If that were the only way to achieve a livable environment, it would be justifiable. But in the last part of the twentieth century, it is a counsel of despair. It was shown in the previous subsection that environmental damage depends on not only the amount but also the form of returns.

In addition, it *is* in fact possible to reduce the withdrawals and discharges necessary to achieve a given living standard. Indeed, that is a normal characteristic of technological progress. For 150 years or so, total output per unit of material extraction has risen gradually in the United States. This is because an important characteristic of technological progress is learning how to make more efficient use of materials. For example, in the early years of the century, much of the content of crude oil was returned to the environment after fuel was refined out. Now a wide range of products—plastics, chemicals, and medicines, for example—are made from materials previously discarded.

Another way to reduce the materials withdrawals and discharges necessary to produce a given living standard is to reuse materials. For example, trees are felled and processed into newspapers and petroleum is pumped from the ground and processed into fuel for thermal electric generators. Newspapers are usually returned to the environment by placing them in landfills. A day or so after publication, a newspaper's consumption value is gone, although its physical condition is unchanged by consumption. Petroleum is mostly returned to the environment in the form of heat and gases released by combustion. Production and consumption of newspapers and electricity can be maintained, while reducing the withdrawal and discharge of petroleum, by burning used newspapers as fuel in thermal electric plants. The return of newspapers to the environment is thereby unchanged, but the form of the return is altered.

The point of this example is that *materials reuse depends on both technical and economic variables.* Many materials can be reused, but some only at great cost. The cost depends on the nature of the material and on the nature of the product in which it is incorporated. Other materials are easy to reuse and are reused in large quantities. The greater the reuse of materials, the smaller is the volume of materials withdrawal and discharge required to maintain given living standards.

Absorptive Capacity of the Environment

Finally, every aspect of the environment has considerable capacity to absorb waste and regenerate itself. A stream can dilute any waste and it can degrade and render organic wastes innocuous. But if a stream is overloaded with organic wastes, it loses its capacity to degrade organic material. The extreme form of overloading occurs when so much organic material is discharged into the stream that it becomes *anaerobic* (i.e., loses all its dissolved oxygen). Its regenerative capacity is then virtually destroyed and may take a long time to return. An anaerobic stream cannot support fish life, and it stinks from the hydrogen sulfide gas it produces.

Chemical and other processes in the atmosphere also permit it to absorb limited amounts of waste without damage. For example, much of the sulfur discharged into the atmosphere is eventually converted to sulfuric acid and other compounds, and is returned to the earth by precipitation. Particles discharged into the air eventually settle back onto the earth's surface. But much less is known about the chemical and other processes by which air restores its quality than about those by which water restores its quality. Although hydrocarbons from automobile exhausts seem certainly to be a major factor, it is still not known, after many years of intensive study, just how smog is produced in Los Angeles and other cities. This is unfortunate since, as Allen Kneese, the leading economist who specializes in environmental problems, put it, "We are in somewhat the same position in regard to polluted air as the fish are to polluted water. We live in it."[1]

The environment can also degrade limited amounts of solid waste. Organic materials eventually rot, and ferrous metals rust. But problems arise when the environment is overloaded. And modern technology produces materials, such as glass, pesticides, and plastics, that do not degrade.

Pollution of all forms is most serious in urban areas because the overloading and subsequent impairment of the environment are most serious there. The concentration of people and affluence produces much more waste than the environment can absorb.

Unfortunately, it is not known how large parts of the materials withdrawn from the environment are returned. Most are returned as solid wastes. But most environmental damage is done by the relatively small amounts returned to air and water environments.

AMOUNTS AND EFFECTS OF POLLUTANTS

Air Pollution

Some materials discharged to the atmosphere are innocuous, at least in the short run. Most important is carbon dioxide, discharged in large volumes by combustion of fossil fuels. Combustion has measurably increased the carbon dioxide content of the atmosphere during the twentieth century. Further increases may have adverse influences on weather and vegetation, but there is no evidence that present levels are harmful. Of the materials discharged to the atmosphere, five are likely to have adverse effects on people and property: particulates, sulfur oxides, carbon monoxide, hydrocarbons, and nitrogen oxides. Table 11.2 shows sources and amounts of these discharges for 1974.

Total discharges in Table 11.2 are nearly a ton per capita. About half is carbon monoxide; sulfur oxides and hydrocarbons are about 15 percent each, and particulates and nitrogen oxides are about 10 percent each. Most of the carbon monoxide comes from automobile exhaust. Diesel engines, used in some trucks, buses, and cars, produce negligible amounts of carbon monoxide. Most sulfur oxide discharges are from combustion

---

1. Quoted in Wolozin, p. 33.

Table 11.2.   AIR POLLUTION EMISSIONS, 1974 (MILLIONS OF TONS PER YEAR)

Pollutants and Sources	1974
Particulates	
Transportation	1.3
Fuel combustion in stationary sources	5.9
Industrial processes	11.0
Solid-waste disposal	0.5
Miscellaneous	0.8
Total	19.5
Sulfur oxides	
Transportation	0.8
Fuel combustion in stationary sources	24.3
Industrial processes	6.2
Solid-waste disposal	0.0
Miscellaneous	0.1
Total	31.4
Carbon monoxide	
Transportation	73.5
Fuel combustion in stationary sources	0.9
Industrial processes	12.7
Solid-waste disposal	2.4
Miscellaneous	5.1
Total	94.6
Hydrocarbons	
Transportation	12.8
Fuel combustion in stationary sources	1.7
Industrial processes	3.1
Solid-waste disposal	0.6
Miscellaneous	12.2
Total	30.4
Nitrogen oxides	
Transportation	10.7
Fuel combustion in stationary sources	11.0
Industrial processes	0.6
Solid-waste disposal	0.1
Miscellaneous	0.1
Total	22.5

Source: Council on Environmental Quality, *Environmental Quality*, 1975, p. 440.

of fossil fuels in electric power plants, factories, and homes. Hydrocarbons are discharged by many industrial processes, but nearly half comes from automobile engines. Particulates are small bits of solid matter, such as dust and ash, which come mostly from industrial processes. Nitrogen oxides come mainly from combustion in vehicles and stationary combustion systems.

What are the effects of these pollutants on people and property? Property damage by pollutants can be studied in laboratory experiments. But health damage must be inferred from laboratory experiments on small mammals or from data on the health of people variously exposed to the pollutants in their normal lives. Lave and Seskin have undertaken the best of the second kind of study. Most of the substances in Table 11.2 are deadly in high concentrations, but average exposures are far below such levels, and the challenge is to estimate chronic health effects of low-level exposures.

Evidence of chronic health effects is strongest for sulfur oxides and particulates. Lave and Seskin estimate that 50 percent reductions in ambient concentrations of these pollutants from their 1970 levels over the average metropolitan area might add a year or so to life expectancy there. It is a striking conclusion and, if correct, justifies a large government air pollution abatement program. Health effects from the other three pollutants, for which the auto is the main culprit, are much less well established.

Carbon monoxide appears to do no property damage at existing concentrations. Hydrocarbons and nitrogen oxides probably do no more than slight property damage. They interact to form smog in the presence of sunlight. Although smog has no discernible long-term health effects, it irritates and annoys people.

Most estimates of the benefits of the air pollution abatement mandated by existing laws place the benefits at about $20 billion per year in the mid-1970s. About $15 billion of the total is health benefits. It is a substantial total, approaching 1.5 percent of GNP. Although the methods and data employed in most estimates can be severely criticized, the frequency of such studies suggests that the estimate of total benefits is at least in the ball park.

Costs of abating polluting discharges by a specified change in production technology are relatively easy to estimate. For example, a frequently used air pollution abatement strategy has been substitution of oil for coal in thermal electric plants. It is not difficult to calculate the costs of such a substitution. The difficult task is estimating what changes in technology will be required to accomplish mandated discharge abatements. Both government and private estimates of the costs of achieving the discharge abatement mandated by existing laws are available. For the mid-1970s, they cluster around $10 billion per year, about half for motor vehicles and half for stationary sources.

Putting together benefit and cost estimates suggests that benefits exceed costs for existing air pollution control programs. That by no means proves that the programs are the best that could be devised, but it suggests that they aim at roughly the right amount of abatement.

Water Pollution

Humans have no feasible alternative to breathing air. Therefore all of it should be fit to breathe. But they drink only a small part of the available water, so not all of it needs to be fit to drink. When the layman thinks of water shortages and water pollution, he thinks of water for drinking and other domestic purposes. But domestic use is only a small part of the water story.

The most important distinction regarding water use is between instream and withdrawal uses. **Instream uses** are those for which the water remains in its natural channel. The most important examples are commercial and sport fishing, pleasure boating, navigation, swimming, hydroelectric generation, and aesthetic use. The last example refers to the fact that many recreational activities, especially hiking, picnicking, and camping, are enhanced by proximity to bodies of water.

Withdrawal uses are those for which water must be withdrawn from its natural channel. The major purposes of withdrawal are municipal use, industrial processing, cooling, and irrigation. Water withdrawn by municipalities for public water supply is for domestic, commercial, and public (e.g., fire protection) uses. Industrial processing refers to a variety of industrial uses, many of which involve the washing away of wastes. Cooling means the use of water to dissipate heat, by far the most important example being thermal electricity generation. Irrigation refers to the withdrawal of water for farm animals and crops.

Water quality is a complex notion with many dimensions, and quality requirements vary enormously among the many uses of water. For pleasure boating and aesthetic uses, the major quality requirements are the absence of odors, discoloration, and floating solids. Quality requirements vary among industrial processing uses, but for most the major requirement is the absence of salts that corrode pipes. Noncorrosive properties are also important for cooling uses, as is temperature. Different kinds of fish can live in water of different qualities, and much is known about the effects of water quality on game fish.

The highest quality requirements are for municipal water, since it must be fit to drink. Stringent quality standards are set by public health authorities in the United States, although there are many unanswered questions about the effects of relaxing one or more standards. But the United States has largely avoided water-borne diseases endemic in countries that apply less strict standards for drinking water.

Swimming water is something of an enigma. Authorities set the same requirements for swimming as for drinking water. But swimmers need not drink the water they swim in, and many people swim in water they should not drink. Various afflictions can result from swimming in poor quality water, but little is known about the likely incidence at different quality levels. Chlorine used to purify water in swimming pools may cause ear and other afflictions. With swimming, as with other water quality requirements, there is an important subjective element, in that people simply find it distasteful to swim in dirty water.

The subjective element in water quality standards causes much confu-

Table 11.3.   ORGANIC WASTE DISCHARGES IN THE UNITED STATES, 1973

Source	Waste (billions of pounds of BOD)
Municipal	5.6
Industrial	4.3
Nonpoint	45.0
Total	54.9

Source: Council on Environmental Quality, *Environmental Quality*, 1976, p. 257.

sion. It is often claimed that people do not like to drink reused water, regardless of its quality. To the extent that the reason is a misunderstanding about its quality, presumably people's feelings can be changed by education. But to the extent that subjective feelings represent genuine tastes, they should not be ignored. It is not proper to ignore the fact that some people pay $100 more for color TV than for black and white, although the preference is certainly subjective. But with water use, the wish is often for someone else to pay the cost. For example, New York City has long urged the federal government to build it a plant to desalt sea water, so that New Yorkers can avoid reusing Hudson River water. No New York mayor has yet seen fit to ask the city's residents whether they are willing to pay for high-cost desalted water. If they are, outsiders should not object.

Not only do the various water uses have different quality requirements, but they also have various effects on water quality. In the course of using water, humans discharge an enormous variety of wastes into streams and estuaries. The most important and best documented category of waste discharge is organic material. Although organic materials are of many kinds, most share the important characteristic that they use the dissolved oxygen in the water as they are degraded. The dissolved-oxygen content determines the kinds of fish and other life that can survive in the water, and affects virtually every use of water. An anaerobic stream is useless for almost all the purposes that have been discussed. Thus, the most significant measure of water pollution is the rate at which organic discharges use oxygen, referred to as **biochemical oxygen demand** (BOD). The quality of the water in a stream is determined by the BOD of wastes discharged into it and by the rate at which the stream can replenish its oxygen from the atmosphere, called its **reaeration rate.**

Table 11.3 shows estimates of BOD discharges into water bodies in the United States in 1973. The table includes only wastes actually discharged into bodies of water. Thus, it excludes BOD wastes that were generated but then removed from wastewater by treatment. It also excludes wastes discharged into the ground, as in septic tanks. Most of the municipal and industrial waste in Table 11.3 is urban. Some of the **non-**

point sources are urban, for example, pollutants washed off city streets into drains that empty into nearby streams. But most wastes from nonpoint sources are agricultural.

Table 11.3 shows that more than 80 percent of organic waste discharges are from nonpoint sources. The national pollution-control program has greatly reduced organic waste discharges from municipal and industrial sources since the 1960s. But further progress will require reductions from nonpoint sources. Wastes from city streets can be collected and treated, although only at considerable cost. But organic wastes from fertilizer and other agricultural sources cannot. For these, discharge reduction requires either erosion control or reduction in the organic wastes produced.

Suspended solids such as salts and silt are the second important type of pollutant. Salts are corrosive, and affect fish life in streams. Irrigation leaches salts from the soil, and irrigation return flow is the major source of harmful salts in western rivers. Silt is mainly runoff from farmland and construction projects. Since slowly moving water allows silt to settle, it fills up navigational channels and water supply reservoirs. It also changes the color of water, affecting its aesthetic use. Most important, silt reduces light penetration in water, impairing its ability to degrade organic materials.

Heat is another major polluting waste. A large thermal electricity plant may withdraw most of the water in a moderate-size stream and raise its temperature 10 or more degrees. Atomic plants tend to be larger than the largest conventional plants, and they operate at lower efficiency levels. They therefore discharge enormous amounts of heat. Water temperature affects fish life. In winter, fish that have disappeared from other parts of streams can be caught near the outfalls of electric plants. But in summer, heat discharge may raise water temperature above the survival level. Most important, high temperature speeds the process of organic degradation, thus reducing the stream's ability to cope with organic pollutants.

Nutrients, such as phosphates and nitrates, are an increasingly serious source of water pollution. Nutrients are the major constituents of agricultural fertilizer, are an important part of detergents, and are produced by degradation of organic material whether it takes place in a body of water or in a sewage treatment plant. Nutrients thus enter bodies of water by degradation of discharged organic material, by the effluent from municipal treatment plants, and by runoff from fertilized farmland. Nutrients fertilize water as they do land. In water, fertilization causes algae growth, which affects the appearance, taste, and odor of the water. Fertilization, or **eutrophication,** of water from treatment plants is most common in estuaries or downstream from large cities. But eutrophication from agricultural runoff is of course most common in rural areas.

A large variety of long-lived chemicals is discharged into water bodies by the chemical and other industries. But chemicals also enter water

Table 11.4.   SOLID WASTE DISCHARGES IN THE UNITED STATES, 1969

Source	Waste (millions of tons)
Residential, commercial, institutional	250
Collected	190
Uncollected	60
Industrial	110
Total	360

Source: Council on Environmental Quality, *Environmental Quality*, 1970, p. 107.

bodies inadvertantly. DDT and other powerful pesticides enter water from agricultural runoff. A particularly perplexing problem is acid drainage from mines. When coal mines are abandoned, they typically fill with water. As ground water passes through them, sulfuric and other acids are formed. Some of the acid eventually seeps into streams. The effects of chemical discharges vary from chemical to chemical. Some are poisonous to fish, wildlife, and humans. Others cause odors and discoloration.

Solid-Waste Pollution

By volume, most of the materials in Table 11.1 are returned to the environment as solid wastes. But most are discharged at the point of extraction. In this subsection, attention will be focused on solid wastes that are wholly or partly processed into products. Most such solid wastes are discharged in urban areas.

Some data on solid-waste discharges are in Table 11.4. The total in the table comes to more than ten pounds per person per day. Somewhat more than half the total is collected by government and private municipal refuse collection agencies. About 80 percent of the collected refuse is combustible, consisting of paper, cardboard, garbage, wood, leaves, and grass. The remainder is mostly glass, metal, and plastic. Industrial solid waste is known to be more variable than domestic waste. Much is either noncombustible or releases toxic fumes when burned.

About 75 percent of collected solid waste is disposed of in nearby open dumps. About 13 percent is placed in sanitary landfills, where each day's waste is covered with a layer of soil to prevent odors, fires, eyesores, and vermin. About 8 percent is incinerated, thus converting solid waste into airborne waste and an unburned residual solid waste.

What harm is done by the various means of solid-waste disposal? The question is surprisingly difficult to answer. Most sources present lists of qualitative and potential damages, but quantitative evidence is almost nonexistent. The most prominent effect of poor solid-waste disposal is aesthetic. Open dumps are terrible eyesores. So are the bottles, cans, and papers discarded on streets, parks, and beaches. But much of the harm from open dumps comes from the air and water pollution they cause. Dumps frequently burn, causing air pollution. In addition, organic wastes leak into streams, adding to BOD discharges from other sources.

ALTERNATIVE GOVERNMENT POLICIES

It is easy to understand the fundamental reason for the pollution problem. Polluting discharges to the environment are an **external diseconomy,** as the term was defined in Chapter 6. As has been shown, many kinds of production can use combinations of inputs that generate a range of kinds and amounts of waste.

In many cases productive techniques that generate large amounts of harmful wastes are cheaper than others. Furthermore, wastes can be discharged to the environment in many forms, depending on ways they are treated. But all forms of treatment require valuable resources. Finally, the extent to which used products are recycled or discharged into the environment depends on the relative costs of new and used materials. As has also been seen, people value a high quality environment for health, aesthetic, and recreational reasons.

Producers can keep costs low by large and relatively harmful discharges to the environment. The cost of the resulting deterioration in environmental quality is borne by those whose use of the environment is impaired, but those who make the decisions regarding harmful discharges fail to take account of the costs that discharges impose. Although a high quality environment is valuable, its value does not get counted in market transactions. Thus, too few resources are devoted to the reduction of waste discharges by recycling and to the treatment of wastes.

Why do producers and users of the environment not make private agreements to optimize discharges? Sometimes they do. Many agreements are made regarding waste disposal on private land. But air and flowing water are **fugitive resources.** Their movements are hard to predict, and it is extremely difficult to compute the damage done to them by each discharger to the environment. Transaction costs of private agreements are so great for many environmental problems that private agreements are rare. The history of government policy toward the environment has been a history of search for policies that regulate discharges to the environment without large transaction costs to the government and private sectors.

It has never been legal to discharge wastes freely into the air and water. The common law has long placed restrictions on activities that create nuisances. State water-rights laws have always provided some protection for the rights of downstream users. And public health laws have long imposed stringent restrictions on discharges into water used for domestic water supply. These laws have been important, especially in protecting public health. But from the point of view of optimum resource allocation, they are a patchwork created at different times and for many purposes, and they are extremely resistant to change. In the postwar period, the need for special laws aimed squarely at pollution has become clear.

Government Collection and Disposal

The most straightforward government policy is government construction and operation of facilities to collect, treat, and dispose of wastes. Public facilities are the predominant method of handling household and commercial sewage and solid wastes. Scale economies make it desirable for a single organization to perform these services for an entire metropolitan area. Such an organization should either be publicly owned, or privately owned and publicly regulated. Both methods are employed in the United States, but the former predominates.

Regulation and Enforcement

Aside from construction and operation of disposal facilities, the most common government antipollution program in the United States is discharge regulation. After more than a decade of experimentation with alternative approaches, the present program was laid down in laws passed in the early 1970s. These laws established the Environmental Protection Agency (EPA) and empowered it to control air, water, and solid-waste discharges.

For air and water discharges, the procedure is similar. EPA is instructed to calculate total discharge volumes into a stream or into the air over a metropolitan area that keep environmental quality at levels that protect public health and welfare. This is an enormous task, especially for the large numbers of wastes discharged into water. Any firm or municipality that wishes to discharge wastes into air or water must apply to EPA for a permit to do so. EPA attempts to restrict the total allowed by the permits issued to discharge volumes that meet their ambient environmental quality goals.

For motor vehicle emissions to the air, the procedure is somewhat different. Unlike other environmental provisions, the 1970 law specifies permitted automotive discharges; permitted discharges were to decrease gradually until, in 1976, discharges per car were no more than 5 percent of discharges by the last uncontrolled cars, in 1967. The goals have since been postponed several times because of energy crises and other events, but standards in effect in the late 1970s entail about 85 percent abatement from 1967 discharge levels.

Control of solid-waste discharges is still mainly the responsibility of states, which delegate most responsibility to local governments. The federal program is restricted to research and development, data collection, and encouragement to state and local governments to upgrade disposal facilities.

There can be no doubt that the government program has improved environmental quality since the early 1970s. Air and water discharge volumes shown in Table 11.2 and 11.3 are smaller than those in earlier years, and ambient environmental quality measures show improvement. Nevertheless, almost all economists who have studied the programs are highly critical of them. They are very expensive, and *economists conclude that the benefits could have been obtained more cheaply.*

The permit systems have become extremely complex. EPA is now our largest regulatory agency, with more than 10,000 employees. The law requires EPA to issue permits fairly, but *literally every industrial, commercial, and government discharge facilitity is unique.* The result is that there are rooms full of regulations about what facility can discharge what wastes. Inevitably, permit levels are negotiated between industrial and government officials. This means that government officials become partners in major business decisions: new plant construction, expansion or redesign of existing plants, design of new products, and important changes in industrial technology. As a result, business decision making is slower, more bureaucratized, less innovative, and less responsive to market signals.

Inevitably, EPA ends up issuing permits if specific devices have been installed: secondary treatment plants, catalytic converters on cars, and so forth. The procedure emphasizes known and conventional devices, not devices designed to optimize a particular situation. Most important, it emphasizes installation instead of operation of abatement devices. Two examples will illustrate.

For the most part, EPA issues organic-waste discharge permits to municipalities if they construct secondary treatment plants, which can remove about 90 percent of organic wastes before discharge. Municipalities are happy to construct such facilities: most of the money is provided in grants by federal and state governments, and local governments win the favor of construction contractors and unions by the resulting business. But municipalities have no incentive to operate the treatment plants efficiently once they are built. The result is that many are operated at about half their potential effectiveness.

New cars must meet stringent discharge limits stipulated in the law.

But once cars are on the road, emissions are not checked except in a few states, notably New Jersey, that check emissions at annual safety inspections. Emission-control devices do not continue to function properly longer than two or three years unless they are serviced and maintained. Furthermore, the car owner has a disincentive to maintain the devices, since the car's fuel mileage improves if the devices fail. The result is that *new cars have technically sophisticated and expensive emission-control devices on them, but most cars on the road do not meet the legal standards.* Much of the money spent to make the car meet extremely high standards when new is wasted.

Economists believe that the federal discharge-abatement program should encourage flexibility and innovation in the means by which discharge goals are met and in the precise times at which goals are met. Most important, they believe the program should permit decentralized and market-oriented decision making, in which businesses can make discharge decisions on the basis of economic criteria, and without negotiating every major decision with government officials.

Subsidies

A federal grant program to subsidize construction of municipal sewage-treatment plants is a major part of the U.S. pollution-abatement program. Annual appropriations were in excess of $4 billion in the late 1970s. It has resulted in treatment plant construction all around the country, and has certainly reduced the volume of organic discharges to streams and estuaries by municipalities. It has already been pointed out that the discharge-abatement program places too much emphasis on facility construction and not enough on operation. The purpose of the subsidy program is political. In principle, the federal government should issue discharge permits and the required abatement should be at the expense of those who generate the wastes. In the case of municipal sewage, the expense would be borne by local taxpayers. In fact, the federal government has almost no way to force local governments to comply with permits they issue. Local officials cannot be fined and jailed. About the only possibility is for the federal government to withhold grant funds for other purposes, such as housing subsidization, in the event of noncompliance. Such funds are given for urgent purposes, mostly to benefit the poor, and to withhold them would be unpopular. In the absence of large federal construction subsidies, many hard-pressed local governments would probably just not comply with federal permits.

Public officials frequently propose broad-based discharge-abatement subsidies. The proposal most studied is simple: a payment to all dischargers proportionate to the amount by which they abate discharges. Economists oppose such proposals on both efficiency and equity grounds. On efficiency grounds, *subsidies do not achieve desired abatement economically.* Subsidization would reduce discharges per unit of output, but the firm's improved revenue position would motivate it to increase output. The net effect could be an increase in polluting discharges. On equity grounds, *subsidies are, in effect, payments to those who pollute by the remainder of society.* It hardly seems like a desirable way to redistribute income.

Such a subsidy scheme would be an administrative nightmare. It would require estimation of discharge volumes in the absence of subsidy payments. Dischargers would be motivated to exaggerate the volume of discharges they would have had. Especially with new or expanded production facilities, or new or modified products, estimation would be extremely difficult.

Effluent Fees

Almost all economists who have studied the subject favor a partial or total dismantling of the permit program and its replacement by an **effluent fee.** Effluent fees are extremely simple: dischargers are permitted to discharge whatever quantity of wastes they wish, but they must pay the government a fee per unit of waste discharged. The fee for each major waste would be set by the government at the level the government estimates would result in discharge volumes that equate marginal benefits and costs of abatement.

Settling effluent fees requires the same data and calculations that issuing permits requires—no more and no less. The government must estimate benefits and costs of abatement for either program; and it must meter actual discharges at least on a sample basis. The great advantage of effluent fees over the permit program is that the government would be removed from business decision making and environmental decisions would be placed within the market context that firms are motivated to use and are experienced in using. Firms could design whatever abatement devices appeared to them to be the most economical means of achieving each abatement level. They would not need to obtain government permission for devices or discharge volumes.

Dischargers would be motivated to seek economical means of abatement as long as they discharged any wastes. Under a permit system, dischargers have no incentive to discharge less than the level provided by their permit.

Effluent fees have been better studied than almost any government program, actual or potential. Their advantages in comparison with alternatives are overwhelming. They have been advocated by economists, business groups, and environmental groups. They have been tried successfully in other countries, especially Germany and France. Why have they not been tried in the United States? The existing environmental program was put in place during the zenith of the environmental movement in the early 1970s. The mood of the country was similar to that of a crusade—not a time when the political process wants to listen to economists talk about the dangers of government intrusion into business. Since then, an enormous amount of human and physical capital has been invested in the permit program: designing it, implementing it, and learning to live with it. And the focus of people's attention has shifted elsewhere: to fuel and other material shortages.

In fact, interest in introducing economic incentives into the environmental program is growing. Government officials are more interested in economic arguments now than they were a decade ago, the problems with the permit program have become more obvious, and more is known about practical aspects of effluent-fee programs. EPA is moving to introduce better economic incentives into the program.

Materials Reuse

Although air and water pollution control is a cooperative federal-state program, its basic characteristics have been federal initiatives since the 1950s. But solid-waste disposal, and hence reuse, is still mainly a state and local responsibility. Furthermore, most of the used products from which reusable materials come are in urban areas. Thus, solid-waste disposal and materials recovery are of great interest to urban governments.

Materials reuse responds strongly to prices of new materials. During times such as the early 1970s, when newly extracted materials—from food to metals to fuel—were scarce and expensive, recovery and reuse flourished. When new materials become relatively cheaper, as they did in the mid-1970s, recovery and reuse languish.

Some materials are much easier to recover and reuse than others. Virgin copper is expensive, and much of it is used to such products as copper wire from which the copper can be recovered easily. An automobile, by contrast, is a complex product containing many materials. Materials recovery and reuse require sophisticated technology.

Many government actions—mostly having to do with the tax system —favor the use of virgin instead of used materials. If so, there is justification for government programs to promote reuse. Unfortunately, nobody knows how much bias toward virgin materials is introduced by governments. In addition, solid-waste disposal is a chronic problem for local governments in metropolitan areas. Especially in central cities, land that can be used for landfills is almost nonexistent. And local governments appear to be unable to contract with each other so that, for example, central-city governments can dispose of solid wastes in distant suburbs.

During the 1970s several cooperative federal-state-local solid-waste recovery and disposal experiments were carried on. Typically, a central facility was established to which municipal and industrial wastes could be brought. At the facility, materials would be separated and processed for reuse. Those for which there was no demand would be disposed of in landfills or incinerators. A typical activity of such facilities is preparation of organic wastes to be used as fuel in thermal electric plants. Such experiments have met with mixed success. But experience and high fuel prices will presumably guarantee eventual success.

A special local government solid-waste problem arises with **sludge** from municipal treatment plants. Traditionally sludge has been burned, disposed of in landfills, or hauled to sea and dumped there. But dumping at sea has been banned, creating a crisis in coastal cities. Promising experiments have been tried to process sludge into fertilizer that can be used on farms and lawns. Easy processing results in an inexpensive and high quality fertilizer. Surprisingly, the biggest problem is caused by heavy metals that are discharged into the sewage system by industry and remain intact through treatment. Heavy metals in sludge that is processed into fertilizer may be taken up by plants and ingested by persons who eat them. Americans have fortunately been free of heavy-metals poisoning, but experience elsewhere, especially in Japan, shows that heavy-metals poisoning can lead to incurable illnesses and death.

Many questions are raised about cooperative solid-waste recovery and disposal facilities. Are they successful? To what extent is success the result of the large subsidies that facilities receive and to what extent is it the result of their innovative activities? Should they be government run? It is too early to answer such questions.

SUMMARY

Pollution is defined as deterioration of the environment resulting from the return of materials to the environment. The materials balance is an exhaustive list of sources and dispositions of materials used in economic activity. The practical ways to abate polluting discharges are to recycle more materials and to alter the form of discharges by process changes and by treatment of wastes.

Pollutants are discharged to the environment as gases, liquids, or solid wastes. There is considerable evidence that air pollution affects mortality and morbidity as well as property. Water pollution affects a large variety of water uses. Inadequate methods of solid-waste disposal mar the landscape and impair many uses of land.

Economic theory shows that excessive pollution results unless discharges are controlled by government policy, because pollution costs are not borne by those who discharge wastes. Government policies to abate pollution may entail public collection and disposal of wastes, regulation of discharges, subsidies for waste treatment, or fees for the discharge of wastes. In the United States, government pollution-abatement programs consist mainly of government collection, treatment, and disposal of wastes, and of an elaborate permit program to regulate discharges. Only recently have governments shown interest in introducing economic incentives into pollution-control programs.

Solid-waste recovery and disposal are mainly local government responsibilities. Implementing effective recovery programs is a challenge to both government and private sectors.

QUESTIONS AND PROBLEMS

1. What would be the effects on income distribution between rich and poor of more stringent controls on air and water pollution?

2. How would the following be affected by a fee levied on discharge of sulfur to the atmosphere: Regulated electric utilities? Manufacturers of atomic reactors? Sulfur mining companies?

3. Evaluate the contention that polluters should be jailed as common criminals instead of being slapped on the wrist by effluent fees.

4. Depletion allowances are percentages of gross revenues that mining firms are permitted to subtract before computing federal corporate profits taxes. Suppose that, instead, they were required to depreciate their holdings like any other capital asset. What would be the effect on materials reuse?

5. How would you modify the materials balance to account for material and commodity imports and exports?

REFERENCES AND FURTHER READING

Allen Kneese, Robert Ayres, and Ralph D'Arge, *Economics and the Environment*, 1970. *A basic data source for the materials balance.*

William Baumol and Wallace Oates, *The Theory of Environmental Policy*, 1975. *A technical, theoretical analysis of environmental economics.*

William Baumol and Wallace Oates, *Economics, Environmental Policy and the Quality of Life*, 1979. *A nontechnical and practical analysis of environmental programs.*

Council on Environmental Quality, *Environmental Quality. The annual report of the federal executive-office agency that advises the President on environmental issues.*

Allen Kneese and Charles Schultze, *Pollution, Prices and Public Policy*, 1975. *A careful analysis of the use of economic incentives in government policy making.*

Lester Lave and Eugene Seskin, *Air Pollution and Human Health*, 1977. *A careful statistical analysis of health effects of air pollution.*

Edwin Mills, *The Economics of Environmental Quality*, 1978. *A textbook on environmental economics.*

Harold Wolozin (editor), *The Economics of Air Pollution*, 1966.

THIS CHAPTER RETURNS TO THE SUBJECT MATTER OF CHAPTER 3: the sizes and structures of urban areas. Whereas Chapter 3 traced historical trends, this chapter analyzes government policy issues related to urban size and structure. This chapter draws on both the factual material presented in Chapter 3 and the positive and normative theoretical analysis in Chapters 5 and 6.

12

Government Policies Toward Urban Sizes and Structures

The contention to be analyzed in this chapter is that market, and perhaps government, decision making produces urban sizes and structures that represent inefficient uses of scarce and valuable productive resources. It follows from this contention, and from the notion that governments have responsibility to correct resource misallocation, that governments should attempt to improve the size distribution and structures of urban areas.

Theoretically, there are many ways in which the size distribution of urban areas could be askew. In practice, *it is invariably contended that the largest urban areas are too large and the smallest are too small.* The belief may be more widely held than any other regarding social problems. It is held by city planners, government officials, journalists, and scholars. It is held in rich and poor countries, in capitalist and socialist countries; it is held in African countries, where the largest urban area has only a few hundred thousand people, and in Japan, which has the world's largest urban area, of some 25 million people. Many countries in Europe and Asia have official, although mostly ineffectual, policies of discouraging growth of the largest urban areas.[1]

Also widely held is the view that U.S. metropolitan areas are excessively spread out or suburbanized. It was seen in Chapter 3 that suburbanization proceeded rapidly and far after World War II. Most metropolitan suburbs are dominated by single-family houses on large lots. Journalists and planners complain that such low-density suburbs make wasteful use of land and fuel for heating, cooling, and transportation, and that they lead to undesirable life-styles. The phrase "slums and suburban sprawl" conveys the feeling of antipathy held by many toward suburbs. Most literature on the subject, however, leaves unclear whether the alleged deficiencies of suburbs are matters of efficiency or equity or whether they result from market failure, from preferences of which authors disapprove, or from misguided government policies.

Although the beliefs analyzed in this chapter are widely held, they are less coherent than the problems analyzed in earlier chapters. An important task of the chapter will be to ask exactly what the alleged problem is; why it is a problem; and, finally, what—if anything—should be done about it.

THE SIZE DISTRIBUTION OF URBAN AREAS

Data and analysis on the size distribution of urban areas were presented in Chapter 3. What reasons are there to believe that the size distribution resulting from residents' and firms' location decisions might not represent an efficient use of productive resources? Mainly as a result of work by Tolley and others, a coherent analysis of this subject is now available. Much of the following is based on the Tolley analysis. It relies on the notion of market failure because of external diseconomies. The basic theoretical analysis of market failure was presented in Chapter 6. Chapter 11 applied the analysis to pollution problems. To build on that analysis, the urban size distribution problem will be introduced in the context of environmental problems. It will then be shown how the analysis can be applied to other causes of market failure.

As was pointed out in Chapter 1, input productivity varies among urban areas because of differences in comparative advantage and other considerations. If the sizes of urban areas matter, it means that input productivity also depends on the size of the urban area. Some inputs, notably labor, are mobile among urban areas. Massive urban migrations observed in the United States and elsewhere, discussed in Chapter 2, represent input movements to the most advantageous locations.

The simplest situation to analyze is one in which there are two urban areas, one large and one small. The same product is produced in each

1.   See Sundquist.

Figure 12.1

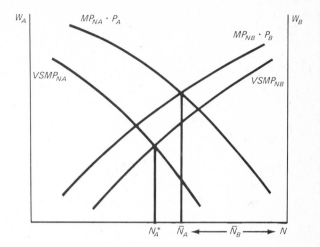

urban area. A given labor supply consisting of N identical workers is to be allocated between the two urban areas. In Figure 12.1, A is the large, and B the small, urban area. The number of workers in A is measured on the horizontal axis with origin at the left vertical axis. Since N is fixed, N_B, *the number of workers in B is* $N_B = N - N_A$. The length of the horizontal axis is N, so N_B is the distance from the right vertical axis to $N_A \cdot MP_{NA} \cdot P_A$ measures the value of the marginal product of workers in A, and $MP_{NB} \cdot P_B$ measures the value of their marginal product in B. Each MP is labor's marginal product and each P is the local product price. $MP_{NB} \cdot P_B$ is measured from the right vertical axis, so it falls to the left. Assume that the labor market is competitive within and between urban areas. As was shown in Chapter 5, the wage rate equals the value of the marginal product in competitive equilibrium. Assume for the moment that workers care only about the local wage rate in choosing between A and B. Then, the labor force is in **locational equilibrium** when the wage rate is the same in both urban areas. That occurs when $\bar{N}_A$ workers work in A and $\bar{N}_B$ workers work in B.

Now suppose that not only commodity production, but also pollution discharges, say to the air, increase as employment increases in each urban area. Assume for the moment that each firm's discharge damages the plant of other firms in the same urban area. (For example, discharges may peel paint from walls.) Then, as was shown in Chapter 11, the social value of extra production from each firm is worth less than its market value; *from the market value of the marginal product must be subtracted the market value of the resulting additional pollution.* $VSMP_A$ and $VSMP_B$ show the social value of the marginal product of labor in A and B as functions of

N_A and N_B. $VSMP_{NA}$ is below $MP_{NA} \cdot P_A$ at each value of N_A, and $VSMP_{NB}$ is below $MP_{NB} \cdot P_B$ at each value of N_B, showing that each additional polluting discharge does harm.

Now make the crucial assumption: that incremental damage from additional discharges is an increasing function of total discharges and hence of total output and labor input. For example, the incremental damage of the third ton per day of sulfur oxide discharge might be slight, but the incremental damage of the tenth ton per day might be much greater. The assumption implies that the vertical distance between $MP_{NA} \cdot P_A$ and $VSMP_{NA}$ increases with movement to the right, and that the distance between $MP_{NB} \cdot P_B$ and $VSMP_{NB}$ increases with movement to the left. Furthermore, at $\bar{N}_A \cdot VSMP_{NA}$ is further below $MP_{NA} \cdot P_A$ than is $VSMP_{NB}$ below $MP_{NB} \cdot P_B$. A socially efficient labor force allocation between the two urban areas requires that $VSMP_{NA} = VSMP_{NB}$, that the value of the social marginal product of labor be the same in the two areas. This follows from the result, established in Chapter 6, that social efficiency requires the (social) marginal product of an input to be the same in all uses. This occurs when N_A^* workers live and work in A in Figure 12.1. If $N_A^* \neq \bar{N}_A$, market failure occurs in the form of labor misallocation between the two urban areas. Since A is larger than B, $VSMP_{NA}$ is below $VSMP_{NB}$ at $\bar{N}_A$. It follows that efficient labor allocation requires a movement of workers from A to B, that workers be shifted from the large to the small urban area.

The common sense of the above result is as follows. *If incremental pollution damage increases with the size of the urban area, then market equilibrium causes too many workers to locate in the large urban area and too few to locate in the small urban area.* Before discussing the implications of the analysis for government attempts to improve resource allocation, it is important to explore the limits of the formal model in a less formal fashion.

The first comment is that the theoretical model is not applicable only to pollution. Suppose, for example, that road congestion is an increasing function of an urban area's population. The analysis in Chapter 9 makes that a plausible assumption. Then, assumptions analogous to those made above imply that **unpriced congestion** *also causes large urban areas to be too large and small urban areas to be too small.* Certain other types of market failure may have similar implications for the relative sizes of urban areas. The possibility will be explored below.

Second, in the formal model it was assumed that the polluting discharges did not directly affect residents' welfare. It might be thought that, since polluting discharges do reduce residents' welfare, the fact that the large urban area is more polluted than the small one would prevent excessive population in the large urban area. But the congestion example shows that the conclusion is false. In Chapter 9 it was shown that congestion is not deterred by the fact that underpriced travel causes travelers direct welfare loss. Even though congestion hurts only those who travel in congested conditions, underpricing nevertheless causes excess crowding on roads. Likewise, in the pollution example, the fact that the large urban area is more polluted than the small urban area deters some, but not enough, people from living in the large urban area. Thus, wages are higher in the large than in the small urban area, inducing more production to locate in the small urban area than if pollution did not affect wages. But it does not cause an optimum distribution of population between the two urban areas, any more than the disutility of congested travel prevents congestion.

Third, the analysis does not depend on there being only two urban areas. Imagine an entire distribution of urban sizes, as discussed in Chapter 3. Then, if the marginal damage from increased population in an urban area increases with the population of the urban area, it follows that a set of the largest urban areas are too large and the remaining smaller urban areas are too small. In practice, damages from pollution are by no means uniquely correlated with the size of the urban area. They also depend on natural conditions (such as weather), on the industrial structure of the urban area, and on other variables. But there is a tendency for large metropolitan areas to be more polluted than small metropolitan areas.

GOVERNMENT POLICIES TOWARD URBAN SIZE DISTRIBUTION

What can governments do to remove the resource misallocation that results in an inappropriate urban size distribution? The immediate reaction of many people is to urge government to undertake a variety of ad hoc programs to deter growth of large metropolitan areas. Many such programs would do great harm. In fact, the policy analysis is complex and must be undertaken with care.

If an external diseconomy were *technologically* linked to population, then the policy solution would be simple. Suppose, for example, that pollution discharges were proportionate to population in an urban area. Then the correct government policy would be a tax on each resident in each urban area equal to the difference between $MP_N \cdot P$ and $VSMP_N$, evaluated at the optimum population N^*. The tax would be higher in larger urban areas, given the assumptions made in Figure 12.1.

Even in this simple situation, inappropriate policies are frequently urged on governments. The most common error is to urge taxes or other controls only on newcomers, say on those who come to reside in the urban area after its population passes N^*. *But newcomers are no more polluting than older residents; pollution is proportionate to total population.* The tax should exclude those to whom residence in the urban area is least valuable, and should be levied on all residents. Taxes for the privilege of residing in large urban areas are understandably unpopular. Thus, government officials commonly think of indirect ways of discouraging growth of large urban areas. For example, steering federal defense and other contracts away from large urban areas is frequently proposed. All such proposals interfere with optimum distribution of particular industries among urban areas, and are therefore undesirable.

The key point, which is misunderstood in almost all discussions of government policies to change the urban size distribution, is that *external diseconomies are by no means technologically linked to urban population.* It was shown in Chapter 11 that polluting discharges depend on how resources are allocated, not just on total population. Wastes can be treated before discharge, production processes and products can be modified so as to produce less waste, wastes can be transported to discharge points where they do less harm, and so forth. The appropriate government policy toward polluting discharges is controls or, better yet, effluent fees, on discharges.

It is likely that effluent fees should be higher, or controls more stringent, in large urban areas than elsewhere. The result may indeed be to shift population and employment somewhat from large to small urban areas. But the main result would be to reduce the polluting discharges resulting from a given total population and employment in an urban area. Any effect on total population in an urban area would be incidental and probably small. In fact, pollution levels are not much higher in large urban areas than in much smaller urban areas. It would take an enormous cut in the population of the New York metropolitan area to improve its air quality much. Population redistribution is about as costly a pollution-control program as could be imagined.

If the analysis is taken a step further, it even becomes unclear that an optimum pollution-control program would shift people and jobs from large to small urban areas. In Figure 12.1, it was assumed that polluting discharges affected production costs in the urban area, but did not directly affect residents' welfare. In fact, pollution affects both people and property, but the most important effects are on health. Consider a large, badly polluted urban area, and suppose an optimum effluent fee is levied on discharges in the urban area. The effluent fee has two effects. First, it makes living and working in the urban area more expensive, inducing people to live and work elsewhere and thus shifting population to smaller urban areas. Second, it makes the urban area more attractive as a place to live. In fact, an optimum set of effluent fees would probably improve environmental quality in large urban areas relative to that in small urban areas. This second effect tends to increase population and employment in the large urban area. Thus, the two effects are offsetting, and it appears not to be possible to predict their net effect on the urban area's population without detailed data for the particular urban area.

The same analysis applies to every alleged external diseconomy. It was shown in Chapter 9 that road congestion depends not only on the total population of an urban area, but also on the allocation of resources in the urban area. Congestion depends on the mix of automobile and public transit investments, on charges that discourage urban travel, and on locations of residences and workplaces. As with environmental problems, a government policy to reduce congestion by reducing the total population of an urban area would be about the most inefficient policy to reduce congestion that could be imagined. Appropriate programs to control congestion are directed at transportation resource allocation, not at the urban area's total population. As with environmental programs, appropriate transportation programs to control congestion may have effects on the total population of an urban area, but the effects would be incidental and probably small.

The implication of this section can be summarized briefly: *if an activity causes distortions in urban sizes, the activity should be controlled directly.* Urban size distortions are no more than symptoms of resource misallocation. To attack the urban size distribution directly is to attack the wrong variable. Tolley et al. analyze a variety of causes of urban size distortions and propose remedies for some.

SUBURBANIZATION AND GOVERNMENT POLICY

In Chapter 3, changes in the percentage of metropolitan residents living or working in central cities or suburbs were employed as measures of suburbanization. It was pointed out that the measure is a poor one because central cities vary as a share of metropolitan areas from one place to another, because central-city boundaries are moved occasionally, and because independent suburban local government jurisdictions are virtually unknown in most countries.

The analysis in the Appendix suggests a measure of suburbanization that does not depend on locations of local government jurisdictional boundaries. There it is shown that urban population density can be approximated by an exponential function,

$$D(u) = D_0 e^{-bu} \tag{12.1}$$

where $D(u)$ is population per square mile u miles from the urban center, e is the base of the natural logarithm, and D_0 and b are constants to be estimated from the data for each urban area. Equation 12.1 is an exact density function in special circumstances and an approximation otherwise. Putting $u = 0$ shows that D_0 is the density at the urban center. It is an artificial notion, since few people live within a short distance of most urban centers, where most land is used for employment. But for most urban areas, Equation 12.1 is a good approximation for distances more than half a mile or so from the center. The term *b* is positive if density decreases with distance from the urban center. Equation 12.1 has the general shape shown in Figure 12.2. The density function is flatter at each *u* the smaller is *b*. It can be shown by differentiating Equation 12.1 with respect to *u* that 100*b* is the percentage by which population falls per mile of distance from the urban center. For example, a *b* of 0.3 implies that density falls 30 percent per mile of movement from the center. The constant *b* is referred to as the **gradient** of the density function.

A final property shows the relationship between the exponential density function and suburbanization. If an urban area's population grows by increasing D_0, leaving *b* unchanged, the percentage of the urban population living within a fixed distance of the center remains unchanged. For example, the percentage living within the central city remains unchanged. It is therefore natural to say that, of two exponential density functions, that with the smaller *b* represents the more **suburbanized** urban area. The basic advantage of using *b* as estimated from Equation 12.1 as a measure of suburbanization is that the measure does not depend on the location or movement of central-city boundaries.

In fact, the most common method of estimating exponential density functions makes no use of central-city or suburban population data. SMSAs are divided into census tracts with a few thousand residents in each. Thus, an SMSA of even one or two million people would cover several dozen census tracts. It is easy to draw a random sample of census tracts from a metropolitan area, record the population of each from census data, and estimate the area of the census tract and its distance from the urban center

Figure 12.2

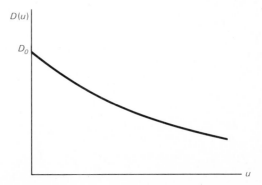

Table 12.1.   AVERAGE DENSITY GRADIENTS FOR SELECTED U.S. AND JAPANESE METROPOLITAN AREAS

U.S. Year	Average Gradient	Japan Year	Average Gradient
1960	.199	1965	.457
1970	.123	1970	.391

Source: Mills and Ohta.

from census maps. Then natural logs can be taken of both sides of Equation 12.1 and log D_0 and b can be estimated using linear least-squares regression.

Equation 12.1 has been estimated for many dozens of metropolitan areas in several dozen countries, some for years as long ago as early in the nineteenth century. Table 12.1 presents averages of density gradients estimated for a sample of U.S. and Japanese metropolitan areas in recent census years. The sample consisted of about 20 representative metropolitan areas in each country.[2]

The data in Table 12.1 are typical of results obtained in many studies in many countries. First, the U.S. metropolitan areas are extremely decentralized. No other country appears to have average density gradients as low as those typical in the United States. Low average b values imply that density falls only slightly with distance from the urban center. Together with low average D_0 values characteristic of U.S. metropolitan areas, they imply low average population densities in U.S. metropolitan areas. There can be no doubt that U.S. metropolitan areas are more suburbanized and have lower average population densities than do metropolitan areas in most countries.

Second, the average density gradients decrease through time, indicating that the metropolitan areas are becoming more suburbanized as time passes. Studies have shown that U.S. metropolitan areas have been decentralizing at least since about the middle of the nineteenth century. Fragmentary evidence indicates that European metropolitan areas have been decentralizing since early in the nineteenth century. Much more plentiful evidence indicates that the trend to decentralization has been pervasive in non-Communist developed and developing countries during the post–World War II period. Decentralization has gone less far in other countries, but the speed of decentralization is greater in many countries, including Japan, than in the United States.

The fact that decentralization pervades so many countries and so

2. The unit distance for the gradients in Table 12.1 is one kilometer, not one mile.

many decades indicates that its basic causes are not the provincial postwar U.S. conditions that have been studied in previous chapters: central-city racial tensions; high central-city tax and crime rates; central-city road congestion, pollution levels, and so forth. This is not to say that problems peculiar to postwar U.S. metropolitan areas have not affected decentralization. They probably have, and may be one reason that U.S. metropolitan areas are more decentralized than those elsewhere.

What then are the basic causes of decentralization that operate in disparate countries and in different time periods? Most of the important reasons can be inferred from the model in the Appendix, but are also commonsensical. Equation A.14b implies that the population density function becomes flatter as income rises or as transportation cost falls. The point is that, as shown in the Appendix, suburban land is cheaper than land near an urban center. As income rises, housing demand rises. The more housing one consumes, the farther it is worthwhile to commute in order to live in a house on cheap land. Likewise, as transportation cost falls, the farther out in the suburbs one can go to obtain housing on cheap land for a given expenditure on commuting.

Rising real incomes have been the norm in northern Europe and North America for at least one or two centuries. As a result, metropolitan areas have gradually spread out. The same has been true in many developing countries during the postwar period. Likewise, technology has gradually lowered the real cost of commuting for at least a century. Before steam railroads, the only feasible commuting modes were foot, horse, and bicycle. By the middle of the nineteenth century, at least a few people could commute by steam railway. By the end of the nineteenth century, electrified street railways were introduced and caused massive suburbanization. After about 1920, increasing numbers of people commuted by car. In the postwar period, increasing availability of cars and dramatic improvements of roads, especially because of the interstate highway system, further reduced commuting costs.

The automobile is by no means unique in causing urban decentralization. Any mode that reduces radial travel costs has a similar effect. In many countries in which cars are rarely used for urban commuting, suburbanization has proceeded rapidly. But in the postwar United States, the automobile has been properly associated with suburbanization.

A third cause of urban decentralization is growth of the total population of the urban area. An urban area with a small population can support only one major concentration of employment and shopping, the central business district (CBD). But larger urban areas generate enough employment and shopping so that suburban subcenters can be supported. Industrial parks and shopping centers are examples. The more shopping and employment available away from the CBD, the further out people can live, taking advantage of cheap land, without incurring high transportation costs. Thus, *large urban areas tend to have flatter density functions than small urban areas.* The growth of large urban areas has thus been a fourth cause of flattening density functions.

In order to discuss market failure as a cause of excessive urban decentralization, it is important to know how much decentralization can be accounted for by the three prosaic market forces just enumerated. Unfortunately, no one knows. It is known that U.S. density functions are somewhat flatter, and average urban densities somewhat less, than in Europe. As Table 12.1 shows, U.S. density functions have gradients less than half those in Japanese urban areas.

However, another market difference between the U.S. on the one hand and northern Europe and Japan on the other has an enormous effect on urban population densities and decentralization: land values. In the inflationary late 1970s home buyers find it hard to believe, but *U.S. land values are low, compared to those in almost any other industrialized country.* It has been estimated that the market value of land in Japan is more than three times GNP; the comparable figure in the U.S. is about two-thirds GNP.[3] In relation to incomes, land values are five times as high in Japan as in the United States. Inevitably, the result is that Japanese economize on urban land. Homes, factories, and offices are built on tiny lots. The result is that metropolitan areas are much higher in density and less decentralized than here. Typical conditions in northern Europe are probably somewhere between those in Japan and the United States. The only industrialized countries in which densities and land values are as low as in the United States are Canada and Australia. In both of those countries, much of the land is more or less uninhabitable.

International and intertemporal comparisons of urban population density functions are instructive. They make clear that urban decentralization is not mainly the result of central-city problems that are peculiar to postwar United States. However, neither data nor theory provides an accurate guide to measures of how much decentralization is consistent with efficient market performance and how much might be the result of market failure. The most that can be done is to discuss each of several causes of excess decentralization that have been alleged by commentators on the urban scene.

GOVERNMENT POLICY ISSUES

Pollution.   This is the easiest kind of market failure to analyze as a cause of excess decentralization. Suppose that air-polluting discharges are concentrated near the centers of urban areas. It is certainly true of discharges

3.   See Mills and Ohta.

from motor vehicles and from combustion from space heating. Pollutants diffuse throughout the metropolitan area according to wind patterns, but become less concentrated further from discharge points. That is why air quality tends to improve somewhat with distance from CBDs in most urban areas.

Improvement in air quality adds another benefit to falling land values as one moves away from the urban center. The sum of the two benefits must be set against increased transportation costs in determining the optimum density pattern. It is intuitively obvious that the resulting population density function indicates more decentralization than the model in Chapter 5 that ignored air pollution.

It is doubtful that the decentralizing effect of air pollution is very important. The United States now has stringent controls on air-polluting discharges. Discharges are nevertheless somewhat greater near urban centers than in suburbs. It seems unlikely, however, that the difference in air quality is great enough to have much effect.

Transportation underpricing. It was suggested in Chapter 9 that urban transportation, especially by automobile, is consistently underpriced in the United States. The effects of increased transportation costs on urban density functions are easy to calculate.

If the price elasticity of housing demand is about minus one, Equations A.14b and A.11 imply that the density gradient b in Equation 12.1 equals tE. E is defined on p. 227 and is a collection of constants that depend on, among other things, units of measurement. The symbol t is the round-trip cost of one mile of commuting. Take the average b of .123 reported in Table 12.1 for U.S. metropolitan areas in 1970. In the example on p. 147 of Chapter 9, it was assumed that urban auto commuting cost was $.25 per mile, $.10 per mile of time cost and $.15 per mile of ownership cost. That implies $t = .50$, and $b = .123 = tE$ implies $E = .25$. Assume that automobile ownership cost should be $.05 per mile greater than in the example. This implies an increase in the gasoline tax of about $.75 (= $.05 × 15 miles per gallon), a drastic increase indeed. Then b would be increased only to .148, still closer to the 1970 than to the 1960 average in Table 12.1.

Of course, all changes in density gradients are long run in nature, requiring construction and alteration of dwellings. Presumably, the effect of an increase in urban travel cost to correct underpricing would be to slow down the decreases in gradients that occur for market reasons. But no one should think that even drastic increases in urban travel costs would dramatically reverse the long-term trend to decentralization.

Land-use controls. In Chapter 10, land-use controls for fiscal or exclusionary purposes were discussed. Although there is a wide range of such controls, zoning is perhaps the most important. An important zoning provision is exclusion of all dwellings but single-family detached houses on lots no smaller than a stipulated minimum. Frequent minima are one or two acres, but some are much larger. The purpose of such controls is to exclude dwellings whose real-estate taxes would not pay the cost of local government services provided to their residents. Their mechanism is to require all residents' housing to be of as high a quality and as low a density as is appropriate for a group of residents able to control zoning provisions. The typical procedure is for the initial residents to have relatively high incomes and to establish zoning provisions appropriate to their housing demand. But as the metropolitan area grows and decentralizes, lower-income residents who would move in if the zoning provisions were absent are precluded from doing so. The result is inevitably to cause suburbs to be lower density than they would be in the absence of zoning.

How large is the excessive decentralization resulting from low-density zoning? Nobody knows. Beyond a doubt, suburban zoning provisions are consistent with the housing demands of most of the people who would live there even in the absence of zoning restrictions. A sudden removal of all controls on the types and densities of suburban housing would probably slow the speed of metropolitan decentralization, but would not reverse the direction.

The most important evidence that distortions from land-use controls are of modest proportions is that urban density functions show little evidence of discontinuity as central-city boundaries are crossed. As was seen in Chapter 10, zoning controls on dwellings are much less important in central cities than in suburbs. If low-density zoning caused large resource misallocation, discontinuities in density functions would be expected at central-city boundaries. But such discontinuities appear to be either nonexistent or small.

Subsidization of owner-occupied housing.   It is frequently claimed that government actions make owner-occupied housing cheaper than it should be. The two government programs most frequently referred to are FHA and VA mortgage insurance and the federal income-tax treatment of mortgage interest and real-estate taxes. Both programs were explained in Chapter 8.

FHA and VA mortgages certainly place emphasis on owner-occupied housing. But it was explained in Chapter 8 that their effects on housing prices and demand are small. Although the tax reduction resulting from deductibility of real-estate taxes and mortgage interest for owner-occupiers is large, it was conjectured in Chapter 8 that the deductibility provisions are probably of about the same magnitude as the neighborhood effect, or external economy, from housing investment. Furthermore, in suburbs real-estate taxes more nearly approximate prices paid for local government services than in central cities, as was shown in the discussion of the Tiebout hypothesis in Chapter 10. The implication of the foregoing considerations is not so much that owner-occupied housing is too cheap as that *unsubsidized rental housing is more expensive than it should be to promote socially efficient resource allocation.*

Extending a deductibility or tax-credit provision to renters would reduce the cost of rental housing and would, if anything, reduce densities and increase decentralization of metropolitan areas. In Chapter 8, it was indicated that a credit of about 15 percent would make rental housing comparable with owner-occupied housing. If the price elasticity of housing demand is as large as unity, the effect would be at most a 15 percent increase in housing consumption for the one third of urban residents who are renters, or a total increase in urban housing demand of about 5 percent. It would have only a small effect on density functions.

Energy costs. The latter part of the 1970s was a period of rapidly rising fuel costs. Many people are deeply concerned that low-density suburbs may be an inappropriate form of urban resource allocation in a period of high energy costs. The issue is not one of market failure, but rather one of adjustment from a form appropriate to low energy costs to one appropriate to high energy costs. Issues fall into three categories.

First is space heating and cooling costs. It requires only about one third as much fuel to heat and cool a high-rise apartment as it does to heat a single-family detached house. Of course, energy requirements are less the better constructed and insulated any dwelling is, but the two-thirds saving is about the same for all construction materials, insulation types, regions of the country, and fuel types, provided similar dwellings are compared. For example, the two-thirds saving is about the same in the cold North as in the warm South. Space heating and cooling are lost through outside walls, windows, doors, and roofs. The saving comes from shared walls, ceilings, and floors. Other housing types, such as garden apartments, are between the extremes for high-rise apartments and single-family detached houses.

The large fuel saving is no argument for requiring or subsidizing attached dwellings or for taxing or preventing detached dwellings. Provided fuel prices are at equilibrium levels, markets provide adequate incentive for fuel-efficient dwellings. But *high fuel prices are a powerful reason for local governments to abolish land-use controls that prohibit multifamily housing.* As was seen in Chapter 10, the main purpose of land-use controls is exclusionary, and of doubtful social benefit. In an era of high fuel prices, restrictions on multifamily housing are unforgivable.

Second is gasoline consumption from automobile use. Low-density suburbs probably entail somewhat longer trips for work and shopping. But the fact of low density does not necessarily mean that jobs and shops are far away. The characteristic of U.S. suburbs that requires long commuting and shopping trips is the extreme segregation of commercial and industrial land uses from residential areas. Excessive segregation results from local land-use controls. In many communities, it is illegal to locate even a single shop in residential areas. And some communities exclude shopping and employment centers altogether. The subject is controversial because many kinds of employment impose undesirable nuisances on nearby residents. But it seems clear that some land-use controls that segregate nonresidential activities could be weakened without substantial damage to residents.

Third, and most complex, is public transit. Beyond doubt, buses and subways require less energy per passenger-mile than do cars. A passenger-mile of car transportation requires at least 10 times as much fuel as a passenger-mile in a nearly full bus. Thus, the higher are motor-vehicle fuel prices, the lower is the relative price of public transit compared with automobiles, and the greater the shift of demand to public transit travel.

Once again the magnitudes are important. Return to the example on p. 147. Even at a price of nearly $1.00 per gallon, the gasoline required for the 5-mile trip considered there costs only about $.25 or $.05 per mile. Suppose fuel prices rise by 50 percent. That would raise the cost of the trip by auto by $.15 to $1.90. It might raise the bus fare by $.02, increasing the cost of the bus trip to $1.85. The bus becomes the cheaper mode in the example, but it is clear that even a drastic increase in fuel costs would have only a modest effect on modal choice.

There can be no doubt that low-density suburbs make it difficult to operate economical public transit systems. It was shown in Chapter 9 that public transit systems require large numbers of travelers between particular origin-destination pairs. Relaxation of land-use controls on multifamily housing and small lots would help. But a modal shift toward public transit commuting will be a gradual process in U.S. metropolitan areas, barring catastrophic fuel shortages.

CONCLUDING COMMENTS

The basic conclusion of this chapter is simple: phenomena that lead to an inappropriate urban size distribution or to excessive suburbanization should be attacked in straightforward fashion. *It is unjustifiable to impose direct controls on urban sizes or on urban decentralization.* They would result in great inefficiency and hardship and would do little to solve the underlying problems. If the problem is pollution, it should be attacked with discharge controls or effluent fees, not with controls on urban sizes or structures. The same conclusion applies to all causes of inappropriate urban sizes and structures.

SUMMARY

There is widespread concern among government officials, scholars, and the public that the largest metropolitan areas are too big and that most urban areas are excessively decentralized. In both cases, much of the concern is misplaced. It is unlikely that any appropriate government intervention would have much effect on urban sizes or structures.

Large metropolitan areas are thought to be too large because it is believed that environmental, congestion, and other externalities increase in importance with urban size. But it does not follow that appropriate intervention to solve the underlying problem would reduce the sizes of the largest urban areas. Whether government attacks on the problem would reduce the sizes of large urban areas or not, changes in urban sizes would be incidental to solution of the problem. The effect of government actions would be to alter resource allocation in metropolitan areas of given size.

U.S. suburbs are thought to be excessively decentralized for several reasons: centrally concentrated pollution discharges, underpricing of urban transportation, land-use controls, subsidization of owner-occupied houses, and high energy costs. Thinking is confused on several issues, and resolution of the problems would be unlikely to have large effects on urban densities. Urban areas have decentralized in the United States and elsewhere for decades because of powerful market forces. To reverse the process would be unjustified and probably impossible.

QUESTIONS AND PROBLEMS

1. In most countries, the share of the urban population living in the largest urban area falls as real income rises. Why do you think that is?

2. During the 1970s, the share of the urban population in the East and North Central regions has decreased, and the share in the South, West, and Rocky Mountain regions has increased. What effect has the regional shift had on the size distribution of urban areas? What effect has it had on energy use?

3. Suppose all residential land-use controls were abolished. How many more people would live in multifamily housing by the end of the century? How much energy would be saved?

4. Suppose that government programs returned typical U.S. density functions to their 1960 forms by the end of the century. What would be the percent saving in energy use?

5. Do you think that density gradients will continue to decline until metropolitan densities are uniform at all distances from the center?

REFERENCES AND FURTHER READING

Martin Beckmann and John McPherson, "City Size Distributions in a Central Place Hierarchy: An Alternative Approach," *Journal of Regional Science*, Vol. 10 (1970), 25–77. *A theoretical model of the urban size distribution.*

J. Vernon Henderson, *Economic Theory and the Cities*, 1977. *An advanced theoretical treatise of urban economics, including analysis of distortions within and among urban areas.*

Edwin Mills and Katsutoshi Ohta, "Urbanization and Urban Problems," in *Asia's New Giant* (Henry Rosovsky and Hugh Patrick, editors), 1976. *A study of urban problems in Japan.*

Richard Muth, *Cities and Housing*, 1969. *Contains a careful analysis of density functions.*

Real Estate Research Corporation, *The Costs of Sprawl*, 1974. *A study of all costs, government and private, of suburban developments at various densities.*

James Sundquist, *Dispersing Population*, 1975. *An analysis of European population-dispersal programs.*

George Tolley, Philip Graves, and John Gardner, *Urban Growth in a Market Economy*, 1979. *Technical analyses of distortions in urban sizes.*

A WAG HAS SAID THAT AN URBAN ECONOMIST HAS THE SAME professional advantages as a dermatologist: his patients never die and never get well. That urban areas have serious ills, or problems, can hardly be disputed. But if the urban ills of the 1980s are serious and difficult to treat, they are far from fatal. Despite the protestations of big city mayors, neither urban areas in general nor central cities in particular are near death. In fact, rapid urbanization during recent decades has produced substantial improvement in the economic and social conditions of both the poor and others who are increasingly concentrated in urban areas.

13

Government and Urban-Area Prospects

This hint of optimism is likely to be such a shock to newspaper readers of the 1980s that it requires elaboration. Urban areas in the United States were crowded with desperately poor immigrants in the nineteenth century and the early decades of the twentieth century. Although immigrants were often oppressed and treated with callous indifference, nobody thinks that the cities caused their poverty and misery. On the contrary, immigrants came here to escape much worse poverty and oppression in Europe and Asia. Although they lived badly enough in U.S. urban slums, their migration was successful in that they achieved better lives for themselves and their children. The urban economy generated higher and more rapidly rising standards of living than were possible in their native lands. And the U.S. political system enabled them to organize to demand their rights.

In the middle decades of the twentieth century, there has been a similar migration of poor and, in the case of blacks, oppressed people to the cities. But this time they have come from the rural South, Appalachia, and midwestern farms. They too have improved their lives by migration. The urban economy has generated higher living standards than did the miserable areas they left, and blacks have been more successful in demanding political rights in the cities than they were in the rural South. Evidence for this was presented in Chapters 7 and 8. The foregoing is not to say that urban migration of blacks from the rural South and of whites from Appalachia has ended poverty and oppression. To claim that a black resident of a northern city has equal economic opportunity or equal protection of the laws is an insult to common observation. But recognition of the existence of urban misery and oppression should not hide the fact that post–World War II urbanization of the poor has been part of a historic and successful struggle for economic and political improvements. As in earlier periods, urban areas have had a remarkable capacity to absorb large numbers of poor and to enable them to improve their economic and political conditions.

Each large influx of poor people into urban areas has generated social conflict, stress, and trauma. Undoubtedly, the influx of blacks has been the most traumatic of all. Racial prejudices are stronger than ethnic prejudices. Equally important, whereas earlier migrants had been oppressed by foreign despots, recent black migrants have been oppressed by their fellow American citizens. Most of our serious urban ills are the ills of the society transferred to urban areas. Far from having made the ills worse, urbanization has contributed more to their cure than was previously possible.

No one can survey the urban scene without being impressed with racism as a cause of urban ills. Poverty, poor housing, crime, drug abuse, fiscal problems of central cities, and other problems are caused or worsened by discrimination against blacks in every aspect of life. How much progress has there been? Statistical evidence has been presented in Chapters 7 and 8. Here, two vignettes are presented.

Kluger presents a devastating picture of blacks' lives in a small town in South Carolina in the 1920s and 1930s. Almost every avenue of improvement was closed to blacks. No employer would hire them except in approved menial occupations. A black farmer who stepped out of line would lose access to credit, supplies, and markets for his products. An employed black and other employed family workers would lose their jobs if any one of them stepped out of line. They received almost no public services: water supply, waste disposal, or paved streets. Their children received abysmal public educations, and could not afford to attend school for more than a few years. They received no government transfers. They had no access to legislative, administrative, or judicial remedies for wrongs against them. The police would not protect them. An "uppity nigger" or his family might be beaten or his house might be burned, or, in extreme cases, he might be lynched.

During the intervening half century, much has changed. The lives of the most able and best educated blacks have been transformed and now do not differ greatly from those of comparably placed whites. But some of the poorest blacks, comparable to those in small towns in South Carolina half a century ago, probably live in the South Bronx, the West side of Chicago, or one of the worst sections of Cleveland or Newark. There they have the advantage of anonymity and cannot be the victims of a boycott organized by all the whites they might go to for employment. Housing is certainly better. Public education for their children, although nothing to brag about, is probably better. They have minimal public services. They receive rather elaborate transfers: welfare, food stamps, and medicaid. They are members of, or are represented by, groups that provide at least minimal access to legislative, administrative, and judicial remedies. They have minimal police protection, but robbery, violence, drug abuse, and arson are rampant. Courts have become much more sympathetic.

Each reader may draw his or her own inference from the two vignettes. It seems clear that living conditions are better in the second than in the first, although by a much smaller margin than most whites would like to believe.

What has caused the considerable improvements in the lives of most blacks, and the modest improvement in the lives of the most poorly placed blacks? Urbanization has been an important cause. It has provided needed variety in access to jobs, better educations, and anonymity. Concentrated numbers have permitted political organization and influence. But a pervasive decline in racial prejudice has also contributed; polls and other evidence show steadily decreasing racial antagonisms on the part of whites. The passage of a number of federal civil rights laws and dramatically improved transfer programs has been partly a cause and partly an effect of other improvements. It is impressive that almost all government programs that have improved living conditions of blacks and other poor people have been federal. Nearly all transfer programs are federal, the initial impetus for civil rights laws has been federal, and most important judicial decisions have been federal.

What about the future? In the late 1970s, a wave of conservative and antigovernment sentiment seemed to be sweeping the country. If it means an end to compassion for the needy, it will presumably slow progress. But if it means a determination to simplify government and to remove waste and unnecessary intrusion by government into personal and business life, it could benefit the poor as much as others.

Government transfer programs are unnecessarily complex and intrusive. A wide range of welfare, unemployment, food stamp, and other programs could be replaced by a single negative income tax, integrated with the ordinary income tax. It would be better focused on the poor, less intrusive and no more expensive to taxpayers. Extremely complex housing-assistance programs could be replaced by a simple housing allowance or rental credit with the same beneficial effects. The poor would also benefit from removal of excessively stringent regulatory programs. Much of the armada of land-use controls should be at the top of that list. Removal of rent controls would certainly improve housing choices of the poor, and elimination of minimum-wage laws would improve job choices.

It is tempting to speculate that the present generation of college students will witness the end of the last great urban crisis caused by the influx of poor and different people to urban areas. Urban migration from rural areas is now slow and cannot become much more than a trickle in relation to the current urban population. The percentage of the population that is urban simply cannot increase much. And given present and prospective immigration laws, a large urban migration from abroad is unlikely. One who is even moderately optimistic can predict that the postwar urban crisis, viewed as a crisis of racial hostility and oppression, will fade into benign oblivion during the next half century.

REFERENCES AND FURTHER READING

Anthony Downs, *Urban Problems and Prospects*, 1970. *An enlightening survey of prospects for solving urban problems.*

Richard Kluger, *Simple Justice*, 1977. *A historical account of Brown vs. Board of Education.*

Thomas Sowell, *Race and Economics*, 1975. *A historical and analytical discussion of the positions of racial groups in the U.S. economy.*

THIS APPENDIX INTRODUCES SOME OF THE MATHEMATICAL techniques that have proven useful to urban economists as well as to researchers in other specialties. One of its purposes is to prove some of the statements made in the text. A much more important purpose is to show that mathematics is a useful tool in understanding urban processes and problems. The fundamental characteristic of an urban area is that many forces interact to determine land rents, land uses, and other interesting urban characteristics. In other words, an urban area is a system with a large amount of simultaneity. Mathematics is indispensable in analyzing such systems.

Appendix:
A Simplified
Mathematical Model
of Urban Structure

It is not necessary to be a professional mathematician to be an urban economist. In any specialty in economics, it is desirable to have a mixture of scholars with different levels of mathematical interest and background. But a specialist in any branch of economics ought to be able to follow the relevant literature. For that purpose the minimum requirement is a knowledge of elementary calculus. That background is sufficient to follow this appendix and, indeed, practically all the important work in urban economics. Anyone lacking that background should try to understand the assumptions and conclusions in this appendix, but should not be concerned with derivations.

A MODEL OF URBAN STRUCTURE

The model analyzed here[1] is mainly concerned with the urban area residential sector. It is the most important urban sector and the one that has been studied most carefully. Most models that include more than one sector are too large to present here and require the help of a computer to solve.

Assume that the urban area has a predetermined center, perhaps at a port or railhead. At each distance from the center, ϕ radians of a circle are available for urban uses. Since a circle has 2π radians, ϕ must not exceed 2π. The rest of the land, $2\pi - \phi$ radians, is either unavailable for urban use, perhaps because of topographical characteristics, or is used for transportation, parks, and other public purposes.

Assume that all the urban area's employment is located in a semicircular central business district (CBD) with a radius of $\underline{u}$ miles. Thus, the CBD has an area of $(\phi/2)\underline{u}^2$ square miles, and it is assumed that N people work there. The terms ϕ, $\underline{u}$, and N are given from outside the model.

The available land outside the CBD is used for housing as far away from the center as is necessary to house the N workers employed in the CBD. The total amount of land available for housing within u miles of the city center is $(\phi/2)u^2 - (\phi/2)\underline{u}^2$.

Housing Supply and Demand

Equations can now be introduced that express the conditions for location equilibrium in the residential sector. It is assumed that commuting cost depends only on the straight-line distance between place of residence and the city center. It follows that land rent and the intensity of land use also depend on straight-line distance, so that all the land u miles from the center commands the same rent and is used with the same capital/land ratio. This is an important simplification in urban models, since it implies that activities can be located with only one variable, distance from the center, rather than two, distance and direction. The value of each variable at a distance u miles from the center is designated with a u in parentheses following the variable. For example, $K(u)$ and $L(u)$ represent inputs of capital and land in the production of housing services u miles from the center. This notation shows that the variables are functions of u, and solving the model consists in deducing from the equations in the model the functional relationship between the variables and u.

It is also assumed that housing services are produced with land and

1.   The model is a simplified version of those analyzed by Mills and Muth.

capital inputs. The production function is assumed to be the **Cobb-Douglas function**, which economists have used to study many production activities. Using this function, the output of housing services at u, $X_s(u)$, depends on the inputs of land and capital employed at u in the following way:

$$X_s(u) = AL(u)^\alpha K(u)^{1-\alpha} \tag{A.1}$$

where A and α are constants. A is a scale parameter and depends on the units in which inputs and output are measured. The term α is called the distribution parameter, and must lie in the interval $0 < \alpha < 1$. (It is discussed later.) It can be verified that Equation A.1 has constant returns to scale, so that competitively priced input payments exhaust firms' revenues.

It is assumed that input and output markets are perfectly competitive, so that firms use amounts of inputs equating VMP to input rental rates at each u. It is assumed that the market for housing capital is national, so that its rental rate r is independent of both u and the amount used in the entire urban area. Land rent $R(u)$ and the rental rate for housing services $p(u)$ are determined by the model, and of course depend on u.

If Equation A.1 is differentiated, it is seen that the MPs of land and capital are

$$MP_{L(u)} = \alpha AL(u)^{\alpha-1}K(u)^{1-\alpha} = \alpha X_s(u)/L(u)$$

and

$$MP_{K(u)} = (1 - \alpha)AL(u)^\alpha K(u)^{-\alpha} = (1 - \alpha)X_s(u)/K(u)$$

Therefore the equations relating factor VMPs to their rental rates are

$$\frac{\alpha p(u)X_s(u)}{L(u)} = R(u) \tag{A.2}$$

and

$$\frac{(1 - \alpha)p(u)X_s(u)}{K(u)} = r \tag{A.3}$$

If Equations A.2 and A.3 are multiplied by their respective input amounts and divided by $p(u)X_s(u)$, they show that the ratio of each input's remuneration to total revenue equals the input's exponent in Equation A.1. These ratios are the shares of the inputs in housing rental revenues; thus, it can be seen why α is called the distribution parameter. The value of α determines the distribution of housing rental revenues between the two inputs.

A typical house may be worth four times the land it occupies, which suggests that α might be about 0.2.

It is assumed that all workers receive the same income w, determined outside the model, and that all have the same tastes. The demand function for housing services per worker living at u, $x_D(u)$, is assumed to be

$$x_D(u) = Bw^{\theta_1}p(u)^{\theta_2} \qquad \text{(A.4)}$$

where B is a scale parameter, and depends on the units in which housing services are measured. The terms θ_1 and θ_2 are the income and price elasticities of demand for housing, as can be verified by computing the elasticities from Equation A.4. Unlike other demand functions, Equation A.4 assumes the elasticities to be constant, and has been used in many applied studies of demand theory. Housing per worker depends on u, as Equation A.4 indicates. Housing is not an inferior good; hence, $\theta_1 > 0$. The housing demand function slopes downward; hence, $\theta_2 < 0$. Recent studies of housing demand suggest that θ_1 may be about 1.0 and θ_2 about -1.0. $X_D(u)$, total housing demand at u, is housing demand per worker multiplied by $N(u)$, the number of workers living at u:

$$X_D(u) = x_D(u)N(u) \qquad \text{(A.5)}$$

In equilibrium, housing demand and supply must be equal at each u:

$$X_D(u) = X_s(u) \qquad \text{(A.6)}$$

In addition, it was shown in the text that locational equilibrium in housing requires that Equation 5.6 be satisfied. That equation can be written

$$p'(u)x_D(u) + t = 0 \qquad \text{(A.7)}$$

Here $p'(u)$ is the slope of $p(u)$, and t is the cost per two miles of commuting. Equation A.7 says that families are unable to increase utility by moving their households if the change in the cost of housing from a move is just offset by the change in commuting cost.

Other Equilibrium Conditions

It has already been assumed that ϕ radians of land are available for housing at each u, so that ϕu is the length of the semicircle available for housing u miles from the city center. Land used for housing cannot exceed what is available, and no available land can be left unused out to the edge of the urban area. Thus

$$L(u) = \phi u \qquad \text{(A.8)}$$

It is assumed that nonurban uses of land command a rent $\bar{R}$. Therefore, the urban area can extend only as far as households can bid land away from nonurban uses. Thus, the distance from the center to the edge of the urban area is $\bar{u}$ miles, where

$$R(\bar{u}) = \bar{R} \qquad \text{(A.9)}$$

Finally, the land available for housing must house all N workers in the urban area. If $N(u)$ workers live u miles from the center, the total number of workers in the urban area is the sum or integral of $N(u)$ for values of u from $\underline{u}$ to $\bar{u}$, that is

$$\int_{\underline{u}}^{\bar{u}} N(u)du = N \qquad \text{(A.10)}$$

The model is now complete. The first eight equations relate the eight variables $X_s(u)$, $L(u)$, $K(u)$, $p(u)$, $R(u)$, $x_D(u)$, $X_D(u)$, and $N(u)$ at each value of u. Their solution provides the value of each variable at each u between $\underline{u}$ and $\bar{u}$. Equation A.7 contains a derivative of $p(u)$ with respect to u. A differential equation, its solution requires a predetermined value of the variable at some u. It is shown below how Equation A.7 can be expressed as a differential equation in $R(u)$. Equation A.9 then provides the required value of $R(u)$ at $\bar{u}$, known as an initial condition for the differential equation. Finally, Equation A.10 can be solved for the variable $\bar{u}$.

Once the model is solved, it shows a complete picture of the housing sector of the urban area. For each value of u, it shows land rent and the rental rate of housing services. From the solution for $K(u)$ and $L(u)$, it is easy to compute the capital/land ratio at each u. From the solution of $N(u)$, population density can be computed at each u.

SOLUTION OF THE MODEL

The land-rent function is the key to the foregoing model. Once it has been found, all the other variables can be calculated easily. The first step in solving $R(u)$ is to derive a well-known relationship between input and output prices for the Cobb-Douglas production function. Solving Equations A.2 and A.3 for $L(u)$ and $K(u)$ gives

$$L(u) = \frac{\alpha p(u)X_s(u)}{R(u)} \qquad K(u) = \frac{(1 - \alpha)p(u)X_s(u)}{r}$$

Substituting these expressions for $L(u)$ and $K(u)$ in Equation A.1 and rearranging terms gives

$$p(u) = [A\alpha^{\alpha}(1 - \alpha)^{1-\alpha}]^{-1}r^{1-\alpha}R(u)^{\alpha} \tag{A.11}$$

which shows that $p(u)$ is proportionate to $R(u)$ raised to a power between zero and 1. Thus, housing prices are high wherever land rents are high, but housing prices rise less than proportionately with land rents because of input substitution. If α is 0.2, then a 10 percent rise in land rent will lead to a 2 percent rise in housing prices.

The derivative of Equation A.11 with respect to u is

$$p'(u) = A^{-1}\left(\frac{\alpha r}{1 - \alpha}\right)^{1-\alpha} R(u)^{-(1-\alpha)} R'(u) \tag{A.12}$$

where $R'(u)$ is the slope of $R(u)$. Now substitute Equation A.4 for $x_D(u)$ in Equation A.7, substitute Equation A.11 for $p(u)$ and Equation A.12 for $p'(u)$ and collect terms. The result is

$$E^{-1}R(u)^{\beta-1}R'(u) + t = 0 \tag{A.13}$$

where E and β stand for collections of constants,

$$E^{-1} = \alpha B w^{\theta_1}[A\alpha^{\alpha}(1 - \alpha)^{1-\alpha}]^{-(1+\theta_2)}r^{(1-\alpha)(1+\theta_2)}$$

and

$$\beta = \alpha(1 + \theta_2)$$

Equation A.13 expresses the differential Equation A.7 in terms of $R(u)$. Using the initial condition of Equation A.9, the solution is

$$R(u) = [\bar{R}^{\beta} + \beta t E(\bar{u} - u)]^{1/\beta} \qquad \text{if } \beta \neq 0 \tag{A.14a}$$

and

$$R(u) = \bar{R}e^{tE(\bar{u}-u)} \qquad \text{if } \beta = 0 \tag{A.14b}$$

In Equation A.14b, the term e is the base of the natural logarithm. This equation therefore indicates that, when β is zero, land rent decreases exponentially as u increases. Both equations indicate that $R(u)$ equals $\bar{R}$ when u equals $\bar{u}$. Both have the characteristic shape established in the text and illustrated in Figure 5.1. It can be seen from the definition of β

that β = zero, and Equation A.14b thus applies, when θ_2 = -1. But it was indicated earlier that θ_2, the price elasticity of demand for housing, is probably about -1, and the exponential function of Equation A.14b should therefore be a good approximation of urban land-rent functions. The term β is positive if θ_2 > -1, that is, if housing demand is price-inelastic. Regardless of the sign of β, $R(u)$ is steep at small values of u and flat at large values of u.

Equations A.14a and A.14b contain the variable $\bar{u}$, representing the radius of the urban area. So far, Equation A.10 has not been used and $\bar{u}$ has not been computed. Using the equilibrium condition of Equation A.6, Equation A.5 can be written:

$$N(u) = \frac{X_s(u)}{x_D(u)} \tag{A.15}$$

Taking the ratio of Equation A.2 to Equation A.3, $K(u)$ can be expressed in terms of $L(u)$:

$$K(u) = \frac{1-\alpha}{\alpha r} R(u)L(u)$$

Now substitute this expression for $K(u)$ in Equation A.1. The result is

$$X_s(u) = A\left(\frac{1-\alpha}{\alpha r}\right)^{1-\alpha} R(u)^{1-\alpha} L(u) \tag{A.16}$$

Substitute Equation A.11 for $p(u)$ in Equation A.4. Then, in Equation A.15, substitute Equation A.4 for $x_D(u)$ and Equation A.16 for $X_s(u)$. Rearranging terms gives

$$\frac{N(u)}{L(u)} = ER(u)^{1-\beta} \tag{A.17}$$

If both sides of this equation are multiplied by $L(u)$, Equation A.8 is substituted for $L(u)$, and the result is integrated from u to $\bar{u}$, an expression for the left-hand side of Equation A.10 results. Equating it to N provides the equation from which $\bar{u}$ can be calculated. The result, however, is cumbersome and so is not presented here.

Equation A.17 shows how the number of resident workers per square mile varies with u. Except for a multiplicative factor equal to the reciprocal of the labor-force participation rate, it is the same as population density, and so will be referred to as "population density" from here on. Equation A.17 expresses a remarkable result: *population density is proportionate to land rent raised to the power $1 - \beta$*. The term $1 - \beta$ must be positive, since θ_2 is negative. Thus, as would be expected, population density is high wherever land rent is high. More important, if $\beta = 0$, so that Equation A.14b applies, population density is proportionate to land rent, and therefore declines exponentially with u just as land rent does. Exponential functions have been used in many applied studies of urban population density (some of which are reported in Chapter 12) and have been found to fit the data very well. Thus, Equation A.17 provides a link between theory and observation.

A universal conclusion of urban population-density studies is that density functions become flatter through time. Many writers have guessed that increasing incomes and falling commuting costs have caused the density functions to flatten. The mathematical model here shows that the guess has a theoretical basis. The population density function of Equation A.17 will be flatter, the larger is the coefficient of u in Equation A.14a or A.14b; that is, the closer the coefficient is to zero. Both increases in w and decreases in t flatten the density function by increasing the coefficients of u in Equations A.14a and A.14b.

It is easy to see that finding $R(u)$ is the key to solving the mathematical model. Many of the other variables have already been expressed as functions of $R(u)$; the term $p(u)$ can be calculated from Equation A.11; the term $L(u)$ is given by Equation A.8; the term $X_s(u)$ can be calculated from Equation A.16; and the term $N(u)$ can be calculated from Equation A.17. As an exercise, calculate $x_D(u)$, which shows how housing demand per worker varies with u, and prove that it is exponential if $R(u)$ is exponential.

TWO HOUSEHOLD SECTORS

In this section, the mathematical model is generalized to study the effects of income differences on the household location pattern. In particular, a proof is provided for the statement in the text that, under realistic conditions, high-income households live farther from the city center than do low-income households.

Until now, the time cost of travel has simply been included in t. In this section, it is assumed that commuters value travel time proportionately to the wage rate w. Thus, t is written

$$t = t_o + t_w w \tag{A.18}$$

where t_o represents operating cost per two miles of travel, about 25–35 cents if travel is by automobile; t_w represents the time cost or disutility of two miles of travel per dollar of income; and t_w is inversely proportional to travel speed. For example, suppose commuting speed is 25 miles per hour. Then two miles of travel require $2(1/25) = 0.08$ hours (4.8 minutes). If travel time is valued at the wage rate, $t_w = 0.08$. If the wage rate is \$7.50

Figure A.1

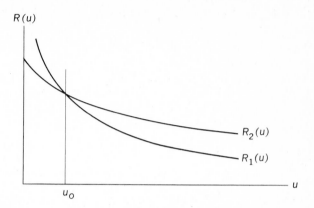

per hour, the time cost of two miles of commuting is 60 cents. If t_o is 30 cents, two miles of commuting have a total cost of 90 cents. In this example, location equilibrium requires that the worker's housing expense must fall by 90 cents per day, or about $20 per month (assuming a 22-day working month), if he moves one mile farther from the city center.

If travel time is valued at less than the wage rate, t_w is less than in the example. If commuting speed is faster than 25 miles per hour, t_w is also less than in the example. As was indicated in the text, the assumption that the marginal disutility of commuting is independent of commuting distance is a special case. It is shown later that the assumption is crucial to the results obtained here.

Suppose there are two household sectors, distinguished only by income. Household sector 1 has income w_1, and household sector 2 has income w_2. All households have the same tastes and therefore the same housing demand function, but the amount of housing demanded differs from one sector to another.

For convenience, the household sector closer to the city center is designated number 1, and its rent-offer function as $R_1(u)$. The sector farther from the center is number 2, and its rent offer $R_2(u)$. Then the two rent-offer functions must be as shown in Figure A.1. If sector 1 is to be close to the center, its rent-offer function must be above that of sector 2 for small values of u. Household sector 1 occupies the available land at values of u between $\underline{u}$ and u_o, and sector 2 occupies the land between u_o and $\bar{u}$. Suppose u_o and $\bar{u}$ satisfy all the equilibrium conditions.

$R_2(u)$ has the initial condition $R_2(\bar{u}) = \bar{R}$, and its solution is Equation A.14a if $\beta \neq 0$; that is,

$$R_2(u) = [\bar{R}^\beta + \beta t_2 E_2(\bar{u} - u)]^{1/\beta} \qquad (A.19a)$$

where w affects E and t, but not β. Therefore, E_2 and t_2 designate the values of E and t when the wage rate is w_2.

$R_1(u)$ has the initial condition $R_1(u_o) = R_2(u_o)$, and its solution is

$$R_1(u) = [\bar{R}^\beta + \beta t_2 E_2(\bar{u} - u_o) + \beta t_1 E_1(u_o - u)]^{1/\beta} \quad \text{(A.19b)}$$

It can be verified that Equation A.19b satisfies its initial condition, and that $R_1(u)$ and $R_2(u)$ can have only one intersection.

Is sector 1, close to the center, the high-income or the low-income sector? The condition that $R_1(u)$ be greater than $R_2(u)$ at values of u less than u_o is

$$[\bar{R}^\beta + \beta t_2 E_2(\bar{u} - u_o) + \beta t_1 E_1(u_o - u)]^{1/\beta} > [\bar{R}^\beta + \beta t_2 E_2(\bar{u} - u)]^{1/\beta} \quad \text{(A.20)}$$

for $u < u_o$. If β is positive, Inequal. A.20 reduces to the condition that the term in square brackets on the left-hand side exceed the term in square brackets on the right-hand side; that is,

$$\bar{R}^\beta + \beta t_2 E_2(\bar{u} - u_o) + \beta t_1 E_1(u_o - u) > \bar{R}^\beta + \beta t_2 E_2(\bar{u} - u)$$

for $u < u_o$, or

$$t_1 E_1 > t_2 E_2 \quad \text{(A.21)}$$

If β is negative, Inequal. A.20 reduces to the condition that the term in square brackets on the left-hand side be less than the term in square brackets on the right-hand side; that is,

$$\bar{R}^\beta + \beta t_2 E_2(\bar{u} - u_o) + \beta t_1 E_1(u_o - u) < \bar{R}^\beta + \beta t_2 E_2(\bar{u} - u)$$

Canceling terms and remembering that $\beta < 0$, this inequality also reduces to Inequal. A.21.

Thus, it is only necessary to establish the relationship between w_1 and w_2 that is equivalent to Inequal. A.21. The following theorem provides the key relationship: If $\theta_1 \geq 1$, then Inequal. A.21 holds if and only if $w_2 > w_1$. To prove the theorem, first note that E is w^{θ_1} multiplied by terms that cancel on both sides of Inequal. A.21, which therefore can be written

$$\frac{t_o + t_w w_1}{t_o + t_w w_2} > \left(\frac{w_1}{w_2}\right)^{\theta_1} \quad \text{(A.22)}$$

by substituting Equation A.18 for t.

1. Suppose $w_2 > w_1$. Then Equation A.22 holds for $\theta_1 = 1$, since

$$\frac{t_o + t_w w_1}{w_1} = \frac{t_o}{w_1} + t_w > \frac{t_o + t_w w_2}{w_2} = \frac{t_o}{w_2} + t_w$$

reduces to $w_2 > w_1$. But the right-hand side of Inequal. A.22 becomes smaller as θ_1 becomes larger than 1. Therefore, $w_2 > w_1$ implies Inequal. A.22.

2. Suppose $w_2 < w_1$. The left-hand side of Inequal. A.22 has a maximum value of w_1/w_2 when $t_o = 0$, and decreases asymptotically to 1 as t_o becomes large. But the right-hand side of Inequal. A.22 exceeds w_1/w_2 if $\theta_1 > 1$. Therefore, Inequal. A.22 cannot hold.

This proves the theorem. Using Equation A.14b, the theorem can be verified if $\beta = 0$. Thus, in this model, an income elasticity of demand for housing of at least 1 implies that low-income workers live closer to the city center than high-income workers. Generally, any number of household sectors, differing only in income, will be ranked by distance from the city center inversely to their rank by income.

The theorem proves that low-income groups live close to the city center only if $\theta_1 \geq 1$. It does not prove that they will live elsewhere if $\theta_1 < 1$. Inequal. A.22 may still hold for $w_2 > w_1$ even if $\theta_1 < 1$. For example, suppose that t_o and t_w have the values 0.30 and 0.08 used in the foregoing example. Suppose further that $w_1 = \$2$ and $w_2 = \$4$. Then Inequal. A.22 holds if $\theta_1 \geq 0.54$.

It is easy to see that the theorem may not hold if high-income workers value travel time higher in relationship to the wage rate than do low-income workers, or if the marginal disutility of commuting increases with the amount of commuting. In the former case, t_w is larger for the high-income group than for the low-income group. In the latter case, t_w is larger for the sector residing farther from the city center. It can be easily verified that the theorem does not hold if either change is made in the model. But it is still true that a sufficiently large income elasticity of housing demand results in the location pattern implied by the model.

Index